23812

13-95

KEY TO
INTRODUCTORY HEBREW GRAMMAR

KEY

TO THE EXERCISES

in the Twentyfifth and Twentysixth editions of

The Late Professor A. B. DAVIDSON'S

INTRODUCTORY HEBREW GRAMMAR

WITH EXPLANATORY NOTES

Third Edition

BY

JOHN MAUCHLINE, D.D.

Professor of Old Testament Language and Literature
University of Glasgow and
Principal of Trinity College, Glasgow

EDINBURGH : T. & T. CLARK, 38 GEORGE STREET

Copyright © T. & T. Clark 1967

PRINTED IN GREAT BRITAIN BY
MORRISON AND GIBB LIMITED
EDINBURGH AND LONDON
FOR
T. & T. CLARK, EDINBURGH

First Edition, J. E. McFadyen   1924
Second Edition, J. E. McFadyen   1929
Third Edition, John Mauchline   1967

PREFACE

There are arguments for and against the publication and use of such a Key as this. To learn a language under the instruction of a tutor has the advantage that the student's questions can be answered as they arise and he may be saved from being troubled with answers to questions which he has not yet asked. Normally the tutor will prefer that a student should not use the Key but should work his passage through the Grammar, learning from his own mistakes. But even when a student is working on his own, he would be well advised when he attempts the exercises in the Grammar to lay the Key aside in the first instance and to use the instructions given in the Grammar as his aid in translation.

With regard to the translations given in the Key, those in the earlier sections keep close to the original in order that the student may follow them as easily as possible. In the later sections a freer style is adopted with the aim of inducing the student to use idiomatic Hebrew or English, as the case may be. *Thou* and *thee* have been retained in use in the Key as in the Grammar, with the exception that, in some conversational pieces which do not easily tolerate the use of these pronouns, the singular *you* has been used.

It is hoped that the notes provided in the Key deal with the questions which students really ask, and seldom waste time expounding the obvious. They are commonly shorter than those in the former edition and, in particular, care has been taken to avoid as far as possible notes which themselves require considerable annotation. In other words, the Key has been planned to be subsidiary to the Grammar and not a related manual giving a more advanced course of instruction.

I am especially indebted to two former students for their aid. Dr. H. C. Thomson made for me the initial translation of the exercises and later examined with great care and skill the finished typescript of the Key, and the Rev. Wm. Johnstone (with the co-operation, I have no doubt, of his wife) also read through the typescript and made many valuable suggestions, and, in particular, indicated points at which, he recommended, additional notes might be provided. To these scholars I am very much indebted. Dr. Thomson and the Rev. James D. Martin greatly aided me in the laborious task of checking the proofs.

The following abbreviations and means of reference used in the Key should be noted. Reference to the Grammar is made in the form : § 24.1.(a).i, and to the Key it is in the form : Key § 24B, note 2. The abbreviation Syn. signifies A. B. Davidson, *Hebrew Syntax* (3rd edition, 1901. T. and T. Clark), and G.K. signifies Gesenius-Kautzsch, *Hebrew Grammar* (2nd English edition (1910) by A. E. Cowley. Clarendon Press, Oxford).

Since the 26th edition of the Grammar has had to be prepared before the publication of this Key, it has been possible to take note in the Key of modifications made in the Exercises for the 26th edition of the Grammar.

JOHN MAUCHLINE

The University,
Glasgow, W.2.

KEY TO THE HEBREW GRAMMAR

§ 1.

A.

First line : by<u>th</u>, d<u>bh</u>r, yr<u>dh</u>, yr<u>kh</u>, gn<u>bh</u>, zqn, ymṭ, ṭ'm, m't, 'ṣh, ḥḥ<u>škh</u>.

Second line : qṣ<u>ph</u>, k<u>ph</u>ym,[1] mg<u>h</u>n, mym, rṣḥ, kn'n, '<u>thh</u>, 'zn.

[1] This is the only transliteration which the student can give at this stage. In actual fact the transliteration of this word is kppym.

B.

First line : ב, ב, ל, ל, לם, מל, סט, שן, לך, גד, דג, קום, רץ,
כף, צו.

Second and Third lines : הם, מץ, מט, עץ, רע, אם, יין, נגן, מים, עופף,
חמס, ציץ, תמם.

§ 2.

A.

If the student gives *any one* of the transliterations set out below for a Hebrew form in this Exercise in the Grammar, that is enough for the present purpose.

First line : mā[1] ; mê or mî ; mêmê, mêmî, mîmê or mîmî ; lê or lî ; lô or lû ; lên or lîn ; lôn or lûn ; šêrô, šîrô, šêrû or šîrû ; qômā or qûmā[1] ; lôlê, lôlî, lûlê, lûlî ; šêrô<u>th</u>, šêrû<u>th</u>, šîrô<u>th</u>, šîrû<u>th</u>.

Second line : hênêq, hênîq, hînêq or hînîq ; hôšê'ā, hôšî'ā, hûšê'ā or hûšî'ā ; sôsêm, sôsîm, sûsêm or sûsîm ; hôrê<u>th</u>ê, hôrê<u>th</u>î, hôrî<u>th</u>ê or hôrî<u>th</u>î[2] ; qôl or qûl ; qôlô<u>th</u>ênô, qôlô<u>th</u>ênû, qôlô<u>th</u>înô or qôlô<u>th</u>înû[2] ; 'ô<u>ph</u> or 'û<u>ph</u> ; hô<u>bh</u>êšô, hô<u>bh</u>êšû, hô<u>bh</u>îšô or hô<u>bh</u>îšû[2] ;

Third line : hêlêlê, hêlêlî, hêlîlê, hêlîlî, hîlêlê, hîlêlî, hîlîlê or hîlîlî ; hôlê<u>kh</u>ô, hôlê<u>kh</u>û, hôlî<u>kh</u>ô or hôlî<u>kh</u>û[2] ; nâ.[3]

[1] The vocalization of final **ה**, for the purpose of this Exercise, is confined to the common *ā*.

[2] In addition, **ו** may theoretically be written as *û* in each case.

[3] This gives an illustration of the use of **א** as a vocalic consonant ; it represents chiefly *â*. Since in this final position (cf. § 1.2.(f)) it is used here as a vocalic consonant, it is not represented in transliteration by **י**.

All the alternative forms given above are theoretically possible, but only some of them are transliterations of words found in use (*e.g.* mê, *the waters of*, and mî, *who ?* (§ 10.3) ; hêlîlî, *howl*, is an imperatival form). To use artificial forms in this way together with forms which are found in use as words provides a convenient way of illustrating the possible range of vocalization of the forms used. Transliterated words in the rest of the Exercise, as printed in the Grammar, are Hebrew words which are found in use.

Note that the vowels in the above Exercise, except in the case of **ה**, are all marked with the circumflex accent. This is because they are pure long (i.e. by nature long and, therefore, unchangeable) and are usually represented by vocalic consonants. To mark them with a horizontal stroke above (*e.g.* *ā*) instead of with a circumflex accent (â) would imply that they were merely tone-long vowels, in which case they would not have had consonantal representation (cf. § 2.6,7.(b)).

B.

First line : קוּם, קוֹם, שִׁיר, שִׁירִים, סוּס, סוּסוֹתֵינוּ, קוֹץ, לִי,
לוּ, לוֹ, מִי.

Second line : [1]מֵישִׁיב, מוּת, הֵילִיל, חוּל, חִילָה, הוֹצִיא, צִיף,
[1]מֵיקִיץ, טוּבִי, נִירִי.

Third line : הוֹשִׁיבוּ, הוֹלִיכוּ, לוּלִי, מֵינִיקוֹתֵינוּ:

[1] With a pure long vowel in the first syllable, this form is not a Hebrew word ; but, with a tone-long vowel in it, it is. This difference will be explained in § 5.

§ 3.

A.

First line : yā<u>dh</u>, gêr,[1] ḥēn, ḥōq, gam, ʿal, śûm, ʾim, ʾa<u>ph</u>, ʿᵃb<u>h</u>ō<u>dh</u>, bᵉ<u>kh</u>ā,[2] dō<u>bh</u>, ṣar,

Second line : ṣārā, ʿîr, ʾᵉ<u>kh</u>ōl, ḥᵃzaq, ʾᵃšer, rᵉ<u>ph</u>oś, šô<u>ph</u>ēṭ,[3] qûm (or qum), rāṣ, rûṣ, hᵃ<u>gh</u>am,

Third line : wāw, dᵉ<u>bh</u>ar, ʾᵉme<u>th</u>.

[1] In terms of § 2.6,7 a reader would naturally assume that the vowel in גֵּר, being without a vocalic consonant, is tone-long, but it is unchangeably long by etymology.

[2] For this form cf. § 3.7.(a) final sentence.

[3] The first vowel in this form would be assumed to be tone-long, but this word is sometimes written as שׁוֹפֵט. Note the final sentence in § 2.7.(b).

The short vowels are left unmarked in transliteration, e.g. a ; the naturally long vowels, which are represented by vocalic consonants, have the circumflex accent, e.g. â ; the merely tone-long vowels are marked by a horizontal stroke above them, e.g. ā.

B.

First line : גַּם, בּוֹר, בּוֹשׁ, שׁוּב, שִׁיר, שׁוֹר, שָׁם, חֹק, אִם, עָם, כֹּל.

Second line : קוֹל, עַם, הַר, רֹב, רוּץ, הֲרֹג, צֵל, חֵיק, מָשָׁל, מְשַׁל, קוֹטֵל.

Third line : שָׁלוֹם, יָרוּץ, קוֹמָם, פָּעֳלוֹ, אָסֹף, הֶחֱזִיק:

In the above transliterations the vowel with circumflex accent, as indicating a pure long vowel, has been invariably represented by the appropriate vocalic consonant. In actual Hebrew usage, however, as has been said above, this is not invariable (cf. § 2.7.(b)). To mark in this way the distinction between a pure long vowel and a tone-long vowel may serve as a convenient general rule.

§ 4.

A.

First line : ᵓelô-hîm, ḥolî, ḥᵃmôr, ᵓᵃrî, mer-ḥāq, hᵃlā-hēn, niš-qᵉlû, mᵉṣaph-ṣᵉphîm.

Second line : qam-nû, qᵉṣîr, lā-ᵓᵃnā-šîm, hoq-ṭᵉlā,[1] hiq-ṭîl, yapht.

[1] The first vowel of הָקְטְלָה, as it is the vowel of a short and unaccented syllable, must be *short*, therefore *o*, not *ā* (cf. § 4.4.(a) ; the accented syllable here, as usually, is the *final* one).

B.

First line : קוֹטֵל, קָם, אֶכְתֹּב, מָקוֹם, וְלוֹ, מִזְמוֹר, קְטָלוֹ, שָׁמַיִם.

Second line : קוּמוּ, לְמִינֵהוּ, וּלְיָמִים, יֶרֶק, לִלְקֹט, מַמְלָכָה, לְשָׁלוֹם.

Third line : שְׁמוֹנִים, שְׁנֵי, מְקוֹמִי, יוֹרְשִׁים, נִלְחַם, יִשְׂרָאֵל, שְׁמוֹ, נַעַר.

Fourth line : חֲמוֹרִים, לֶאֱסֹף, עֲמַלְנוּ׃

Here, as in § 3, the vowel with the circumflex accent, being pure long, has uniformly been represented in Hebrew by a vocalic consonant.

The word וּלְיָמִים *ûlᵉyāmîm*, which seems to violate the rule that every Hebrew word or syllable must begin with a consonant (cf. § 4.2), is justified by the principle explained in § 11.II(c).

§ 5.

לְבָבִי, מִדְּבָרִים, זְקֵנִים, חֲדָשִׁים, כּוֹכָבִים, קְטָלוֹ, קְטַלְתֶּם, קְטָלָנוּ, קָטַֽלְנוּ, סְפָרִים, עֲנָבִים, צִדְקָתֵנוּ, דְּבָרֶיךָ, גְּדוֹלִים, הֲקִימוֹתֶם, שָׁמַיִם, חָכְמָה, אֲלָפִים, תָּשׁוּב, יָקִים׃

Note :

(i) That the long vowel *qāmeṣ* is required in the open pretonic syllable (cf. § 5.2.(b)) in the case of כּוֹכָבִים, מִדְבָּרִים and

קְטָלוֹ of the first line, עֲנָבִים, קָטַלְנוּ and צִדְקָתֵנוּ of the

second line and שָׁמַיִם, חָכְמָה and יָקִים of the third line.

(ii) The rule that the vowel in the syllable before the pretonic one must be reduced, wherever possible (cf. § 5.2.(c).i), to a hurriedly pronounced vowel (a vocal sh[e]wa) is illustrated in the corrections required in such forms given in the Grammar as קְטַלְתֶּם, חֳדָשִׁים, זְקֵנִים, לְבָבִי and קְטָלוֹ of

the first line, דְּבָרֶיךָ, עֲנָבִים, סְפָרִים, קְטָלְנוּ and גְּדוֹלִים

of the second line and אֲלָפִים and הֲקִימוֹתֶם of the third

line. In כּוֹכָבִים of the first line the vowel of the first

syllable is pure long (note the use of the vocalic consonant) and so unchangeable.

(iii) For the *paṭḥaḥ* under the tone in קָטַלְנוּ (second line), see

§ 5.2.(f), second para., and for the vocalization of קְטָלָנוּ

see the final sentence of that para. שָׁמַיִם (third line) is

observably different in form from סְפָרִים (second line) or

אֲלָפִים (third line) ; its final syllable is יִם, but the tone

is on the preceding open syllable מַ ; cf. § 4.4.(a), second para.

§ 6.

1 גַּם, כֹּל, דָּם, בֵּן, אֵת, מוֹת, פַּת, כַּף, כֶּלֶב, תִּכְתֹּב כָּתַבְתָּ,

בְּכוּ, לְבַד, דָּבָר, מִשְׁפָּט, מִדְבָּר, בְּתוֹךְ, מַלְכִּי, יַבְדֵּל, כּוֹכָבִים,

כְּבַדְתֶּם, תִּכְבְּדִי, כַּסְפְּךָ, חֶלְקֶךָ, יֹלֶרֶדֶת יַֽרֵב, יֶֽיבְךָ, גְּדוֹלִים:

¹ The accent on רֶדֶת is on the penult; hence the vowel of the first syllable of לָרֶדֶת, which is pre-tonic and open, is long (cf. § 5.2.(b)).

² In יִרְבְּ and יֵבְךְ the first syllable is closed (cf. § 4.3). Therefore, the following consonant, בּ in the one case and ךְ in the other, not being preceded by a vowel, takes *daghesh lene*.

2 ¹מְבַקְשִׁים, חַלּוֹן, הַמַּיִם, ²וַיִּנָּגְפוּ, לְמַדְתָּ, דִּבֶּר, מְדַבָּר, סָפְדוּ, מִסְפֵּד, בְּכַסְפְּכֶם, שַׁבָּת, מִבְּנֵי, צִפּוֹר, יִכְתֹּב, בִּקְצַרְכֶם, בַּדָּם, בּוֹדֵד, יִתְּנוּ, לְבַדּוֹ:

¹ In actual fact the common practice is to omit the *daghesh forte* from certain letters, including ק, when they are followed by vocal sheʷwa, as ק is here (cf. § 6.5).

² wayyinnāgpû cannot be rendered into Hebrew as וַיִּנָּגְפוּ (with *daghesh lene* in the פ) since that would give a long vowel ā in its pre-tonic closed syllable (נָגְ; cf. § 5.2.(b), final sentence). For the sake of the long vowel ā the syllable in which it occurs must be open (נָ); that in turn makes the final syllable גְפוּ (ghephû) with vocal sheʷwa.

§ 7.
A.

הִשְׁמִיעַ, פֶּשַׁע, עֶבֶד, לַאֲרִי, שָׁמֹעַ, ¹אָמֹר, יִשְׁחֲטוּ, שָׂרִים, ²נֶאֱמַר, חֲזַק, שָׁלוּחַ, ²יֶאֱהַב, יַעֲמֹד, טַעֲמוּ, בַּחֲמֹר, ³גָּלָה, ⁴יֶהֶפֵּךְ, ⁵יִמְצָא, ⁶יַעַמְדוּ, מָצָאתָ, ⁵גָּבוֹהַּ, ⁷יֹאכַל, ⁷הֶאֱרִיךְ, רוּחוֹ, נָקִיא:

¹ For the *hateph seghôl* in this form, cf. § 7.1.(b).
² Cf. § 7.5.(a),6.(b).ii.

[3] For *qāmeṣ* in the final syllable, cf. § 7.6.(b).i.

[4] This is an example of compensatory lengthening of the vowel before ה ; cf. § 7.7.(b).

[5] For the *qāmeṣ* following the צ in this form, cf. § 7.6.(b).ii.

[6] In the uncorrected form יַעֲמְדוּ in the Grammar the *sh*ᵉ*wa* following the *mêm* cannot be silent, since that would require a full *pathaḥ* in the preceding closed syllable (עַמ) and *daghesh forte* in the *dāleth* following that closed syllable. Therefore, in the uncorrected form two vocal sh*ᵉ*was (one composite and the other simple) stand together ; in consequence, the first must become a full vowel, a *pathaḥ* (cf. §§ 3.6 ; 7.1.(c)), which is the component short vowel of the composite sh*ᵉ*wa.

[7] In יֹאכַל, as given in the Grammar, the *ḥôlem*, a long vowel, shows that the first syllable must be open (cf. § 5.2.(b)) ; hence the 'āleph must be quiescent, so that silent *sh*ᵉ*wa* cannot be written to it (cf. § 7.6.(b).ii). But in הַאְרִיךְ, the *ḥîreq*, a short vowel, indicates that the first syllable (הַא) is closed, so that the 'āleph in this case has consonantal value. The *ḥîreq* in the first syllable is depressed to *s*ᵉ*ghôl* (§ 7.2) and a helping vowel is introduced after the 'āleph (§ 7.5.(a)) to yield the form הֶאֱרִיךְ.

B.

עֲמֹד, יִשְׁחֲטוּ, בֶּאֱמֶת, לָעֲבֹד, נֶעֱמַד, שֶׁרֶשׁ, ²שׁוֹלֵחַ, יֵעָבֵר, יֶחְדַּל, בַּעֲלִי, פַּחְדוֹ, ³מֵאֲנָה, ⁴נָקִי, עֶזְרִי, פָּעֳלִי, ²שָׁכוּחַ, שְׁכוּחִים, ³כֹּהֲנִים :

[1] In the transliterated form in the Grammar, yišḥᵃṭû, the syllable division is yiš-ḥᵃṭû. Therefore, in יִשְׁחֲטוּ the sh*ᵉ*wa written to שׁ is silent.

[2] Cf. § 7.4.

[3] Cf. § 7.3.(a).

[4] Or נָקִיא

§ 8.
A.

1. The night and the day. 2. The man and the woman.
3. The great darkness. 4. The firmament is high. 5. The silver
is good. 6. The evening and the morning. 7. The darkness is
great on the waters. 8. The man is good.

9. הַיּוֹם הַגָּדוֹל׃   The great day.

10. הָאוֹר עַל־הַשָּׁמַיִם וְהַחֹשֶׁךְ עַל־הַמַּיִם׃

The light is on the heavens, and the darkness is on the waters.

B.

1 הַיּוֹם׃ 2 הַבֹּקֶר׃ 3 הַלַּיְלָה׃ 4 טוֹב הָאוֹר or ¹הָאוֹר

טוֹב¹׃ 5 הָאוֹר הַטּוֹב׃ 6 הָרָקִיעַ הָרָם׃ 7 הָאִישׁ ²וְהָאִשָּׁה׃

8 גָּדוֹל הַחֹשֶׁךְ or ¹הַחֹשֶׁךְ גָּדוֹל¹׃ 9 הָאִישׁ הַטּוֹב׃ 10 הָאִישׁ

הַגָּדוֹל וְהַטּוֹב׃ 11 יוֹם גָּדוֹל׃ 12 טוֹב הַזָּהָב or ¹הַזָּהָב טוֹב¹׃

13 הֶעָפָר עַל־הַמַּיִם׃ 14 אִישׁ טוֹב׃

¹⁻¹ In such a sentence the noun or the adjective may come first.

² Note that the fem. of אִישׁ *man* is not אִישָׁה but אִשָּׁה. The *daghesh
forte* in אִשָּׁה is owing to the assimilation to the שׁ of a נ of which there is
no trace in the masc. אִישׁ (cf. § 42).

§ 9.
A.

1. Yahweh is God.[1] 2. The famine is[2] [3]heavy in[3] the earth.[4]
3. The boy came to the palace, and [5]the king did not know (it)[5].
4. The man took the gold and the silver. 5. God created the
heavens and the earth. 6. The boy called to the wise man, and
[5]the man did not hear[5]. 7. God created the light and the
darkness. 8. The boy spilt the water on the ground. 9. The
powerful and great people. 10. The king took the sword.

[1] The article before אֱלֹהִים suggests *the one true God* ; e.g. the contest on Carmel between Yahweh and the Phoenician Baal ends with the triumphant words יהוה הוא הָאֱלֹהִים " *Yahweh is* (the true) *God* " (I Kings 18.39 : cf. 2 Chr. 33.13). But when the article is omitted, the word may mean *God* (as distinct from man) ; but e.g. אֱלֹהִים צַדִּיק *righteous God* probably conveyed the meaning of *the one righteous God*.

[2] *or* was (according to the context).

[3–3] כָּבֵד *heavy* means here *severe, serious*. The introduction of the preposition בְּ here is premature ; in the next printing of the Grammar עַל will be used in place of it (i.e. עַל־הָאָרֶץ).

[4] *or* land. Commonly it is clear whether הָאָרֶץ in any particular use of it means " earth " or " land ", but occasionally the reader may be left in doubt as to which is meant.

[5–5] Note how the subject is placed first ; probably the clause should be understood as a circumstantial one (cf. § 9.2) rather than as one in which the subject is placed first for emphasis (cf. § 9.1).

B.

1 הָאִישׁ הַטּוֹב : 2 ¹רָם מְאֹד הַהֵיכָל¹ : 3 שָׁמַע הַמֶּלֶךְ הַטּוֹב אֶת־הָאִשָּׁה וְלֹא לָקַח אֶת־הַכֶּסֶף וְאֶת־הַזָּהָב : 4 יָשַׁב הָאִישׁ הֶחָכָם עַל־הֶעָפָר וְלֹא שָׁמַע : 5 ²הַחֹשֶׁךְ עַל־הַבֹּקֶר ³וְעַל־הָעֶרֶב ²וְהָרָעָב עַל־הָאָרֶץ ⁴וְהוּא כָּבֵד מְאֹד⁴ : 6 יהוה הוא ⁵הָאֱלֹהִים : 7 הָאִישׁ הַטּוֹב הוא הָאִישׁ הֶחָכָם : 8 הָעָם הַטּוֹב ⁵וְהַגָּדוֹל : 9 קָרָא הַיֶּלֶד אֶת־הָעָם אֶל־הָהָר :

[1–1] Or הַהֵיכָל הוּא רָם מְאֹד ; cf. § 8.5, rule 4 ; § 9.1.

[2] In such cases, where a type or class or unparticularized whole is referred to, especially in comparisons, Hebrew uses the article generically (cf. § 12.2.(b)).

[3] Notice how the preposition is repeated ; this is the common practice in Hebrew in such a construction as this.

[4] Or וְכָבֵד מְאֹד הוּא

[5] Cf. note 1 in A above.

[6] Notice that the article is repeated in Hebrew before the second adjective.

§ 10.

A.

1. The mountain is very high.[1] 2. Thou art (the) God. 3. The sword is on the dust. 4. The people are very powerful. 5. I am the wise man. 6. Who are you ? 7. This mountain is very high. 8. This is the day which God made.[2] 9. This powerful people. 10. This is the boy who heard the voice. 11. The man came[3] who had poured[4] the water on the ground.[5] 12. How good is this day ! 13. One called to the other [6]and said[6] : " Holy is Yahweh ".

14. לָקַח הַמֶּלֶךְ אֶת־הַחֶרֶב : The king took the sword.

15. זֶה הַמֶּלֶךְ הֶעָצוּם : This is the powerful king.

[1] Lit. *the mountain, it is very high*—an idiomatic Hebrew mode of expression. But the Hebrew רָם מְאֹד הָהָר would also serve the purpose (cf. sentences 2, 3 and 4).

Note that the adjective רָם is pointed with *qāmeṣ* (cf. the noun יָד) while the adjective רַע (cf. Voc. § 9) is pointed with *paṯaḥ* (cf. the nouns פַּר and חַג, עַם, הַר mentioned in footnote (i) to the Voc. § 9). The reason for the difference in vocalization lies in the fact that רָם belongs to one type (cf. § 31) and רַע to another (cf. § 40).

² The verb בָּרָא means *to create*, יָצַר means *to form, to shape*, and both are often translated as *to make*. עָשָׂה *to make* emphasizes the act, i.e. the fact that he did it.

³ בָּא, used as here without extension defining the man's point of departure or arrival, must be interpreted as meaning *came upon the scene*, *arrived* or *came back*.

⁴ In Hebrew there is no special form for the pluperfect; the purpose is served by the perfect (cf. §§ 11.5; 43.I.1.(a)).

⁵ אֶרֶץ has more than one meaning as it is used in the Old Testament: *earth*, e.g. בְּכָל־הָאָרֶץ *in all the earth*; *land*, referring to a particular land or country, e.g. אֶרֶץ כְּנַעַן *the land of Canaan*; *ground* (with the same meaning as אֲדָמָה *ground, soil*), e.g. the use of אֶרֶץ here in sentence 11.

⁶⁻⁶ The use of וְאָמַר in sequence after קָרָא, i.e. " called . . . and said " is a simple form of expression sometimes found in Hebrew, usually when the two verbs are more or less synonymous (cf. § 20.5.(b)). But the normal construction for such a narrative sequence is different and will be explained in § 20.4.

B.

1 הָהָר הוּא רָם מְאֹד: 2 ¹הֶעָפָר עַל־הַמַּיִם הוּא: 3 אֲנִי הָאִישׁ: 4 אֲנַחְנוּ הָעָם: 5 הָעָם הַטּוֹב יוֹהְעֲצוּם: 6 הָהָר הַגָּדוֹל וְהָרָם: 7 מִי אֵלֶּה: 8 מָה־הֶם: 9 מִי הָאִשָּׁה הַזֹּאת: 10 אֲנִי הַמֶּלֶךְ הַגָּדוֹל אֲשֶׁר עַל־²הָאָרֶץ: 11 הַיּוֹם הַגָּדוֹל הַהוּא: 12 זֶה רֹאשׁ טוֹב: 13 טוֹב הָרֹאשׁ הַזֶּה: 14 הָרֹאשׁ הַטּוֹב הַזֶּה: 15 זֶה הַיֶּלֶד ³הָרַע אֲשֶׁר שָׁפַךְ אֶת־הַמַּיִם עַל־הָאָרֶץ: 16 אֵלֶּה הַשָּׁמַיִם וְהָאָרֶץ ⁴בָּרָא אֲשֶׁר אֱלֹהִים ⁵הַיּוֹם הַזֶּה⁵: 17 מַה־גָּדוֹל הַהֵיכָל הַהוּא:

¹ Students should not worry about using me<u>th</u>eg<u>h</u> as yet in the English–Hebrew exercises, but it will be used in the Key, as here, in order that they may become acquainted with the use of it. Note the variety in order of expression illustrated in sentences 1 and 2.

² No me<u>th</u>eg<u>h</u> with the *qāmeṣ* written to the הַ because, although it is in an open syllable, it is pretonic (הָאָ֫רֶץ).

³ Cf. Key § 10A, note 1.

⁴ See note 2 in A above.

⁵⁻⁵ Or simply הַיּוֹם ; cf. § 8.1.

§ 11.

A.

1. Yahweh said to the woman. 2. God and Moses. 3. To God they cried, and¹ the famine was on the land. 4. David and Jonathan. 5. Israel and Judah. 6. The war was heavy on the people, and they² sold the cattle. 7. I am the man whom you sold into Egypt.³ 8. God saw what he had made, and behold it was very good.

9. וּבַיּוֹם הַהוּא כָּתַבְתִּי אֶת־הַסֵּפֶר׃

And ⁴in that day⁴ I wrote the book.

10. מֹשֶׁה וּמִרְיָם׃   Moses and Miriam.

11. יוֹם ⁵וָלַיְלָה׃   Day and night.

¹ The second clause in this sentence has the value of a circumstantial clause, so that it may be translated as " *while the famine was on the land* ".

² This use of the pronoun הֵם which refers to the people just mentioned, and not to others, is not normal Hebrew usage. It has to be used at this stage because it is not possible to use simply וּמָכְרוּ and translate that as " and they sold ". This is dealt with in § 20.

³ The form of מִצְרַ֫יְמָה, of which the pausal form appears here in the Grammar, is explained in § 14, 5 ; meantime it should be noted that the termination הָ denotes *motion towards* and does not carry the tone.

4-4 The form בַּיּוֹם comes in here prematurely in the Grammar (cf. § 12), but the same meaning is gained by the use of הַיּוֹם which will be used in place of it in later editions.

5 וְלַיְלָה is the pausal form of וְלַ֫יְלָה; the *qāmeṣ* is pre-tonic (cf. § 11.II.(e)).

B.

1 אָמַ֫רְתִּי אֶל־הָאִישׁ: 2 יָשְׁבוּ ¹הַיּוֹם ¹הַשְּׁבִיעִי¹: 3 צָעַ֫קְנוּ
אֶל־אֱלֹהִים וְהוּא שָׁמַע ²אֹתָ֫נוּ: 4 מָחָה אֱלֹהִים ³אָדָם וּבְהֵמָה³
עַל־²הָאָ֫רֶץ: 5 עַם ⁴וָמֶ֫לֶךְ 6 מִי שָׁפַךְ אֶת־הַמַּ֫יִם עַל־
²הָאָ֫רֶץ: 7 אָמַ֫רְתָּ קָדוֹשׁ יהוה: 8 לַ֫יְלָה ⁴וָבֹ֫קֶר: 9 ⁵שָׁפַטְתָּ
אֶת־הָעָם הַזֶּה: 10 יָשַׁ֫בְנוּ עַל־הַיַּבָּשָׁה ⁶וְשָׁם שָׁבַ֫תְנוּ מְעַט:
11 ⁷אֶת־הַבְּהֵמָה אֲשֶׁר מָכַר דָּוִד לָקַח הַיֶּ֫לֶד אֶל־הָעִיר⁷:
12 בָּרָא אֱלֹהִים אֶת־הַיּוֹם וְאֶת־²הַלַּ֫יְלָה: 13 רָאָה הַמֶּ֫לֶךְ
⁸אֶת־אֲשֶׁר ⁹עָשָׂה וְהוּא טוֹב מְאֹד:

1-1 This is an adequate way of expressing in Hebrew *on the seventh day*, but *on* can be, and often is, explicitly expressed by the preposition בְּ (§ 12.1).

2 Students should not attempt as yet to use *sillûq* in their English–Hebrew exercises ; but they should study the note following the Exercise in the Grammar and observe the examples of its use in the Hebrew–English Exercises in the Grammar. Where phrases, and not full sentences, are used in these Exercises, pausal accents and vowels are not used.

3-3 This is a simple rendering of *man and cattle* ; another mode of translation may be found in § 12.4.(g).

אָדָם commonly means *humanity*, man in general, although there are occasional cases of its use with reference to an individual ; אִישׁ is the common word for an individual man and for man as distinct from woman (אִשָּׁה).

⁴ For the *qāmeṣ*, not *šûreq*, with וּ before a labial under the tone, cf. § 11.II.(e).

⁵ שָׁפַט *to judge* may mean also *to rule*, and so can fittingly be used here with a direct object. Another possible verb is מָשַׁל (cf. Voc. § 12) but its construction is different.

⁶ The adverb שָׁם is read here immediately after the conjunction וְ and before the verb for the reason given in note 2 of Key § 11A.

⁷⁻⁷ The unusual order of the parts of this sentence, with the direct object of the verb of the main clause placed first, is used to emphasize the fact that it was cattle which David had sold that the boy took into the city.

⁸ § 10.4.(c) speaks of the use of אֲשֶׁר as a correlative : *he who*, *him who*, etc. This is an example of its correlative use with the meaning *him who*, in which it is governed, in its value as antecedent, by רָאָה and is construed with אֶת־ (cf. § 9.4.(a)).

⁹ Note the *qāmeṣ* in this verb with final ה. That is because the final syllable is open, ה having no consonantal value (cf. § 7.6.(b).i). A final ה which has consonantal value is written with *mappîq* : הּ (cf. § 6.8.).

§ 12.
A.

1. God called¹ the light day, and the darkness he called night. 2. God rested on the seventh day from the work which he had done. 3. The man² heard the voice in the garden. 4. The king ruled over the people. 5. The boy dwelt³ in this place. 6. Yahweh blotted out⁴ all that he had made, both man and beast. 7. God made man ⁵out of dust⁵ from the ground. 8. God is in the temple. 9. They shed blood like water.⁶ 10. You burned the temple with fire. 11. ⁷In the days of⁷ David the king. 12. The people, small

and great, fled from the land. 13. Because of[8] the rumour which they had heard they fled[9] from the place.

14. נָתַן אֶת־הַחֶרֶב לַמֶּלֶךְ׃   He gave the sword to the king.

15. כָּתַב הַיֶּלֶד בַּסֵּפֶר׃   The boy wrote in the book.[10]

[1] קָרָא can be used intransitively, meaning *to call, to cry, to cry out*; transitively, meaning *to announce* (e.g. news), *to invite* (*sci.* a person). When קָרָא is used with the meaning *to name* two constructions are possible : (*a*) a direct object and the actual name in apposition, e.g. they called the name (שֵׁם) of the man Jacob.   The Hebrew for that : קָרְאוּ אֶת־שֵׁם הָאִישׁ יַעֲקֹב will be understood when § 14 is reached ; (*b*) with לְ as here : God named the light day.

[2] *The man*, i.e. in the Genesis story, the first man Adam. Without the article, אָדָם is sometimes used as the proper name Adam (cf. Gen. 4.25 ; 5.1).

[3] or *sat*.

[4] מָחָה is suitably rendered as *to blot out, to wipe out*, and has a stronger meaning than some other verbs which mean *to destroy*.

[5-5] In the Hebrew *man* and *dust* are in apposition and there is no word (such as מִן) for *out of*. In such a case the nearer object is usually definite (here אֶת־הָאָדָם) and the more remote (עָפָר) indefinite.

[6] Hebrew uses the generic article in such a case as this : *like water* ; cf. § 12.2.(b).i.

[7-7] בִּימֵי *in the days of* may be learned by sight ; *the form of it* cannot be understood until § 14 is reached ; but the reader will have noted that it is incidentally used in § 12.1.(b).

[8] מִן here does not mean simply *from*, either of time or place ; its use is illustrated in § 12.4.(d).

[9] Nothing in the translation corresponds to לָהֶם in the Hebrew. לָהֶם is a good example of *Dativus Commodi*, Dative of Advantage (§ 12.2.(c).i). It makes the meaning of the sentence *they fled for themselves*, i.e. for their own safety.

10 In Exod. 17.14 where a somewhat similar thing is said, בַּסֵּ֫פֶר is written as here with the definite article, but the translation is *in a book*. This use of the article is found in the first mention, for example, of a book, hitherto unknown, which is to be used for a special purpose or of something which later became important and well known (cf. G.K. § 126. q–s).

B.

1 לָאָֽרִי : 2 נָתַן אֱלֹהִים אֶת־הָאִשָּׁה לָאִישׁ ¹לְאִשָּׁה :

3 בַּבֹּ֫קֶר : 4 בַּשָּׁמַ֫יִם הָאֵ֫לֶּה : 5 בָּאָֽרֶץ : 6 בַּיּוֹם הַהוּא :

7 בְּהֵיכַל הָרָם : 8 קָרָא הָאָֽרִי ²כַּחֲמוֹר : 9 קָרָא אֱלֹהִים

לָרָקִ֫יעַ שָׁמַ֫יִם וְלַיַּבָּשָׁה קָרָא אָ֫רֶץ : 10 הָֽאָדָם עָפָר מִן־

³הָֽאֲדָמָה : 11 אָכַל מִן־הָעֵץ : 12 שָׁבַת הָעָם הֶחָכָם בַּיּוֹם

הַשְּׁבִיעִי : 13 לֶֽעָפָר : 14 בְּהַר הָרָם : 15 ⁴קָרָא זֶה אֶל־זֶה

וְאָמַר⁴ טוֹב יהוה : 16 אָכַל הָעָם ⁵מִצַּדִּיק וְעַד־רָשָׁע⁵ עַל־

הֶהָרִים וְהָרָעָב בָּאָֽרֶץ : 17 שָׁפַךְ אֶת־הַדָּם עַל־הָאָ֫רֶץ

⁶כַּמָּ֫יִם :

¹ This is idiomatic Hebrew, lit. *for wife*, or *as wife*, cf. I will be your God (לָכֶם לֵאלֹהִים) and you will be my people (לִי לְעָם).

² In such a comparison Hebrew commonly uses the generic article (cf. § 12.2.(b).i). The form כַּחֲמוֹר can be construed as having the article or as without it ; Hebrew usage argues for the article.

³ Obviously the whole point of what is said in this sentence would be lost if הָאָ֫רֶץ were used in place of הָֽאֲדָמָה for *the ground*.

[4-4] For the first part of this sentence in Hebrew, cf. § 10.5 ; the plur. form קְרָאוּ may be used as an alternative to the sing. קָרָא. For the use of וְאָמַר (or וְאָמְרוּ if קְרָאוּ is used in the first part), cf. note 6–6 in § 10A of the Key.

[5-5] An alternative rendering would be גַּם צַדִּיק וְגַם רָשָׁע.

[6] A form with the generic article (§ 12.2.(b).i).

§ 13.

A.

1. These are the scraggy[1] cattle which the king saw in the city. 2. Man ruled[2] over the beasts.[3] 3. Those are the princes and the mighty men whom the king set over the people. 4. I said to this people : " You are righteous ".[4] 5. These mountains are very high. 6. Thou hast counted the stars. 7. How high those palaces are in the city ! 8. The king saw that[5] the words which the righteous prince spoke[6] to the people were wise.[7] 9. Good are the songs which I heard in the temple. 10. Haughty[8] eyes, deaf ears and hands which [9]have shed[9] blood.

11. רָאָה הַמֶּלֶךְ בַּחֲלוֹם אֶת־הַפָּרוֹת הַטֹּבוֹת עַל־הַהֵיכָל:

The king saw [10]in a dream[10] the fine[11] cattle by[12] the temple.

12. זָכַר יהוה כִּי עָפָר אֲנָחְנוּ:

Yahweh remembers[13] that we are dust.

[1] רַע, fem. רָעָה (cf. § 9, note (i) to the Voc., and Key § 10A, note 1) obviously does not mean *morally bad* here, but in bad condition physically, i.e. *scraggy, emaciated* (cf. § 9, note (ii) following the vocabulary).

[2] מָשַׁל probably should be given no time reference in this verse, so that the appropriate translation would be *rules*. This use of the perfect is dealt with in § 43.I.2.

[3] בְּהֵמָה is commonly, as here, a collective singular. It signifies beasts as distinct from man, and domesticated animals, cattle, as distinct from wild beasts.

[4] צַדִּיק can mean *in the right* before the law, i.e. blameless, innocent, or *righteous* in the sense of doing what is right as prescribed in the law.

[5] כִּי is a conjunction which has a variety of uses of which only two need be noted now : (*a*) *for, because*, introducing a principal clause ; (*b*) *that*, introducing a noun clause.

[6] or *had spoken*.

[7] In actual fact the adjective חָכָם is used only of persons in the Old Testament and is not used of the words which they spoke, whereas English employs both these uses of the word *wise*.

[8] Literally *high*, but here not in that primary sense but in the obviously related, derivative sense of *proud, haughty*. Note in this sentence the association of dual nominal forms with plural adjectives and verbal forms : cf. § 13.6.(b).

[9–9] or *shed*.

[10] or *in the dream*.

[11] That is, cattle in good condition (cf. note 1 above).

[12] עַל־ can mean *beside, by* as well as *upon*.

[13] not *remembered* in this case (cf. note 2 above).

B.

זָכַרְתִּי אֶת־יהַשִּׁירִים אֲשֶׁר שָׁמַעְתִּי בַּהֵיכָל : 2 הַשָּׁמַיִם 1

הָהֵם רָמִים מְאֹד : 3 אֵלֶּה הַחֲמוֹרִים אֲשֶׁר הֲרָגְוּ : 4 מִי

²הַשָּׂרִים וְהַגִּבּוֹרִים הָאֵלֶּה² : 5 שָׁמַעְתָּ אֶת־הַפָּרוֹת : 6 ³זָכַר

אֱלֹהִים אֶת־הַצַּדִּיקִים : 7 יָשְׁבוּ ⁴עַל־הֶהָרִים⁴ יוֹמַיִם : 8 ⁵לֶחֶם

אָכַל וּמַיִם שָׁתָה⁵ : 9 הַצַּדִּיקִים כַּכּוֹכָבִים אֲשֶׁר ⁶בָּרָקִיעַ⁶ :

10 לָקַח ⁷פָּרִים וּפָרוֹת וְסוּסִים וַחֲמוֹרִים : 11 סָפַרְתִּי אֶת־

הַכּוֹכָבִים אֲשֶׁר נָתַן אֱלֹהִים בַּשָּׁמַיִם : 12 מַיִם ⁸מֵהַבְּאָרוֹת :

13 נָתַן־לִי אֱלֹהִים שִׁיר חָדָשׁ: 14 שָׁפַכְתְּ דָּמִים: 15 יוֹמַיִם
שָׁבַתְנוּ בַּהֵיכָל וְשָׁם זָכַרְנוּ אֶת־הַטּוֹב אֲשֶׁר עָשָׂה לָנוּ
אֱלֹהִים:

¹ The masc. שִׁיר is much commoner than the fem. שִׁירָה.

²⁻² Or הָאֵלֶּה may be read after הַשָּׁרִים; cf. Deut. 10.21 הוּא תְהִלָּתְךָ
וְהוּא אֱלֹהֶיךָ אֲשֶׁר עָשָׂה אִתְּךָ אֶת־הַגְּדֹלֹת וְאֶת־הַנּוֹרָאֹת הָאֵלֶּה *he is
thy praise and he is thy God who has done with thee these great and terrible
things*; Deut. 26.16 יהוה אֱלֹהֶיךָ מְצַוְּךָ לַעֲשׂוֹת אֶת־הַחֻקִּים הָאֵלֶּה
וְאֶת־הַמִּשְׁפָּטִים *Yahweh thy God commands thee to practise these regulations
and rules.*

³ Cf. sentence 12 Hebrew–English above.

⁴⁻⁴ *or* בֶּהָרִים.

⁵⁻⁵ The usual order of the verbal sentence is verb, subject, object
(cf. § 9.1); the changed order here is adopted for emphasis; cf. אֹתִי
אֹתִי זְכַרְתֶּם *me, me, you have remembered*; וְאֶת־קֹלוֹ שָׁמַעְנוּ *and his
voice we heard.*

⁶ In בָּרָקִיעַ, קִיעַ is the final syllable, the *pathah* being only *pathah*
furtive; thus *methegh* is normally placed.

⁷ The nouns in this sentence, being indefinite, have no אֶת־ before
them, since it is used only with definite objects directly governed by an
active verb (cf. § 9.4.(a)).

⁸ בְּאֵר is an example of a feminine noun which does not have the
feminine ending in the singular but assumes it in the plural (cf. § 13.5.(f)).

⁹ Or הַטֹּבוֹת.

§ 14.
A.

1. The law of Yahweh is good for man, and the spirit of God
is powerful for¹ salvation. 2. Yahweh counts² the stars³ of

heaven, and also he knows[2] all the earth. 3. The poor of the people are righteous. 4. We have not kept the law of Yahweh, the God of Israel. 5. The prince did according to the king's command. 6. And in the law of Yahweh thou hast not walked. 7. These are the commands of the God of all[4] the earth which I have written [5]this day[5]. 8. [6]In the days of[6] King David all the people kept the law of Yahweh and the poor trusted in him.[7] 9. There came a great army from the four winds of the heavens. 10. We ate of every tree of the garden. 11. [8]Now the queen of the land was the daughter of [9]a valiant warrior[9]. 12. There was a famine in the land, [10]and Abram went down[10] to Egypt for the famine was severe in the land.

13. תּוֹרַת יהוה טוֹבָה׃   The law of Yahweh is good.

14. בַּיּוֹם הַהוּא עָשָׂה יהוה יְשׁוּעָה [11]בְּיִשְׂרָאֵל׃

In that day Yahweh wrought salvation in Israel.

[1] The use of אֶל־ here is very suitable, since it indicates direction and goal. As a former generation expressed it, the spirit of God is " effective unto salvation ".

[2] For the use of the present tense here, cf. Key § 13A, note 2.

[3] Note the printer's error of a composite sheᵉwa instead of a simple one after the second כ. A simple sheᵉwa is used in the 26th edition of the Grammar.

[4] The phrase *the God of all the earth* is a closely knit one, with the result that no *daghesh lene* is written in the כ of the word כָּל־ owing to the vocalic ending of the preceding word אֱלֹהֵי with which it is in close liaison. The whole phrase is a rhythmic unit. Cf. אֱלֹהֵי פְלִשְׁתִּים *the gods of the Philistines* ; כְּלֵי כֶסֶף vessels of silver. The omission of *daghesh lene* in such cases is not universal (the determining influence was how the passage in which any particular example occurs was meant to be read, and that was indicated by the accents ; cf. § 47) ; but the omission takes place in most cases and the student should follow this practice.

[5-5] הַיּוֹם would also meet the need, since it means *today* as well as *the day*.

6–6 The plural of יוֹם *day* is shown in § 14.5 ; it is יָמִים of which the construct is יְמֵי (cf. § 14.4, rule 2). Note what happens when יְמֵי is preceded by the preposition בְּ : בְּיְמֵי > בִּיְמֵי (because two vocal sheʷas cannot stand together) > בִּימֵי (because the י loses consonantal value in such a position and becomes vocalic ; in other words, it quiesces ; cf. § 12.1.(b)).

7 No *daghesh lene* in the ב of בוֹ because the word is closely associated with the preceding verb בָּטְחוּ (cf. note 4 above).

8 This translation illustrates the fact that the Hebrew וְ is not always to be rendered into English by *and*. Various relationships and shades of meaning are expressed by it, such as may be indicated by *now, then, but, or, nevertheless, so, therefore* and so on.

9–9 גִּבּוֹר חַיִל is *a fighting man, a valiant hero*. חַיִל can mean (a) *army, force* ; (b) *strength* ; (c) *efficiency, valour* ; (d) *wealth* ; (e) *moral worth, excellence of character*. The orthodox doctrine in ancient Israel for a long time was that the good man received God's blessing and prospered ; so we can understand how חַיִל could have the meanings (d) and (e). An אִישׁ חַיִל was a leader in the community in peace and in war. The term גִּבּוֹר in place of אִישׁ emphasizes the warlike qualities.

10–10 The normal rendering of וְאַבְרָם יָרַד would be : *but Abraham had gone down*. The usual way in Hebrew of rendering *and (in consequence) Abram went down* will be explained in § 20.

11 Probably the *daghesh lene* should be inserted in the first consonant in this case because the attachment of בְּיִשְׂרָאֵל to the preceding words עָשָׂה יהוה יְשׁוּעָה is not close.

B.

1 יוֹם יהוה הַגָּדוֹל : 2 גָּדוֹל יוֹם יהוה : 3 מַלְכַּת הָאָרֶץ

¹הַטּוֹבָה : 4 כָּל־עַם הָאָרֶץ : 5 כָּל־חֲמוֹרֵי הַמֶּלֶךְ ²הַטּוֹבִים :

‎6 רָאָה ³הַשַּׂר אֶת־כָּל־גִּבּוֹרֵי הַחַיִל וְאֶת־כָּל־עַם הַמִּלְחָמָה:

‎7 הָלַכְתִּי צָפוֹנָה: 8 יָרַדְנוּ שְׁאוֹלָה: 9 הָלַךְ הָהָרָה: 10 הָרַגְנוּ

אֶת־חֲמוֹר הָאִישׁ: 11 לֹא שָׁתָה הָעָם מִמֵּי ⁴הַיְאֹר כִּי ⁵דָם

הֵם: 12 לֹא שְׁמַרְתֶּם אֶת־⁶מִצְוֹת אֱלֹהֵי כָל־הָאָרֶץ: 13 אֱלֹהֵי

הָאָרֶץ וֵאלֹהֵי ⁷הָרוּחֹת ⁸לְכָל־בָּשָׂר: 14 שָׁמַרְתָּ אֶת־אֶבְיוֹנֵי

הָאָרֶץ מִכָּל־רָע: 15 אָכַלְתָּ מֵעֵץ הַגָּן: 16 שָׁמַע הַנָּבִיא אֶת־

דְּבַר יהוה בַּהֵיכָל וְשָׁם יָשַׁב וְלֹא הָלַךְ בֵּיתָה: 17 בְּנֵי הַמֶּלֶךְ

‎⁹וּבְנוֹתָיו לֻקְּחוּ ¹⁰אֶת־הַמַּטָּן אֶל־אִישׁ הָאֱלֹהִים וְהוּא נָטָה

אֶת־¹¹יָדָיו הַשָּׁמַיְמָה וְלָעָם נָתַן תּוֹרָה מֵאֱלֹהֵי כָל־הָאָרֶץ:

---

[1] The Hebrew of this sentence can also be translated : *The queen of the good land.* If it is desired to express clearly the sense given in the Grammar, all ambiguity can be removed by reading הַמַּלְכָּה הַטּוֹבָה לָאָרֶץ lit. *the good queen belonging to the land.*

[2] In this example there can be no question concerning the noun to which הַטּוֹבִים is related, since the one noun (הַמֶּלֶךְ) is singular and the other (חֲמוֹרֵי) is plural. Note § 14.4, rule 3.

[3] שַׂר retains *pathaḥ* with the article, whereas פַּר *ox* takes *qāmeṣ* (הַשָּׂר, הַפָּר ; cf. § 13, p. 62, footnote to first part of Voc.). שַׂר can mean *prince*, or *captain, commander, officer.*

[4] יְאֹר *river* is commonly used specifically of the Nile. For the omission of the *daghesh forte* in the י, cf. § 6.5.

[5] Notice the *daghesh lene* in דָם in spite of the vocalic ending of the preceding כִּי. This may well mean that the three short words of the final clause were not read as a flowing, closely-knit unit, but that, for emphasis,

each word was sharply and separately enunciated. Cf., on the other hand, the elision of the *daghesh lene* in כָּל־ in the next sentence where it occurs in a closely-knit phrase ; see note 4 in Section A above.

[6] Normally written thus and not מִצְוֹת (sing. מִצְוָה) ; cf. § 2.7.(c).

[7] רוּחֹת and רְחוֹת are both found ; cf. § 2.7.(d).

[8] This is how the phrase occurs in the Old Testament, but it is possible to write כָּל־הַבָּשָׂר (instead of לְכָל־בָּשָׂר) with the constr. רוּחֹת preceding it.

[9] The form required is to be found in § 14.4, rule 2. It has not yet been explained ; it can be noted at present by sight and the explanation will follow in § 16.

[10] This renders *the gift*, not *their gift* (so in the 25th edition of the Grammar), for which the student is not yet ready.

[11] His hands is יָדָיו. This form has been called for prematurely (cf. § 16.2, 3.(a).iv). In the 26th edition of the Grammar this Hebrew word will be supplied in a footnote.

§ 15.
A.

abs. sing.	cstr. sing.	abs. plur.	cstr. plur.
זָכָר	[1]זְכַר	זְכָרִים	[1]זִכְרֵי
דָּבָר	דְּבַר	דְּבָרִים	דִּבְרֵי
מָשָׁל	מְשַׁל	מְשָׁלִים	מִשְׁלֵי
כָּבֵד	כְּבֵד and כְּבַד	כְּבֵדִים	כִּבְדֵי
קָדוֹשׁ	קְדוֹשׁ	קְדֹשִׁים	קְדֹשֵׁי
[1]קָצֵר	קְצַר	[1]קְצֵרִים	קִצְרֵי
מָאוֹר	מְאוֹר	[2]מְאוֹרֹת	[3]מְאוֹרֵי

נָבִיא	¹נְבִיא	⁴נְבִיאִים	נְבִיאֵי
בָּרִיא	¹בְּרִיא	⁵בְּרִאִים	בְּרִיאֵי
תָּמִים	תְּמִים	⁶תְּמִימִים	תְּמִימֵי
שָׂפָה	שְׂפַת	שְׂפָתַיִם (dual)	שִׂפְתֵי (dual)
בְּרָכָה	⁷בִּרְכַּת	בְּרָכוֹת	בִּרְכוֹת
נְקָמָה	נִקְמַת	נְקָמוֹת	³נִקְמוֹת
נְבֵלָה	נִבְלַת	⁸נְבֵלוֹת	⁸נִבְלוֹת

¹ Not found.

² So Gen. 1.15 ; מְאֹרֹת in Gen. 1.14,16.

³ This is the only form of the cstr. plur. which occurs (Ezek. 32.8) ; the implication probably is that both plural forms, masc. and fem., were used.

⁴ Much commoner than נְבִאִים.

⁵ So 1 Kings 5.3 (E.V. 4.23).

⁶ Also written תְּמִימִם.

⁷ Note this form with the *daghesh lene* in the *kaph*.

⁸ Not found. The sing. can be used in a collective sense : *e.g.* Isa. 5.25 נִבְלָתָם *their dead bodies*.

B.

בְּרִיאוֹת abs. or cstr. plur. fem. of בָּרִיא *fat*.

נְבִיאֵי cstr. plur. of נָבִיא *prophet*.

יִשְׁרֵי cstr. plur. masc. of יָשָׁר *upright*.

רְקִיעַ cstr. sing. of רָקִיעַ *firmament*.

לְבָבוֹת abs. plur. of לֵבָב *heart*.

מְאוֹר cstr. sing. of מָאוֹר *luminary.*

מִשְׁלֵי cstr. plur. of מָשָׁל *proverb.*

כְּבַד cstr. sing. masc. of כָּבֵד *heavy.*

לְבַב cstr. sing. of לֵבָב *heart.*

שִׂפְתֵי cstr. dual of שָׂפָה *lip.*

נִקְמַת cstr. sing. of נְקָמָה *vengeance.*

בִּרְכוֹת cstr. plur. of בְּרָכָה *blessing.*

יָדַיִם abs. dual of יָד *hand.*

C.

1. And darkness was upon the surface of the waters. 2. The prophet wrote all the words in the[1] book. 3. [2]The word of Yahweh came[2] to the prophets. 4. The law of Yahweh is in the heart of the righteous. 5. I wrote for this people all the words of the law of Yahweh. 6. None[3] of the elders of Israel was there. 7. God set [4]the two great luminaries[4] in the firmament of heaven. 8. The prince gathered an army, numerous[5] as the stars of heaven or as the [grains of] sand on the seashore.[6] 9. Isaac said : " The voice is the voice of Jacob, but[7] the hands are the hands of Esau." 10. The old prophet lifted the corpse of the man of God [8]on to[8] the ass. 11. The righteousness of Yahweh [9]our God[9] is very great [10]to the broken-hearted[10].

12. כְּבַד לָשׁוֹן אָנֹכִי:

I am heavy of tongue (i.e. slow of speech).

13. קָרָא הֶחָכָם בְּסֵפֶר תּוֹרַת הָאֱלֹהִים:

The wise man read in the book of the law of God.

---

[1] Or *in a book.* Cf. § 12A, note 10, in the Key.

[2-2] The absence of *daghesh lene* from the ד in דְּבַר is owing to the close association of the word with the preceding הָיָה whose final syllable is open, the ה having no consonantal value (cf. § 6.8 and Key § 14A, notes 4 and 7). הָיָה *happened* (to), *occurred* (to) may be rendered suitably as *came* (to).

[3] אִישׁ ... לֹא is a Hebrew way of expressing *no, none*, in a verbal sentence. The point to note is that the negative is used with the verb in Hebrew, whereas in English it is used commonly with the subject or object as the case may be. *Heb. There-was-not one of the elders of Israel there*, i.e. *none of the elders of Israel was there*. (Cf. § 10.5).

[4-4] lit. *the two of the luminaries, the great ones*, i.e. *the two great luminaries*, not *two of the great luminaries* which would appear in Hebrew as שְׁנַיִם מִן־הַמְּאֹרוֹת הַגְּדֹלִים. (This use of מִן in Hebrew is the usual way of defining a part of a greater whole.)

[5] כָּבֵד *heavy*, when used of property and possessions, can mean *much, rich* or as here, *numerous* ; cf. מִקְנֶה כָּבֵד מְאֹד *very much cattle*.

[6] lit. *the lip of the sea.*

[7] The connective וְ is not always to be rendered by *and* in English. In this sentence the contrast between the two clauses demands the rendering *but*, cf. § 14A, note 8, in the Key.

[8-8] lit. *to*. But אֶל־ here has the value of both אֶל־ and עַל־. The full meaning is that the prophet carried the corpse to the ass and laid it upon the ass.

[9-9] The Hebrew form אֱלֹהֵינוּ *our God*, which has a pronominal suffix (cf. § 16) is used prematurely here. In its place אֱלֹהֵי יִשְׂרָאֵל will be used when the Grammar is reprinted.

[10-10] נִשְׁבָּר is a passive ptc. of the verb שָׁבַר *to break* ; cf. § 22. לֵב *heart* is a short form of לֵבָב (cf. § 40.6.(a)). Note the absence of the article with לֵב ; this is a usage frequently found in poetic style.

D.

1 תּוֹרַת יהוה יתְּמִימָה: 2 רָאָה הַמֶּלֶךְ אֶת־הַפָּרוֹת הַבְּרִיאוֹת עַל־שְׂפַת הַיְאֹר: 3 ²אֲכַלְתֶּם בְּשַׂר פָּרִים בְּרִיאִים²: 4 יְשָׁרִים דִּבְרֵי שִׂפְתֵי יהוה: 5 לֹא אִישׁ דְּבָרִים

אָנֹכִי : 6 טוֹבִים דִּבְרֵי תוֹרַת יהוה : 7 הַמַּיִם עַל־פְּנֵי הָאֲדָמָה

8 שָׁמַעְנוּ אֶת־³דִּבְרֵי נְבִיאֵי אֱלֹהֵי כָל־הָאָרֶץ³ : 9 שָׁמַרְתָּ

אֶת־⁴לְבַב הָעָם הַזֶּה ⁵מֵרַע : 10 גְּדֹלוֹת מְאֹד צִדְקוֹת אֱלֹהִים:

11 בְּרוּכִים יִשְׁרֵי ⁶לֵבָב : 12 גְּדוֹלָה ⁷נִקְמַת הָעָם⁷ : 13 תְּמִימִים

מִשְׁלֵי הַמֶּלֶךְ הֶחָכָם : 14 מָחָה אֶת־כָּל־⁸דְּגַת הַיְאֹר :

15 ⁹חֲכָמִים מְאֹד מִשְׁלֵי הַמֶּלֶךְ הַזָּקֵן :

<hr/>

¹ תְּמִימָה fem. of תָּמִים is from the root תָּמַם. Another form of the masc. adjective is in use, תָּם, but it is of a different type from such nouns as יָד and דָּם. The fem. of תָּם is תַּמָּה (the *daghesh forte* being due to the root תָּמַם), but this, and related forms of this type, will be dealt with at a later stage (cf. § 40).

²⁻² Three points should be noted in this sentence : (i) according to § 7.1.(a) and (b), a guttural takes a composite sheʷa instead of simple sheʷa vocal ; א in this case commonly takes ֲ, but may take ֱ, as in אֲכַלְתֶּם, when it is removed from the tone ; (ii) בְּרִיאִם or בְּרָאִים (cf. § 2.7.(d)) ; (iii) *the flesh of fat oxen* seems to raise the question of whether the phrase is to be regarded as definite or indefinite. The genitive *fat oxen* is indefinite and may be taken as determinative in this case.

³⁻³ The object in this sentence illustrates a series of nouns in the cstr. state before the final noun (הָאָרֶץ) in the absolute. The whole phrase is made definite by the noun in the absolute.

⁴ Two points are to be noted here ; (*a*) לְבַב or לֵב may be used. But, as in the case of תָּמִים and תָּם above (note 1), the noun לֵב belongs to the type of nouns dealt with in § 40 ; (*b*) Hebrew uses the sing. *heart* where English uses the plur.

c

⁵ מֵרַע *from evil*; but מֵרָעָה would also be possible. The explanation of the fem. form רָעָה from the masc. רַע (from the root רעע) will be given in § 40.

⁶ In the phrase יִשְׁרֵי לֵבָב (*or* יִשְׁרֵי לֵב) *the upright of heart* we would expect, according to the rules, הַלֵּבָב (*or* הַלֵּב); cf. Key § 15C, note 10–10.

⁷⁻⁷ In נִקְמַת הָעָם the genitive can be a subjective one (*the vengeance taken by the people, sci. on others*) or objective (*the vengeance taken on the people*).

⁸ דְּגַת is the cstr. form of the collective sing. דָּגָה; but דְּגֵי, the cstr. plur. of דָּג, would serve the purpose here equally well.

⁹ For the use of חָכָם in this sentence, cf. Key § 13A, note 7.

§ 16.

A.

His law; his lips; thy (m.) blessings; thy (m.) sons; your (m.) proverbs; her place; from my flesh; your (m.) flesh; before me; before thee (f.); thy (m.) lips; our sons; our heart; their (m.) sons; my hands; his hand; their (m.) law; their (f.) hands.

B.

1. Lot went out to the men at the doorway¹ and shut² the door behind him. 2. He is Yahweh our God; in all the earth are his judgments. 3. He ever remembers³ his covenant which he made with⁴ Abraham. 4. The love of Yahweh is from everlasting to everlasting upon those who fear him,⁵ and his righteousness to children's children. 5. As for me,⁶ in thee have I trusted,⁷ O Yahweh; I have said: "Thou art my God". 6. They passed before the ark of the covenant into the Jordan, and the people picked up stones from the Jordan for a memorial. 7. I made my covenant with this people, and from year to year I have gone before them to this day. 8. They went out from the king's presence, ⁸the men of war following behind them.⁸

9. ‏שָׁמַע יהוה אֱלֹהֵינוּ אֶת־תְּפִלָּתֵנוּ‎:

Yahweh our God has heard our prayer.

10. ‏יָרַד אֶל־בָּנָיו ¹⁰שְׁאוֹלָה‎:

He went down to Sheol to his sons.

¹ Heb. lit. *to the doorway*. For the ending ‏ה‎ *He Locale*, cf. § 14.5. Note that ‏פֶּתַח‎ means *entrance, doorway* (the verb ‏פָּתַח‎ means *to open*), while ‏דֶּלֶת‎ is the *door* which closes the *entrance* or *doorway*.

² The order of obj.-verb normally means that an emphasis on the object is intended. That is not so here. The reason for this order is that we have not yet reached the section (§ 20) which explains the common verbal usage in narrative sequence in Hebrew.

³ The translation : " *He has remembered for ever* " is possible, although obviously stilted (cf. § 19.2.(c)).

⁴ The fact that ‏אֶת־‎ is used both as a sign of the def. accus. and as a preposition meaning *with* may appear confusing to the learner, but there is seldom any uncertainty on this account. ‏אֶת־‎ here is the preposition *with* and not the sign of the definite accusative. The object of the verb ‏כָּרַת‎ is the relative ‏אֲשֶׁר‎ which is related to, and gets its meaning from, the preceding noun ‏בְּרִיתוֹ‎.

⁵ ‏יְרֵאָיו‎ *his fearers*. ‏יָרֵא‎, as used here, is the Qal participle of the verb ‏יָרֵא‎ *to fear*. This participle is declined as a first declension noun ; hence the form with suffix ‏יְרֵאָיו‎ (cf. § 15.1). ‏חֶסֶד‎, which is found at the beginning of sentence 4, means more than *mercy* or *kindness*. It indicates a constant attitude of care and a close bond of association, so that *constant love* or *devotion* is a better rendering.

⁶ ‏וַאֲנִי‎ is for emphasis, the purpose being to define the subject at once before making the statement. This most commonly occurs when a contrast is being drawn, e.g. *You may do what you propose, but, as for me* (‏וַאֲנִי‎), *I will remain faithful*.

[7] בָּטַח is construed with עַל־, as here, in the sense of *to rest on, to rely on*, or with בְּ *to trust in, have confidence in*.

[8-8] This is a common Hebrew form for a circumstantial clause ; the Hebrew connective has no place in the English translation.

[9] In this sentence שמע could be pointed as imperative (שְׁמַע), to give the sense : *O Yahweh our God, hear our prayer*. The imperative will be dealt with when § 18 is reached.

[10] Cf. note 1 above.

C.

1 בִּרְכוֹתֵיכֶם : 2 נְבֵלָתָהּ : 3 מִצְוֹתַי : 4 [1]שְׂפָתֶיהָ : 5 דְּבָרֶיךָ :
6 פָּנָיו : פָּנֶיהָ : פָּנָי : 7 [2]וְאֶת־דְּבָרָיו שָׁמַעְנוּ [3]מִן־הָאֵשׁ :
8 תּוֹרָתְךָ בְּלִבָּבִי אֱלֹהָי : 9 שָׁמַעְתָּ אֶת־קוֹלִי מֵהֵיכָלֶךָ :
10 יָשַׁבְנוּ לְפָנֶיהָ : 11 דִּבְרֵי שְׂפָתֶיךָ כַּחוֹל אֲשֶׁר עַל־שְׂפַת
הַיָּם : 12 בָּא [4]וּבְיָדוֹ חֶרֶב[4] : 13 טוֹבִים מְאֹד מִשְׁלֵי שְׂפָתָיו :
14 אַתֶּם בָּנַי וּבְנוֹתַי אָמַר [5]אֱלֹהֵיכֶם : 15 לְבָבִי בְּתוֹרָתוֹ
[6]תָּמִיד : 16 שָׁמַרְתָּ אֶת־לְבָבָם : 17 לֹא שָׁמַרְנוּ אֶת־בְּרִית
אֱלֹהֵינוּ בְּכָל־[7]לְבָבֵנוּ : 18 שְׁמַרְתֶּם אֶת־תּוֹרָתִי וְאֶת־מִצְוֹתַי :
19 תּוֹרָתְךָ הַתְּמִימָה : 20 בְּכָל־נְבִיאָיו הַגְּדוֹלִים : 21 הָאֲנָשִׁים
אֲשֶׁר שָׁלַח [8]לָנוּ דָוִד מִן־הַמִּדְבָּר הֵם לְחוֹמָה עָלֵינוּ יוֹם
וָלָיְלָה : 22 שְׂמַחְתֶּם שָׁם לִפְנֵי יהוה בְּכָל־לְבַבְכֶם [9]אַתֶּם
וּנְבִיאֵיכֶם[9] :

[1] Dual (abs. שְׂפָתַיִם), not plural, in accordance with § 13.6.(a) ; § 16.2.(b), column 4 of Table of Nouns with pron. suffixes.

² Even when the object precedes the verb as here, for emphasis, אֶת־
may be used with the definite accusative ; cf. also אֶת־קוֹלְךָ שָׁמַעְתִּי *thy
voice I heard* ; but this use is not invariable. Sometimes, as in an example
in Deut. 4.36, אֶת־ is dispensed with.

³ מֵהָאֵשׁ or מִן־הָאֵשׁ.

⁴⁻⁴ Here is a very good example of a circumstantial clause ; lit. *and
in his hand a sword*. This literal translation of the clause is used in the
Grammar in order to enable the student to use the Hebrew idiom ; the
sentence may be freely expressed as : *He came armed with a sword*.

⁵ This form shows *methegh* in the open syllable second from the tone
(cf. § 9, note 2 following Exercise ; § 11, note following Exercise).

⁶ The ת in תָּמִיד may be written with or without *daghesh lene* here.
The fact that it has it means that, when the sentence was read, a slight
pause was made before תָּמִיד, so that it was given some emphasis. But
note the absence of *daghesh lene* from בְּתוֹרָתוֹ which is closely associated
with the preceding לְבָבִי.

⁷ In לְבָבֵנוּ the tone is on the penult, so that the *qāmeṣ* of לֵבָב remains
in the open pretonic syllable of לְבָבֵנוּ and the *ṣērê*, two places from the tone,
is reduced to vocal shᵉwa. Note how Hebrew says *our heart*, and not *our
hearts* (cf. לְבָבָם in sentence 16).

⁸ or אֵלֵינוּ.

⁹⁻⁹ *you and your prophets with you* is adequately translated as shown here.
It is possible, of course, to add a word for *with you*, both אִתְּכֶם and עִמָּכֶם
(§ 40.6.(b)) being available ; but their form and use have not yet been
dealt with.

§ 17.

A.

תִּזְכֹּרְנָה   2 or 3 plur. fem. impf. Qal of זָכַר.

תִּזְכְּרִי   2 sing. fem. impf. Qal of זָכַר.

תִּפְקְדוּ   2 plur. masc. impf. Qal of פָּקַד.

נִשְׁמֹר   1 plur. impf. Qal of שָׁמַר.

יִשְׁמְרוּ   3 plur. masc. impf. Qal of שָׁמַר.

תִּשְׁמֹר   2 sing. masc. or 3 sing. fem. impf. Qal of שָׁמַר.

אֶשְׁמֹר   1 sing. impf. Qal of שָׁמַר.

B.

1. You shall not keep their judgments.[1] 2. We ourselves will cut trees [2]from the mountain[2]. 3. The mighty men of valour will not pursue after thee again.[3] 4. In that day I will pour out my spirit on all flesh. 5. The men of war will pursue the people who went down to the city, and also shed their blood like water.[4] 6. Behold, [5]the two kings did not stand before him[5], and how shall we[6] stand ? 7. All that[7] thou writest in the book we shall keep with all our heart. 8. The old man leans[8] on the wall and he reads in the book of the law before the people while they listen to[9] him. 9. Samuel said to the people : "Whose[10] ox have I taken, or[11] whose ass have I taken, or[11] whom have I wronged, or[11] from whose hand have I accepted a bribe ?" 10. And all the people said : "Thou hast not wronged any man,[12] nor taken anything[12] from the hand of any man."

11. נִרְדֹּף אֶת־הָאֲנָשִׁים מִן־הַמִּדְבָּר [13]אֶל־הָהָרָה[13] וְשָׁם נִשְׁמֹר אֹתָם כִּי רְשָׁעִים מְאֹד הֵם:

We will pursue the men from the wilderness to the hill-country, and there we will keep[14] them, for they are very wicked.

12. יִכְרֹת יהוה לִפְנֵיכֶם אֶת־יְאֹר מִצְרָיִם:

Yahweh will divide before you the river of Egypt.

[1] Lit. *judgments*, but probably *customs* or *practices* would be a more suitable translation in this sentence ; cf. the note on מִשְׁפָּט following Voc. of § 18.

2–2 עֵץ is often used as a collective noun ; the plur. עֵצִים can mean *trees* or *pieces of wood, timber* ; cf. דָּם *blood* and דָּמִים *acts of bloodshed*, or *bloodguiltiness*. הַר, *mountain, hill,* can also mean *hill country*.

3 עוֹד can mean *again* or *still*, the first signifying repetition, the second continuance. In this sentence, therefore, it can be translated by *again* or by *any more, further*.

4 Note the generic article in Hebrew כַּמַּיִם, cf. § 12.2.(b).i.

5–5 לֹא עָמְדוּ לְפָנָיו can be translated in this way, but the meaning is not precisely given. *To stand before a person* commonly means *to present one-self before him* (e.g. to state, or plead, a case), or *to serve* or *to attend upon him* ; but in this sentence the meaning probably is *to stand before* in the sense of *to withstand, to stand up against, to resist*. For the translation *the two kings*, cf. § 15C, note 4, of the Key.

6 The subject here is picked out for emphasis ; hence the use of אֲנַחְנוּ ; cf. sentence 2 above.

7 In the phrase אֶת־כָּל־אֲשֶׁר, אֲשֶׁר is a compound relative, with the value of *that which* (cf. § 10.4.(c)). The syntax of the sentence is that אֶת־כָּל־, together with the substantive value *that* in אֲשֶׁר, is governed by נִשְׁמֹר, while the relative value *which* expressed by אֲשֶׁר is governed by תִּכְתֹּב.

8 The precise rendering given to the imperfects here depends on the context in which this verse is set. E.g., it might be : *the old man would* (or *used to*) *lean on the wall and read in the book of the law before the people while they listened to him.*

9 שָׁמַע governing an accus. means *to hear* ; שָׁמַע בְּ *to listen to, to obey* ; שָׁמַע אֶל־ *to listen to, to give heed to.*

10 *Whose ?* is sometimes rendered by לְמִי ; here מִי is in the genitive in its first two occurrences : *the ox of whom. . . . the ass of whom. . . .* i.e. *whose ox, whose ass.* Similarly later in the sentence : *from the hand of whom,* i.e. *from whose hand* (cf. § 10.3.(b)).

[11] וְ should be rendered as *or* rather than *and* here ; cf. Gen. 26.11 הַנֹּגֵעַ בָּאִישׁ הַזֶּה וּבְאִשְׁתּוֹ *he who touches this man or his wife* ; Exod. 21.17 מְקַלֵּל אָבִיו וְאִמּוֹ *he who curses his father or his mother*.

[12] This is another example of the way in which Hebrew negatives the verb, whereas the English usage is more often to negative the subject or object. The translation in the Key follows the Hebrew mode, but more idiomatic English would be : *Thou hast wronged no man nor accepted a gift from any.* מְאוּמָה is usually found after a negative, so that לֹא · · · מְאוּמָה means *nothing*.

[13] Note the double indication of direction, with אֶל־ and *He locale* ; cf. § 14.5.

[14] Not *keep* in the sense of *maintain*, but *guard, keep watch on*.

C.

1 אֶרְדֹּף אַחֲרֶיהָ : 2 יִשְׁפֹּט יהוה אֶת־הָעָם הַזֶּה : 3 תִּשְׁמְרוּ אֶת־מִצְוֹת אֱלֹהֵיכֶם בְּכָל־לְבַבְכֶם : 4 אֶת־מִצְוֹתָיו וְאֶת־ דְּבָרָיו נִשְׁמֹר : 5 יִשְׁמְרוּ בָנָיו אֶת־בְּרִיתוֹ : 6 [2]וַאֲנִי אֶדְרֹשׁ[2] אֶל־אֱלֹהִים : 7 יִשְׂרֹף אֶת־עִירְכֶם בָּאֵשׁ : 8 נִזְכֹּר אֶת־ [3]חֲסָדֶיךָ יהוה כִּי מֵעוֹלָם הֵם : 9 אָמַר לְזִקְנֵי הָעִיר [4]הָאֲנָשִׁים הָאֵלֶּה חֲכָמִים הֵם [5]וְיִשְׁרֵי לֵבָב : [6]יִשְׁמְרוּ אֶת־תּוֹרַת יהוה [7]וַאֲנַחְנוּ נִשְׁמֹר אֶת־בְּרִיתֵנוּ : 10 שָׁמַעְתִּי אֶת־תְּפִלַּתְכֶם : [8]הַכֹּהֵן יִשְׁמֹר אֶת־הָאֵשׁ עַל־הַמִּזְבֵּחַ [8]וְהָעָם יִזְכֹּר אֶת־תּוֹרָתִי : 11 מִי אֲנִי כִּי אֶשְׁפֹּט אֶת־הָעָם הַזֶּה [9]וּמַה כְּבוֹדִי[9] כִּי יִשְׁמְעוּ אֵלָי : 12 הַיּוֹם תִּזְכְּרוּ לִפְנֵי יהוה אֱלֹהֵיכֶם אֶת־כָּל־ [10]הַדְּבָרִים הַגְּדוֹלִים אֲשֶׁר עָשָׂה [11]לָכֶם בַּמִּדְבָּר וְלֹא תִשְׁכָּחוּ :

[1] Note the characteristic use of the Hebrew sing.; with all your *heart*.

[2-2] Note the use of the connective וְ here to translate *But*. It illustrates the fact that וְ is not always to be translated into English by *and*. Here, used with the personal pronoun אֲנִי, it points a contrast : (You may take your own way), *but* (, if I were in your position,) *I would seek unto God*. בָּקַשׁ (cf. § 23), which is not found in the Qal, is normally used in the sense of *to seek* or *to search for* something which has been lost. דָּרַשׁ means *to resort to* God or a shrine, *to consult* a priest, *to seek God in worship*; that is, it is commonly used in a religious sense. But occasionally בָּקַשׁ has this religious sense (cf. 2 Sam. 21.1); and there are some instances in which דָּרַשׁ means simply *to inquire about, to investigate* (cf. 2 Sam. 11.3). For the emphatic use of the 1st pers. pronoun here, cf. Job 5.8.

[3] In § 16, Hebrew-English Exercise, sentence 6, אֲבָנִים was used and interpreted as the plural of אֶבֶן, a type of noun not yet explained (cf. § 25). Similarly the plur. of חֶסֶד is חֲסָדִים (which is similar in form to First Declension plurals). The plural means acts of חֶסֶד, i.e. of *kindness, love, devotion* (cf. Key § 17B, note 2).

[4] For the form, cf. § 16, footnote 1 to the Exercise.

[5] For the absence of the article before לֵבָב, cf. Key § 15D, note 6.

[6] In Hebrew there would commonly be a connective before a verb like this, but no connective is used here because there are rules about narrative sequence which have to be learned before the *waw* is introduced immediately before verbal forms (cf. § 20).

[7] The use of אֲנַחְנוּ is justified here in the interests of emphasis.

[8] The order here of subj.-verb is used deliberately to distinguish sharply the subjects of the two clauses.

[9-9] *What is my honour?* means : *What honour or standing have I in the community?*

[10] It should be noted that דָּבָר means both *word* and *thing* or *act*.

[11] לָכֶם does not mean here what God did *to* the people in the wilderness (e.g. by way of punishment and discipline) but what he did *for* them. It is an example of *Dativus Commodi*; cf. § 12.2.(c).i.

§ 18.
A.

גָּנוֹב	infin. abs. Qal of גָּנַב.
לִשְׁמֹר	infin. cstr. Qal of שָׁמַר with prepos. לְ prefixed.
שִׁמְרוּ	plur. masc. imper. Qal of שָׁמַר.
שְׁמֹר	sing. masc. imper. Qal of שָׁמַר or infin. cstr.
גְּנוּבִים	plur. masc. abs. of passive ptc. Qal of גָּנַב.
תִּזְכְּרִי	2 sing. fem. impf. Qal of זָכַר.
זְכֹר	sing. masc. imper. Qal of זָכַר. or infin. cstr.
כֹּרְתִים	plur. masc. abs. of active ptc. Qal of כָּרַת.
דֹּרְשֵׁי	plur. masc. cstr. of active ptc. Qal of דָּרַשׁ.
רֹמֶשֶׂת	sing. fem. abs. or cstr. of active ptc. Qal of רָמַשׂ.

B.

1. Pursue after him. 2. I promised[1] to keep thy words. 3. The rulers[2] of this people. 4. Who shall dwell on the hill of Yahweh? He who walks uprightly[3] and[4] does justly and speaks the truth in his heart.[5] 5. Joseph came from the land of Egypt to bury[6] Jacob. 6. They buried the corpse of the old prophet in the grave where[7] the man of God was buried.[8] 7. The sons of Jacob went down to Egypt to buy food. 8. And now gather to me all Israel to mount Carmel,[9] and the prophets of Baal[10] four hundred who eat [at][11] the table of Jezebel. 9. And Deborah, a prophetess,[12] judged[13] Israel at that time, and she used to sit under the palm tree of Deborah in the hill country[14] of Ephraim. 10. God said to Abimelech in a dream by night: "Behold thou art oppressed

[15]because of the woman whom thou hast taken.''[15] 11. Thou art passing this day over the Jordan to find very great nations. 12. And Yahweh thy God is passing over before thee to cut off the people in the land to which[16] thou goest. 13. I dreamed a dream and behold Yahweh was sitting on [17]his glorious throne[17] and all the host[18] of heaven was standing before him.

[1] אָמַרְתִּי, as here, followed by the infin. cstr. with לְ can have one of two meanings of which the first is illustrated here : (a) I (speaking for myself) *said to keep*, i.e. *I said that I would keep, I promised to keep* ; (b) *I said* (to someone else) *to keep*, i.e. *I commanded him to keep*.

[2] מָשַׁל בְּ *to rule*—so says § 12 Vocabulary. But the ptc. מֹשֵׁל is here used as a *noun, in the cstr. plur.*, and not as a *part of a verb governing a noun* ; therefore, we have here a normal cstr.-gen. relationship of two nouns. Note that, while מֹשְׁלֵי is the masc. plur. cstr. of the active ptc. Qal of מָשַׁל *to rule*, מִשְׁלֵי is the plur. cstr. of מָשָׁל *a proverb*.

[3] תָּמִים in Hebrew is not an adverb (like *uprightly* in English) but an adjective. The meaning is : *he who walks [as] an upright man*, as *a man of integrity*. In English such a descriptive phrase is considered to be in nom. case, in apposition to *he* ; but in Hebrew, although it makes no difference *to the form*, we know from the corresponding use in Arabic that it would be regarded by grammarians as an Accus. of Respect.

A second point may be made. The adjective יָשָׁר means *straight, upright, just*, but תָּמִים has the basic meaning of *whole, complete*, and so is exactly rendered by the Latin phrase *integer vitae*.

[4] For the pointing of the conjunction here, cf. § 11.II.(c).

[5] To *speak the truth in the heart* means to harbour no grudge, scandal or misrepresentation and to think no lie, i.e. to be honest and sincere.

[6] The presence of the *daghesh lene* in the *bêth* shows that לִקְבֹּר is composed of two syllables, *liq-bōr* ; cf. § 18.2.(a).iii.

[7] אֲשֶׁר · · · שָׁם (equally good, אֲשֶׁר · · · בּוֹ) together express the relative *where* ; cf. § 10.4.(a).

[8] *was buried* does not here convey the *historical fact* that the man of God had been buried there, but the *circumstance* that he *lay buried* there. Sentence 9 later in this Exercise provides another excellent example of participles used to express circumstances or existing situations ; cf. also sentence 13.

[9] הַכַּרְמֶל *the garden-land* retains the article as a proper noun ; similarly הַיַּרְדֵּן *the down-rusher, the Jordan* and הַבַּעַל, *the owner, the master, Baal.*

[10] Cf. note 9 above.

[11] The constr.-gen. relation covers a wide range of relationship ; cf. אִישׁ דְּבָרִים *a man of words, an eloquent* (or *talkative*) *man* ; שֵׁם כָּבוֹד *a name of honour, an honourable name* ; כְּלֵי כֶסֶף *vessels [made] of silver* ; דֶּרֶךְ הַיָּם *the road of the sea, the coast road,* or *the road to the sea* ; שְׁמוּעַת שֹׁמְרוֹן *the report of (concerning) Samaria* ; דֶּרֶךְ יְרִיחוֹ *the way of (to) Jericho* ; so here *the prophets . . . who eat at Jezebel's table,* i.e. her court prophets who enjoy royal maintenance and hospitality.

[12] Note *a woman, a prophetess.* The first noun seems to be pleonastic, but it is also possible to regard the second, the prophetess, as a *noun of nearer definition,* cf. *an ass, a foal,* Job 11.12 ; *a girl, a virgin,* Deut. 22.23,28 ; *a woman, a widow,* I Kings 7.14 ; *a man, a prophet,* Jud. 6.8.

[13] Cf. note 8 above. The two participles in this sentence express a historical *circumstance* within a historical narrative ; probably that is conveyed suitably in English by translating the second as *used to sit. Used to sit* is doubtless better than *used to dwell* (which is linguistically possible), since the reference is to her giving judgment. שָׁפַט can be rendered as *to judge* or *to rule.*

[14] הָהָר can mean *the mountain* or *the hill country* ; it is in the latter sense that the cstr. form הַר is used here.

[15-15] לָקַח *to take* can also mean, as here, *to marry.* The use of בְּיַד here is not usual. Note first that בְּיַד הָאִישׁ can mean several things : (*a*) lit. *in the man's hand* ; (*b*) in such a clause as *there is no evil in* (or *on*) *the man's hand,*

the original reference was to bloodstains on the hand, so that the meaning
of the clause is : *The man has done no evil* ; *(c) in the power* (or *under the
authority*) *of the man.* Further, בְּיַד commonly means *by the hand of,
through the agency of,* as in the case of *a man killed by* (בְּיַד) *an enemy,* or
the word of God spoken through (בְּיַד) *the prophets.* The use of בְּיַד here
has the force of עַל־דְּבַר *because of the matter of, because of,* and does not
mean *by the agency of.*

[16] אֲשֶׁר · · · שָׁם means *where* (cf. note **7** above) ; here the meaning is
whither or *to which.* The more accurate Hebrew for that would be
אֲשֶׁר · · · שָׁמָּה (cf. § 10.4.(a)).

[17–17] Lit. *the throne of his glory.*

[18] For the *qāmeṣ* in the cstr. form of צָבָא owing to the quiescent final א,
cf. § 7.6.(b).ii.

C.

1 אָמַרְתִּי לִרְדֹף אַחֲרֵיהֶם: 2 רְדֹף (or רָדְפוּ) אַחֲרָיו:
3 נָתַן אֶת־הַכּוֹכָבִים בִּרְקִיעַ הַשָּׁמַיִם לִמְשֹׁל [1]בַּלַּיְלָה: 4 עִיר
שֹׁפֶכֶת דָּם [2]כַּמַּיִם: 5 [3]שְׁמֹר אֶת־לְשׁוֹנְךָ מֵרָע: 6 חָדְלוּ
לִסְפֹּר אֶת־מִשְׁלֵי שְׂפָתָיו כִּי הֵם כַּחוֹל אֲשֶׁר עַל־שְׂפַת הַיָּם:
7 יָדַיִם [4]שֹׁפְכוֹת דָּם: 8 בָּא [4]לִשְׁפָּךְ־דָּם: 9 קָבֹר (or קִבְרוּ)
אֶת־נִבְלָתִי בַּקֶּבֶר [5]אֲשֶׁר הַנְּבִיאִים קְבוּרִים שָׁם:[5] 10 [6]זָכַרְנוּ
כִּי אֱלֹהֵינוּ הוּא אֱלֹהִים [7]גָּדוֹל וְשֹׁפֵט גָּדוֹל: [6]זָכַר הוּא כִּי
אֲנַחְנוּ עָפָר וּבָשָׂר אֲשֶׁר [6]יָרַד אֶל־הַקֶּבֶר: 11 אָמַר לָהֶם
[8]לְבִלְתִּי [9]שְׁכֹן בָּעִיר אֲשֶׁר לֹא שָׁמַר הָעָם אֶת־מִשְׁפָּטָיו שָׁם:
12 [10]בִּשְׁפָטוֹ אֶת־יִשְׂרָאֵל חָדַל הָעָם לִגְנֹב וְהַשֹּׁפְטִים חָדְלוּ
לִשְׁמֹר מֵחוֹמוֹת הָעִיר:

¹ The ordinary form of לַיְלָה is accented on the first syllable, so that in pause the *patḥaḥ* is lengthened to *qāmeṣ*, לָיְלָה.

² The generic article is used here according to the Hebrew idiom ; cf. § 12.2.(b).i.

³ In sentence 2 of this Exercise *pursue* can be translated by the sing. imperat. רְדֹף or the plur. רִדְפוּ ; but here only the sing. imperat. can be used to translate *keep* because of the sing. possessive adjective *thy* following.

⁴ Note (*a*) the plur. שְׂפָכוֹת because there is no dual of the ptc. ; cf. § 13.6.(a),(b) ; and (*b*) how the *ḥôlem* of the final vowel of the infin. לִשְׁפֹּךְ in sentence 8 is shortened because of the tone in דָּם immediately following ; (cf. § 9, note 1 to Exercise).

⁵⁻⁵ Cf. B, notes 7 and 8 above.

⁶ Note the perf. ; cf. Key § 13A, note 2 and § 16B, note 3, and § 19.2.(c) in the Grammar.

⁷ Note the sing. adj. גָּדוֹל with אֱלֹהִים which is plur. in form but sing. in meaning.

⁸ Cf. § 18.2.(a).v.

⁹ The infin. cstr. cf. שָׁכַן (Voc. 17) must be used here ; the infin. cstr. cf. יָשַׁב is of a form quite different from קְטֹל (cf. § 29.2.(2).(b).iii).

¹⁰ Cf. § 18.2.(a).iv.

§ 19.

A.

תִּשְׁפַּלְנָה	2 or 3 plur. fem. impf. Qal of שָׁפֵל.
קָטֹנְתִּי	1 sing. perf. Qal of קָטֹן.
תִּקְטַן	2 sing. masc. or 3 sing. fem. impf. Qal of קָטֹן.
יָכְלָה	3 sing. fem. perf. Qal of יָכֹל.
יְכָלְתֶּם	2 plur. masc. perf. Qal of יָכֹל.

לִבְשִׁי   sing. fem imper. Qal of לָבֵשׁ (or לָבַשׁ).

נִכְבַּד   1 plur. impf. Qal of כָּבֵד.

תִּכְבְּדִי   2 sing. fem. impf. Qal of כָּבֵד.

אֶגְדַּל   1 sing. impf. Qal of גָּדַל.

רָעֵבוּ   3 plur. perf. Qal of רָעֵב (pausal form ; ordinary

form רָעֵבוּ).

B.

1. We shall neither hear the trumpet's call[1] nor shall we be hungry for bread. 2. Thou canst not count the stars. 3. The name of Yahweh is great[2] for ever. 4. Now I know that thou fearest God.[3] 5. O Yahweh my God, thou art very great. 6. The remembrance of the righteous (or of a righteous man) is a blessing,[4] but the name of the wicked (or of wicked men) rots away. 7. Thou art near, O Yahweh, and all thy commands are truth ; my cry will come near[5] to thy presence.[6] 8. The king [7]will read in the book of the law all the days of his life, that he may learn to fear[7] Yahweh his God. 9. [8]No flesh is righteous[8] before thee. 10. Righteous art thou, O Yahweh, who givest bread to the hungry and good things to those who fear thee.[9] 11. I cannot judge this people. 12. Come near to me that thou mayest learn[10] the wisdom which the elders of the nations do not know.[11] 13. Every[12] bitter (thing) is sweet to the hungry. 14. The wicked delight in stolen waters.

15. קָדוֹשׁ אַתָּה יהוה מָלְאָה כָל־הָאָרֶץ כְּבוֹדֶךָ:

Holy art thou, Yahweh ; all the earth is full of thy glory.

[1] Obviously קוֹל should not be translated here as *voice* ; *sound* or *call* is suitable. Occasionally it is used as an interjection ; e.g. the first words of Isa. 40.3 can be rendered as *A voice calls* or *Hark ! someone calling.*

[2] Alternatively, this verse can be translated as : *Let the name of Yahweh be great* (or *be magnified*) *for ever* ! (cf. § 20.1).

[3] Lit. *a fearer of God, a God-fearer.* יְרֵא is the cstr. form of the ptc. יָרֵא ; cf. § 19.5.

[4] This is a characteristic use of the preposition לְ. *The remembrance of the righteous is* or *becomes a blessing* probably means that the influence and effect of his good example lives on in the community. Similarly, such a sentence as *I will be their God and they shall be my people* is rendered into Hebrew as : אֶהְיֶה לָהֶם לֵאלֹהִים וְהֵם יִהְיוּ לִי לְעָם lit. *I will be for God to them and they shall be for people to me.* Sometimes such a לְ is most fittingly translated into English by *as* ; cf. Deut. 6.8. *You shall bind them as a sign* (לְאוֹת) *on your hand*, etc.

[5] Again, as in note 2, the translation of this verse may be given as : *let my cry come near.* . . . רִנָּה can mean a cry of joy or of pain.

[6] That a cry should *come near to God's presence* is a common way of expressing in Hebrew the hope that it should reach God and so be heard by Him.

[7-7] יִרְאָה is the form of infin. cstr. of יָרֵא *to fear* which is in use. Cf. § 19,4. Note that another possible rendering of this sentence is : *The king read . . . that he might learn* (cf. § 17.5.(b)).

[8-8] This sentence should not be translated as : *All flesh is not righteous before thee*. That is not idiomatic English. Cf. Key § 15C, note 3, for the Hebrew practice of negativing the verb where English negatives the subject or object. This is an example of difference of idiom between the two languages. Secondly, in place of *is righteous*, we may give the rendering *can be righteous* : cf. § 17.5.(d).

[9] The ptc. יָרֵא is here used as a noun of the First Declension type ; so יְרֵאֶיךָ is *thy fearers, those who fear thee*. Note the vocalization of this form when preceded by the preposition לְ : לְיִרְאֶיךָ > לִירֵאֶיךָ > לִירֵאֶיךָ (cf. § 12.1.(b)).

[10] Cf. §§ 17.5.(d) and 20.5.(a).

[11] *Do not know* or *have never known*. Both are possible here.

[12] כָּל־מַר *every bitter thing*, a distributive usage. So כָּל־אִישׁ *every man* but כָּל־הַיּוֹם *all the day* ; cf. § 10.5.

C.

1 לֹא יָכֹלְתִּי ¹לִקְרַב: 2 אֶגְדַּל: 3 קָרַב (sing.) or (plur.)

קָרְבוּ: 4 אֶת־הָאֱלֹהִים אֲשֶׁר עָשָׂה אֶת־הַשָּׁמַיִם וְאֶת־הָאָרֶץ

אֲנִי יָרֵא: 5 לֹא יְכָלְתֶּם לִשְׁמֹר אֶת־חֻקּוֹתַי בְּכָל־לְבַבְכֶם:

6 (masc.) קָטֹנְתָּ or (fem.) קָטֹנְתְּ: 7 שְׁמַע לְמַעַן תִּלְמַד לְיִרְאָה

אֶת־יהוה אֱלֹהֶיךָ: 8 לֹא יָכְלוּ לִרְדֹּף אַחֲרַי: 9 יָדַעְתִּי כִּי

מָלוֹךְ ²תִּמְלֹךְ: 10 חִדְלוּ לִקְרֹב לְפָנַי כִּי ³מָלְאוּ יְדֵיכֶם

דָּמִים: 11 מַה־גָּדַלְתָּ אֱלֹהָי: גָּדוֹל כְּבוֹדְךָ ⁴בַּשָּׁמַיִם וּבָאָרֶץ

יָדְעוּ הָאֲנָשִׁים אֶת־צִדְקָתְךָ וְאֶת־כְּבוֹדְךָ: 12 ⁵לִפְנֵיכֶם ⁶שָׂמְחוּ

הַצַּדִּיקִים ⁷בְּבִרְכַּת יהוה וְהָרְשָׁעִים ⁶רָעֵבוּ ⁸לֶחֶם: 13 יָכֹלְתָּ

⁹לַחְפֹּץ בְּחֶסֶד יהוה וְלֹא יָכֹלְתָּ לִסְפֹּר אֶת־הַכּוֹכָבִים:

---

¹ The infin. after יָכוֹל is usually preceded by לְ : cf. § 18.2.(a).iii.α.

² The *δ* vowel in מָלוֹךְ is pure long and so unchangeable, but the
δ vowel in the imperf. form תִּמְלֹךְ is tone-long and so should strictly not be
written as תִּמְלוֹךְ (cf. § 2.7.(b) ; but cf. 1 Sam. 24.21). The fact that the
vowel of תִּמְלֹךְ is tone-long is seen, for instance, in the corresponding plur.
form תִּמְלְכוּ.

³ In Isa. 1.15 the last three words of this sentence occur in the order :
יְדֵיכֶם דָּמִים מָלֵאוּ ; this emphasizes the bloodguiltiness. Note how מָלֵא
takes an accusative after it (דָּמִים, although there is nothing in the Hebrew
form to mark that fact) and not בְּ (i.e. not בְּדָמִים here).

⁴ The opportunity may be taken here to illustrate a valuable use of
aṯnāḥ and *sillûq* (cf. § 11, note following the Exercise). If the whole sentence
were taken as a unit, the *aṯnāḥ* would fall at אֱלֹהָי. But the first three

D

words may be regarded for the present purpose as a separate unit. The effect of placing *athnāḥ* at בַּשָּׁמַיִם is to indicate that the first clause is not : *thy glory is great in heaven and in earth*, but that there is a pause within the sentence at בַּשָּׁמַיִם, and that וּבָאָרֶץ belongs to the second clause.

[5] Or לְעֵינֵיכֶם, cf. § 13.6.(a).

[6] Perfects are in order here (cf. § 19.2.(c)) but participles (שְׂמֵחִים and רְעֵבִים) are possible.

[7] Note the pointing of the cstr. sing. of בְּרָכָה : בִּרְכַּת with *daghesh lene* in the *kaph* (cf. § 15.2.). This is exceptional.

[8] לַלְּחֶם is also found after the verb רָעֵב.

[9] The infin. cstr. of חָפֵץ is not found in the Old Testament. We may assume this form on the analogy of לַחְשֹׁב *to plan, to devise*, לַחְתֹּם *to seal* ; cf. § 7.3.(a),5.(b).

§ 20.

A.

1. I would keep thy law[1] continually. Let us make a covenant, thou and I, and it will be a witness[2] between thee and me.[3] 2. Abraham said to the Hittites[4] : " Sell me a grave that I may bury[5] my dead out of my sight."[6] 3. Be not very[7] angry, O Yahweh. 4. Do not come near here, for the place on which thou standest[8] is holy ground.[9] 5. . . . and he sold[10] him his birthright. 6. Yahweh said : " Behold, the man[11] has become as God, knowing[12] good and evil[13] ; and now, lest he reach out his hand and take of [the fruit of] the tree of life and eat and live for ever . . . "[14] 7. And (the) people will become like (the) priest,[15] and I shall punish it for its deeds[16] ; and they will eat without being satisfied, because they have forsaken Yahweh. 8. The man said to them : " Do not shed blood ; leave him in this pit in the wilderness[17] and [18]do him no violence."[18] 9. Do thou draw near and learn[19] all that our God is saying to us ; and we will learn (it) from thee and will obey.[20] 10. You shall keep all the command which I give you today, in order that you may be holy to Yahweh and inherit the land.

11. נִקְרְבָה אֶל־יהוה וְיִשְׁפֹּט בֵּינִי וּבֵינֶךָ:

Let us come near to Yahweh that he may judge between thee
and me.

12. וַיִּשְׁכְּחוּ בְנֵי־יִשְׂרָאֵל אֶת־יהוה אֱלֹהֵיהֶם וַיִּמְכֹּר אוֹתָם
בְּיַד מֶלֶךְ מוֹאָב:

And the Israelites[21] forgot Yahweh their God, and he sold them
into the hands of the king of Moab.

[1] Or *let me keep thy law.*

[2] Hebrew *for a witness* ; cf. Key § 19B, note 4.

[3] Note two points : (*a*) Hebrew puts the 1st personal pronoun first
(lit. *between me and thee*) ; so in the first part of the sentence ; (*b*) the
preposition בֵּין is repeated.

[4] Lit. *the sons of Heth* ; so בְּנֵי יִשְׂרָאֵל *the sons of Israel, the Israelites* ;
so בְּנֵי אָדָם *human beings.* In these cases בְּנֵי is not used specifically to
mean " sons of a father " ; *children* is a somewhat better translation but is
not sufficiently generalized. Translations such as those given in the example
quoted should be used.

[5] Or *and let me bury* ; but it is probably better to translate the clause as
indicating purpose (cf. § 20.5).

[6] Lit. *away from* (מִן) *before me* (לְפָנַי). Hebrew can conjoin two prepositions in this way ; e.g. מִתַּחַת *from under,* מֵעַל *from upon.* Comparable
usages can be found in English : *he picked up the pencil from under the table ;
he lifted the box on to the platform.*

[7] מְאֹד normally is used as an adverb meaning *very* ; it stands after the
adjective, adverb or verb which it qualifies. It is basically a noun, meaning
" *muchness* ", *strength.* Occasionally it is used explicitly as a noun (e.g.
בְּכָל־מְאוֹדְךָ *with all thy strength*) ; and עַד־מְאֹד *up to muchness, very
much* must be explained in this way.

[8] עוֹמֵד is used here, as the participle is often used, in a circumstantial
clause (cf. § 18.3.(a)).

⁹ Lit. *ground of holiness*—an idiomatic Hebrew expression.

¹⁰ Obviously this is a clause which forms part of a sentence in the narrative from which it is taken. (Gen. 25.29–34). But it must be noted that a paragraph and even a book may begin with such a *waw consecutive* verbal form (cf. § 20.4.(b) final paragraph).

¹¹ הָאָדָם can be translated as *the man*, i.e. *Adam*, but it may be taken for granted that the meaning *man*, i.e. *humanity* was also implied.

¹² It appears that syntactically יָדַע may be construed in two different ways (although the meaning in the two cases is practically the same) : (*a*) as in the translation given, in which it is in apposition to *the man*, i.e. *the man has become like God, knowing, as he now does, good and evil* ; (*b*) *the man has become like God who knows* (lit. *knowing*) *good and evil.* (This meaning could also be expressed by הַיֹּדֵעַ *who knows*, in which case the words טוֹב וָרָע would be construed as in the accus. following the verbal use of the participle.) The second rendering is in order grammatically, since אֱלֹהִים, when it means God, is construed with a singular verbal form.

¹³ For the *qāmeṣ* with the conjunction, cf. § 11.II.(e).

¹⁴ In Gen. 3.23 the expected apodosis after this dependent clause (e.g. *let us now expel him from the garden of Eden*) is not found. But the first statement in the narrative immediately after the dependent clause assumes it. The meaning of the whole is not in doubt.

¹⁵ Lit. *and it shall be, like people, like priest.* The normal meaning of such a Hebrew form of expression is as given in the translation. But the same phrase in Isa. 24.2 seems to mean : " *the priest shall become like the people.*"

¹⁶ פָּקַד עַל־ means *to punish. I shall punish it* (i.e. the people) *for its deeds* is a common singular pronominal reference after the noun עַם (although the plural is also found) and is preferable to making the reference of these suffixes to *the priest*, since the sentence as a whole is speaking about the people. The use of the plural in the verbal forms in the second part of sentence 7 illustrates a fluidity in the use of sing. and plur. in Hebrew which is characteristic of the language.

[17] Lit. *in this pit which is in the wilderness.* The אֲשֶׁר is not wholly necessary; it may well have been introduced to separate בַּבּוֹר הַזֶּה and בַּמִּדְבָּר because of the recurring preposition.

[18-18] Lit. *do not put forth a hand upon* (or *against*) *him*; i.e. *do not lay hands on him.* Hebrew commonly uses a singular like *hand* in this case where the plural is used in English.

[19] וְלָמַדְתָּ *and learn* is idiomatic Hebrew, i.e. a *waw consec.* perf. (cf. § 20.4.(e).ii) and not another imperative following קְרַב

[20] שָׁמַע, as used here, seems to mean *listen* or *obey*, and not simply *hear.*

[21] Cf. note 4 above.

B.

1 לֹא תִשְׁכַּב בַּמָּקוֹם הַהוּא: 2 אֶשְׁכְּבָה: 3 אַל־תִּקְרְבוּ:
4 יִשְׁפֹּט יהוה בֵּינִי וּבֵין הָעָם הַזֶּה: 5 [1]שְׁמַע [2]אֶת־תְּפִלָּתִי
אֱלֹהֵינוּ: 6 אָכַל הָאִישׁ מִן־הָעֵץ אֲשֶׁר בַּגַּן וַיִּקְצֹף אֱלֹהִים
[3]מְאֹד: 7 כֹּה אָמַר יהוה: הִנֵּה אֲנִי [4]נֹתֵן אֶת־הָעִיר הַזֹּאת
[5]בְּיַד מֶלֶךְ מוֹאָב [6]וּשְׂרָפָהּ אֹתָהּ בָּאֵשׁ: 8 וַיִּקְרָא אֱלֹהִים [7]לָאוֹר
יוֹם וְלַחֹשֶׁךְ קָרָא לָיְלָה: 9 וְשָׁמַרְתָּ אֶת־תּוֹרָתוֹ [8]תָּמִיד:
10 וָאֶזְכֹּר אֶת־דְּבָרָיו: 11 וְהָיָה כַּנָּבִיא [9]כַּכֹּהֵן: 12 הֲיֵשׁ־פֹּה
נָבִיא [10]לַיהוה [11]וְנִדְרְשָׁה אֶת־יהוה וְנִשְׁמְרָה אֶת־תּוֹרָתוֹ:
13 אָמַר יוֹסֵף לָעָם מְכַרְתֶּם [12]לִי אֶת־[13]אַרְצְכֶם הַיּוֹם הַזֶּה:
[14]הִנֵּה זֶרַע לָכֶם וּזְרַעְתֶּם אֶת־הַזֶּרַע וַאֲכַלְתֶּם אֶת־תְּבוּאַת
אַרְצְכֶם: 14 [15]אִם תֹּאמַר בִּלְבָבְךָ [16]עָשָׂה־לִי עֹצֶם[16] יָדִי
אֶת־הַחַיִל הַזֶּה וְזָכַרְתָּ אֶת־יהוה כִּי הוּא [17]הַנֹּתֵן לְךָ אֶת־
הַחַיִל הַזֶּה:

¹ Or the emphatic form שִׁמְעָה.

² In poetry (as in the Book of Psalms) the אֶת־ is often omitted (e.g. Ps. 4.2).

³ Or עַד־מְאֹד ; see sentence 3 Heb.–Eng. above.

⁴ This is an example of the futural use of the ptc. : I am *about to give*, or *will give*. The ptc. as such has no temporal value : e.g. הוּא יוֹשֵׁב בַּמָּקוֹם וַיִּקְרָא הָאִישׁ *he was sitting in the place when the man called* . . . ; שָׂרַף אֶת־הַבַּיִת בָּאֵשׁ וַאֲנִי לֹא יוֹדֵעַ *he burned down the house while I was unaware of it* ; הִנֵּה אָנֹכִי הוֹלֵךְ הַיּוֹם בְּדֶרֶךְ כָּל־הָאָרֶץ *behold, I am going today the way of all the earth* (Josh. 23.14), i.e. *I am dying* (cf. § 18.3.(a)).

⁵ The sing. יַד is idiomatic Hebrew usage ; cf. note 18 in section A of this Exercise.

⁶ Or וְהוּא יִשְׂרֹף, with the pron. used because of the change of subject.

⁷ Cf. Key § 12A, note 1.

⁸ For the omission of *dagh. lene*, cf. Key § 16C, note 6.

⁹ Cf. note 15 in section A of this Exercise.

¹⁰ Cf. § 15, note to the Exercise, second paragraph, for the *pathah* following the ל. The *Qᵉrê* of יהוה is אֲדֹנָי which, with ל, is read as >לַאדֹנָי לַאדֹנָי because of the quiescent א : so לַיהוה. Note also נָבִיא לַיהוה a *prophet of Yahweh* ; נְבִיא יהוה means *the prophet of Yahweh*.

¹¹ An example of the simple *wāw* with the Cohortative to express purpose ; cf. § 20.5.(a).

¹² לִי would normally be placed thus, immediately after the verb and before the object.

¹³ The form אַרְצְכֶם illustrates how a 2nd decl. type of noun (cf. § 25) appears with the 2nd. pl. pron. suffix. In future editions of the Grammar *this land* will be read instead of *your land*.

¹⁴ Hebrew uses הִנֵּה in this case, and not הֵנָּה or פֹּה which mean *here* in the local sense.

¹⁵⁻¹⁵ אָמַרְתָּ may be used here suitably ; the impf. תֹּאמַר also would serve the purpose (cf § 29, footnote 2 to Heb.–Eng. Exer.). *To say in the heart* is a Hebrew way of expressing *to think, to consider, to purpose.* This sentence is based on Deut. 8.17 which begins with וְאָמַרְתָּ. This illustrates the Hebrew use of two parallel clauses (וְאָמַרְתָּ . . . וְזָכַרְתָּ) where, as here, English usage makes one of the clauses subsidiary.

¹⁶⁻¹⁶ Two points should be noted here concerning לִי : (*a*) the *daghesh* used is *dagh. forte conj.* (cf. § 6.6) ; (*b*) לִי itself, as used here, illustrates *Dativus Commodi* (cf. § 12.2.(c).i). The cstr. of עֹצֶם being of the same form as the absolute, the student can use this noun, which is masc. in gender, without any difficulty here. But גְּבוּרָה (cstr. גְּבוּרַת) requires the verbal form עָשְׂתָה. Because of this, later editions of the Grammar will substitute *gathered* for *made.*

¹⁷ The participle is used here with verbal force, governing אֶת־ הַחַיִל הַזֶּה ; lit. *he is the one who gives you this wealth.* But the participle can be used also as a noun : e.g. אֲנִי מוֹשֵׁל הָאָרֶץ הַזֹּאת *I am the ruler of this land,* in which case מוֹשֵׁל is a noun in the cstr. state before הָאָרֶץ הַזֹּאת.

§ 21.

Hardly any of the vbs. enumerated is found in all parts. It will be sufficient, for purposes of illustration, to take two—פקד which is found in all forms, and קדשׁ in all but the Hoph‘al.

The feature which beginners are apt to overlook, in pointing, is that, as the first syllable of the pf. Niph‘al, Hiph‘il and Hoph‘al is *closed* (like the first syllable of the impf. Qal), the second letter of the root in these forms, starting as it does a new syllable, will take a *daghesh lene* if it be a *beghadhkephath* letter.

Thus pf. Qal כָּתַב, impf. Qal יִכְתֹּב, pf. Niph. נִכְתַּב.

Pf. Qal מָכַר, impf. Qal יִמְכֹּר, pf. Niph. נִמְכַּר.

Pf. Qal כָּבֵד, impf. Qal יִכְבַּד, pf. Niph. נִכְבַּד.

Pf. Qal גָּדַל, impf. Qal יִגְדַּל, pf. Hiph. הִגְדִּיל.

Of פקד the parts are :

Niph. נִפְקַד, Pi. פִּקֵּד, Pu. פֻּקַּד, Hithpa. הִתְפַּקֵּד, Hiph., הִפְקִיד,
Hoph. הָפְקַד.

Of קדשׁ the parts are :

Niph. נִקְדַּשׁ, Pi. קִדֵּשׁ,[1] Pu. קֻדַּשׁ, Hithpa. הִתְקַדֵּשׁ, Hiph. הִקְדִּישׁ
(Hoph.[2] הָקְדַּשׁ).

---

[1] In point of fact, however, the 3rd. sing. masc. pf. Pi. of קדשׁ always
appears in the form קִדַּשׁ ; see § 23.1.(a).i.

[2] Not found.

§ 22.
A.

נִשְׁמָר	sing. masc. ptc. Niph. of שׁמר, *kept*, *watched*. It might also be the *pausal* form (נִשְׁמָר) of 3 sing. masc. pf. Niph. (נִשְׁמַר) *he* (or *it*) *was kept* (or *watched*).
הִשָּׁפֵט	sing. masc. imperat. Niph. *enter into judgment* or cstr. inf. Niph. of שׁפט *to enter into judgment*.
נִפְקַדְתֶּם	2 plur. masc. pf. Niph. of פקד *you were visited*.
אֶשָּׁבֵר	1 sing. impf. Niph. of שׁבר *I shall be broken*.
נִכְתְּבוּ	3 plur. pf. Niph. of כתב *they were written*.
נִשָּׁפְטָה	1 plur. cohortative (§ 20.2) Niph. of שׁפט *let us enter into judgment*.
לְהִמָּלֵט	cstr. inf. Niph. of מלט, with the prepos. לְ, *to escape*.
יִשָּׁקֵל	3 sing. masc. impf. Niph. of שׁקל *it will be weighed*.
תִּלָּחֵם	2 sing. masc. or 3 sing. fem. impf. Niph. of לחם *she will* (or *thou wilt* f.) *fight*.
נִלְחַמְתִּי	1 sing. pf. Niph. of לחם *I fought*.
תִּזָּכַרְנָה	2 or 3 plur. fem. impf. Niph. of זכר *they* (or *you*) *will be remembered*.

It should be noted that in several cases the translation given is not the only one possible, but it will serve the present purpose.

B.

1. The wicked will not be written[1] in the book of life.[2] 2. The snare is broken[3] and we[4] have escaped. 3. And the earth was corrupted before God, and the earth was filled with violence.[5] 4. He who sheds the blood of man,[6] by man shall his blood be shed. 5. I have been driven out today from[7] the face of the earth, and from thy face shall I be hidden. 6. And Yahweh repented that he had made man upon the earth. 7. The enemy came to the city and was not able to fight[8] against it. 8. In that day Israel will no more lean upon its (own) strength and on its gold, but it will lean on Yahweh the holy one of Israel in truth.[9] 9. Your wickedness will be weighed and your deeds counted,[10] and Yahweh will judge all men in righteousness.[11] 10. In that day Yahweh will remember those who fear him, and the wicked who have hidden themselves from him will flee to the wilderness.

11. ‎¹²וַתִּשָּׂרֵף הָעִיר בָּאֵשׁ:

And the city was burned with fire.

12. ‎¹³הִשָּׁמֶר־לְךָ פֶּן־תִּכְרֹת בְּרִית ¹⁴לְיוֹשֵׁב הָאָרֶץ ¹⁵וְלָקַחְתָּ מִבְּנוֹתָיו לְבָנֶיךָ:

Beware[16] lest thou make a covenant with the inhabitants of the land and take of[17] their[18] daughters for thy sons.

[1] The use of *methegh* in the form ‎יִכָּתְבוּ is interesting and instructive (cf. § 9, note 2 following the Exercise). It is in the *open* syllable two places from the tone, so that both the use of the *methegh* where it is written and the absence of a *daghesh lene* in the ‎ב show that the word is syllabically *yik-kā-tẖᵉḇẖû*.

[2] Alternatively, *the book of the living.* ‎חַיִּים can mean *life* (cf. ‎זְקוּנִים old age, and ‎נְעוּרִים *youth*) ; but it can also be the plural of ‎חַי *living* (the reduplication of the ‎י in the plural ‎חַיִּים cannot be understood until § 40 is studied). In Ps. 69.29, where ‎חַיִּים is paralleled with ‎צַדִּיקִים *the righteous*,

it is to be taken in the sense of *the living*. The book of the living is the book in which are written the names of those who are destined to life ; cf. Exod. 32.32 ; Ezek. 13.9 ; Dan. 12.1 ; Mal. 3.16 ; Rev. 20.12,15.

We would normally expect the article with חַיִּים, whether used in the one sense or the other (i.e. סֵפֶר הַחַיִּים) ; but we have already had יִשְׁרֵי לֵב *the upright of heart* and נִשְׁבְּרֵי לֵב *the broken-hearted* (cf. Key §15C, note 10–10). In terms of actual usage, אֶרֶץ חַיִּים *the land of the living*, is found more often without the article written to חַיִּים than with it. *The tree of life* is found as עֵץ הַחַיִּים three times in the Old Testament (Gen. 2.9 ; 3.22,24) and once as עֵץ חַיִּים (Prov. 15.4).

[3] נִשְׁבַּר is prob. to be construed as the 3 sing. masc. perf. Niph'al, pausal form (ordinary form נִשְׁבַּר), parallel to the perf. Niph'al form נִמְלָטְנוּ in the second part of the sentence. But it could be construed as the Niph. ptc. נִשְׁבָּר ; if so, the meaning would be : *The snare lies broken*.

[4] אֲנַחְנוּ, which is unnecessary since person and number are defined in the verbal form נִמְלָטְנוּ, is introduced for emphasis.

[5] *with violence* is rendered in Hebrew by חָמָס alone (an accusative of respect) and not by בְּחָמָס (cf. Key § 19C, note 3).

[6] *He who sheds the blood of man* is a *casus pendens*, since the subject of the main clause, which follows, is *his blood*. That is the formal analysis of the sentence. Another way to describe the literary usage would be to say that *He who sheds the blood of man* is, indeed, the subject of the sentence, and that *his blood* is a subject of nearer definition in apposition to it (cf. Key § 18B, note 12).

[7] A compound preposition : מִן־עַל > מֵעַל *from upon* (cf. Key § 20A, note 6).

[8] The meaning required here seems to be *fight successfully* (cf. Isa. 7.1).

[9] On בֶּאֱמֶת two comments may be made : (*a*) with regard to accentuation, *sillûq* is written under the מ to indicate the final accented syllable of

the sentence. *Meṯheḡ* is written under the בְ because its vowel occurs in an open syllable and is the second vowel from the tone (even although the intervening vowel is only a vocal shᵉwa ; cf. § 9, note 2 following the Exer.) ; (*b*) as to use, בְ construed, as here, with an indefinite noun in Hebrew has often the value of an English adverb : so בֶּאֱמֶת lit. *in truth* or *in faithfulness*, but idiomatically *faithfully*, *loyally* (cf. בִּצְדָקָה in sentence 9 immediately following).

¹⁰ *counted* or *told.* סָפַר *to count* ; סִפֵּר *to recount, to relate, to narrate, to tell* (cf. § 23). מַעֲלָל *deed* is commonly used in the sense of *misdeed* (cf. Voc. § 20), but here it means simply *deed.* The plur. is מַעֲלָלִים and the cstr. plur. מַעַלְלֵי (< מַעֲלְלֵי) ; hence מַעַלְלֵיהֶם in the Hebrew text.

¹¹ Cf. note 9 above.

¹² Not וַתִּשְׁרֶךְ. The retraction of the accent (with the *waw* consec.) and the consequent shortening of the last syllable described in § 22.2, takes place chiefly where the word following the vb. is a monosyllable (as in the last illustration in § 22.5). There are certain forms, however, in which the retraction has become usual : e.g. וַיִּלָּחֶם *and he fought*, is always thus written, and וַיִּנָּחֶם often (always in the phrase וינחם יהוה *and Yahweh repented*).

¹³ The imper. Niph. of שמר is to be included among the words referred to in the last sentence of the preceding note : it is *always* (except in Isa. 7.4 הִשָּׁמֵר) written in the form הִשָּׁמֶר. But הִשָּׁמֶר is commonly followed by לְךָ. In such a combination the vocal shᵉwa of לְךָ is so lightly touched in pronunciation that לְךָ is virtually monosyllabic. For this reason the accentuation and vocalization of השמר in the phrase הִשָּׁמֶר־לְךָ may be regarded as coming under the principle that the occurrence of two accented syllables in succession is contrary to the rhythm of the Hebrew language.

[14] יוֹשֵׁב collective, as frequently, "inhabitants." Cf. Isa. 5.3 יֹשֵׁב

יְרוּשָׁלַ͏ִם וְאִישׁ יְהוּדָה " ye *inhabitants* of Jerusalem and ye *men* of Judah ".

After כָּרַת בְּרִית " to make a covenant ", *with*, which is here rendered by לְ,

is also commonly rendered by אֶת־ (i.e. the prep.) or עִם (for both words

see § 40.6.(b)). Cf. Gen. 15.18 כָּרַת יהוה אֶת־אַבְרָם בְּרִית *Yahweh made a*

covenant with Abram ; Gen. 26.28 נִכְרְתָה בְרִית עִמָּךְ) עִמָּךְ pausal form of

עִמְּךָ) *let us make* (cohortative) *a covenant* (notice absence of *daghesh* from בּ

after vowel of preceding word with which it so closely goes in sense ; see

Key § 15C, note 2) *with thee.*

[15] Note : *wāw* consec. with the *pf.* after the *impf.* which naturally

follows פֶּן־. Note further, in this contruction, that the accent is normally

thrown forward from the penult to the *last* syllable (תָּ), and that conse-

quently the vowel in the open syllable second from it (לְ) takes the *meṯheḡ*.

[16] Lit. " take heed to thyself ".

[17] " From among " : or it might be the partitive use of מִן " (some)

from ", " some of ". The use of מִן in this latter sense is well established in

the Old Testament (cf. § 12.4.(c)).

[18] Singular suffixes in Hebrew, because יוֹשֵׁב is sing. For בֵּן and בַּת

see § 16.3.(b), rule 2.

C.

1 קָרוֹב יהוה [1]לְנִשְׁבְּרֵי־לֵבָב[2] 2 נִסְתַּרְתִּי מִפְּנֵי אֱלֹהַי:

3 הִסָּתֵר מִפָּנָיו: 4 תִּסָּתְרוּ בַּיּוֹם הַהוּא: 5 וַתִּשָּׁחֵת הָאָרֶץ

וַיִּכָּרֵת כָּל־בָּשָׂר בַּמַּיִם: 6 תִּשָּׁבַרְנָה [2]זְרֹעוֹת הָרְשָׁעִים:

7 אִמָּלְטָה בְּיוֹם הַלֶּחֶם: 8 וַתִּמָּלֵא הָאָרֶץ [3]דָּמִים: 9 נִקְבַּר

מֵתוֹ מִלְּפָנָיו: 10 [4]כֹּה אָמַר יהוה אֱלֹהֵי יִשְׂרָאֵל הִנְנִי נֹתֵן

אֶת־הָעִיר הַזֹּאת בְּיַד מֶֽלֶךְ־בָּבֶל וּשְׂרָפָהּ בָּאֵשׁ ⁵וְאַתָּה לֹא

תִמָּלֵט מִיָּדוֹ כִּי ⁶תִּלָּכֵד ⁷וְנִתַּתָּ בְיָדוֹ⁷ : 11 בְּטַח ⁸בַּיהוה

בְּכָל־לְבָבְךָ ⁹וְאַל־תִּשָּׁעֵן אֶל־בִּינָתְךָ⁹ :

¹⁻¹ In the two places where this phrase occurs in the Old Testament,
it is the short form לֵב which is used for *heart* and not לֵבָב (Ps. 34.19 ;
Isa. 61.1). For the absence of the article from לֵבָב here, cf. Key § 15C,
note 10–10, and § 22B, note 2, in the Grammar.

² In Ps. 37.17, where these words occur, the verb is placed at the end
of the clause for purposes of contrast with the following clause. As to form,
זְרֹעֹת and זְרֹעוֹת are both in order ; זְרוֹעוֹת is not normally found
(cf. § 2.7.(d)). In Ps. 37.17 רְשָׁעִים is used without the article, as is צַדִּיקִים
in the contrasting clause in the same verse (cf. note 1–1 above).

³ דָּם or, better, דָּמִים *acts of bloodshed* (cf. Key § 17B, note 2). For the
use of דָּם or דָּמִים here after the verb מָלֵא, cf. Key § 22B, note 5.

⁴ For this sentence, cf. Key § 20B, notes 4–6.

⁵ The pronoun אַתָּה is introduced here to emphasize particularly the
fate of the person addressed.

⁶ לָכַד is *to capture* persons or cities, booty, etc. ; לָקַח is *to take*
(Lat. *sumere*), or, specifically, *to marry*.

⁷⁻⁷ Sharpness is added to the end of the sentence by reading בְיָדוֹ
before the verb, i.e. וּבְיָדוֹ תִּנָּתֵן ; note that, while the English usage here is
into his hand, Hebrew regularly uses the prep. בְּ. If we were to use the
common order of a verbal sentence or clause and put the verb first, the
form would be וְנִתַּתָּ. The explanation of this form is as follows. The Niph.
Perf. of נָתַן is נִתַּן > נִנְתַּן by the assimilation of the radical נ to the following
תּ. Similarly the 2 s.m. pf. Niph. is נִתַּתָּ > נִנְתַּתָּ by a similar assimilation.

⁸ The verb בָּטַח is commonly construed with בְּ, sometimes with עַל־
which expresses the trust as a *reliance upon* a person, occasionally with אֶל־

which expresses the movement of the trust towards the person considered trustworthy. For the vowel *pathaḥ* following the בּ in בְּיהוה, cf. § 15, note to the Exercise, second paragraph, and Key § 20B, note 10.

[9-9] Or, for emphasis, the verb may be kept to the end : וְאֶל־בִּינָתְךָ

אַל־תִּשָּׁעֵן. Cf. Exod. 3.7 : רָאִיתִי אֶת־עֳנִי עַמִּי וְאֶת־צַעֲקָתָם שָׁמַעְתִּי:

I have seen the suffering of my people and I have heard their cry. The effect of the אֶל־ after תִּשָּׁעֵן is to give the meaning : *do not turn to your own understanding and rely on it.*

§ 23.

A.

1. Hear, O heavens, for [1]Yahweh has spoken[1] : " Sons I have reared and they[2] have rebelled against me." 2. But why do you[3] harden your hearts as Egypt[4] and Pharaoh hardened[5] their hearts? 3. The heavens are telling[6] the glory of God. 4. Remember the Sabbath day to sanctify it.[7] 5. And for the land no atonement[8] shall be[9] made for the blood which has been shed[10] in it except by the blood of him who shed it.[11] 6. What shall we say and how are we to justify ourselves ?[12] 7. The poor seek[13] water and there is none.[14] 8. [There was] a small city and few men in it ; a great king came there and burned it down. 9. But there was found in it a wise man and he by his wisdom saved the city ; yet the men of the city[15] would not remember the wise man nor honour him.

10. אֶת־פָּנֶיךָ יהוה אֲבַקֵּשׁ: Thy face, Yahweh, will I seek.

11. נִמְצְאוּ הַחֲמוֹרִים אֲשֶׁר הָלַכְתָּ לְבַקֵּשׁ:

The asses have been found which you went out to look for.

12. וַיִּקְרָא פַרְעֹה אֶת־כָּל־[16]חַכְמֵי מִצְרַיִם [17]וַיְסַפֵּר לָהֶם אֶת־חֲלֹמוֹ:

Then Pharaoh summoned all the wise men of Egypt and told them his dream.

[1-1] The order (subj.-verb) shows that יהוה is emphasized in this verse. Note also דִּבֵּר, the pausal form of דִּבֶּר (cf. § 23.1.(a).i).

² הֵם *they* (with emphasis) i.e. the people whom Yahweh had reared and from whom he expected obedience and loyalty.

³ *do you harden* (as you have been doing) or *will you harden*.

⁴ מִצְרַיִם, commonly used of *Egypt* the country, can mean *Egyptians*, as we can use *England* to denote the people of that country. But there is a distinctive noun for *an Egyptian* מִצְרִי (pl. מִצְרִים), a form with the so-called gentilic ending (cf. עִבְרִי Hebrew, מוֹאָבִי Moabite, פְּלִשְׁתִּי Philistine, etc.).

⁵ כִּבְּדוּ *hardened*, the historic past, refers obviously to the way in which Pharaoh hardened his heart against the entreaties of Moses and the accusing evidence of the plagues during the Israelite slavery in Egypt.

⁶ The ptc. מְסַפְּרִים expresses a continuing state or activity in the use which is exemplified here. This can also be expressed by the impf., as is illustrated in Ps. 19.2–3.

⁷ *To make* (or *to keep*) *it* קָדוֹשׁ *holy, apart*. *The Sabbath day* is in Hebrew *the day of the Sabbath*.

⁸ *Atonement* or *expiation*. יְכֻפַּר is used impersonally here : *and for the land it shall not be atoned*, i.e. no atonement shall be made for the land.

⁹ *shall be* or *can be*. There seems little doubt that the meaning intended here is better expressed by *can be* than by *shall be*.

¹⁰ As passive to שָׁפַךְ *to pour, to shed*, both the Niph. and the Puʿal are in use. Commonly the Puʿal is pass. to the Piʿel, but the Piʿel of שָׁפַךְ is not found in the Old Testament.

¹¹ שֹׁפְכוֹ *its shedder*, the masc. pron. suff. referring to הַדָּם earlier in the verse. The form of nouns of the type שֶׁפֶךְ when used with pronom. suffixes is dealt with in § 26, but § 18.3 shows that the plur. of שֶׁפֶךְ is שְׁפָכִים ; similarly, the form here with pronom. suffix, שֹׁפְכוֹ.

¹² *to justify ourselves* or *to make ourselves out to be innocent*, cf. § 23.3.(b). צַדִּיק means *right, righteous, innocent*.

¹³ מְבַקְשִׁים ptc.; so *seek*, or *are seeking*. For the omission of the *daghesh forte* from the ק, cf. § 6.5.

¹⁴ Note the lengthening of the *patḥaḥ* of אַיִן to *qāmeṣ* in pause and the pre-tonic *qāmeṣ* in the conjunction; cf. § 11.II.(e).

¹⁵ Subj. precedes verb in this clause for emphasis, to contrast sharply the subject here with the explicit הוּא in the preceding clause. For the translation *would not remember* in this clause, cf. § 17.5.(d).

¹⁶ For the *patḥaḥ* in חַכְמֵי owing to the guttural (cf. דִּבְרֵי), cf. § 5.2.(d).ii.

¹⁷ For the omission of the *daghesh forte* from the י, cf. § 6.5 (cf. note 13 above).

B.

1 אֵלֶּה הַדְּבָרִים אֲשֶׁר דִּבַּרְתִּי: 2 אַל־תְּכַבְּדוּ אֶת־לְבַבְכֶם
פֶּן־יִקְצֹף יהוה אֱלֹהֵיכֶם: 3 ¹בַּקְשׁוּ אֶת־פָּנָיו: 4 הִתְהַלְּכוּ
לְפָנַי ²וְהִתְקַדָּשְׁתֶּם: 5 לֹא יָכֹלְתִּי לְדַבֵּר אֶל־הָעָם הַזֶּה כִּי
כָבְדוּ אֶת־לְבָבָם: 6 שָׁמַעְנוּ אֶת־קוֹל יהוה ³מִתְהַלֵּךְ בַּגַּן
⁴וַנִּסְתַּתֵּר מִפָּנָיו: 7 אָמַר אֶל־הָאִשָּׁה דַּבְּרִי וַתְּדַבֵּר הָאִשָּׁה:
8 אֲכַבֵּד אֶת־⁵מְכַבְּדַי: 9 וְעַתָּה הִנֵּה הַמֶּלֶךְ מִתְהַלֵּךְ לִפְנֵיכֶם
⁶וַאֲנִי ⁷זָקַנְתִּי ⁸וַאֲנִי ⁸הִתְהַלַּכְתִּי לִפְנֵיכֶם מִנְּעוּרַי עַד־הַיּוֹם
הַזֶּה: 10 ⁹גַּדְּלוּ אֶת־יהוה אִתִּי⁹ ¹⁰וּנְרוֹמְמָה אֶת־שְׁמוֹ יַחְדָּו:
11 בִּקַּשְׁתִּי אֶת־יהוה וְהוּא ¹¹הִסְתַּתֵּר מִמֶּנִּי: צָעַקְתִּי אֵלָיו
וְהוּא פָקַד אֹתִי ¹²בִּישׁוּעָתוֹ: 12 יְכַבְּדוּ אֹתִי ¹³בִּשְׂפָתָם
¹⁴וּלְבָבָם רָחוֹק מִמֶּנִּי¹⁴: יִשְׁמְרוּ אֶת־מִצְוֹת ¹⁵הָאֲנָשִׁים אֲשֶׁר
¹⁶לִמְּדוּ בָם¹⁶ וְאֶת־תּוֹרָתִי אֲשֶׁר נָתַנּוּ לָהֶם נְבִיאַי יִשְׁכָּחוּ:
עַל־כֵּן תִּסָּתֵר מֵהֶם חָכְמַת הַחֲכָמִים וְהִסְתַּתַּרְתִּי מִלִּפְנֵיהֶם:

¹ While 3 pl. perf. and impf. Pi‛el and the masc. plur. abs. of the ptc. (מְבַקְשִׁים, יְבַקְשׁוּ, בִּקְשׁוּ) are found without the *daghesh forte* in the קֿ (cf. § 6.5), the *daghesh* is always found in the קּ of the imper. as shown.

² In this form the *pathaḥ* following the דּ is found attenuated to a *ḥireq* ; הִתְקַדִּשְׁתֶּם. For the consec. perf. verbal form following an imperative, cf. § 20.4.(e).ii.

³ *walking* or *as he was walking.*

⁴ For the fact that the ס precedes the ת of the first syllable (הִתְ) of this form, cf. § 23.3.(a).ii.

⁵ *my honourers, those who honour me.*

⁶ The אֲנִי is emphatic here, being used to draw a contrast between the speaker and the king. The contrast in this instance is not of activity or achievement but of condition : *and I am old* or *and I am now old.*

⁷ The repetition of the emphatic אֲנִי is notable, but is quite in order. The contrast is now in respect of what the speaker has done. The king is now ruling and directing public affairs but, it is said, that is what the speaker has been doing from the days of his youth until now. This is stated more forcefully by the use of the second אֲנִי and the following perf. than it would be by the use of וָאֶתְהַלֵּךְ, the *wāw* consec. Impf. construction.

⁸ *to walk before* means *to go about one's daily work, to lead an active life,* even *to live constantly in the midst of the people* with the implied meaning *to commend oneself* by fulfilling one's duty.

⁹ Or עָמִּי. For אֵת‏(אֶת־), cf. Voc. of § 16 ; for the forms of אֵת and עִם with pron. suffixes, cf. § 40.6.(b). The first clause might also be rendered as : גַּדְּלוּ ; Ps. 34.4. reads לַיהוה after the imper. נְגַדְּלָה אֶת־יהוה אֲנִי וְאַתֶּם : but a direct object is used after other Pi‛el forms of this verb in Ps. 69.31 and Job 7.17.

¹⁰ For this form, cf. § 23.5.

¹¹ Cf. note 4 above. In sentence 11 וְהוּא occurs twice for emphasis. Without such emphasis the related verbal forms would be וַיִּסָּתֵר and וַיִּפָּקֵד.

E

[12] יְשׁוּעָה and תְּשׁוּעָה are both used meaning *salvation, deliverance, victory*, as is the masc. יֶשַׁע (§ 25). Note the vocalization here with בְּ : בִּישׁוּעָתוֹ > בִּישׁוּעָתוֹ > בִּישׁוּעָתוֹ ; cf. § 12.1.(b).

[13] It is idiomatic Hebrew to use the sing. שָׂפָה where English uses the plural (cf. sing. לֵבָב later in the sentence) ; but שִׂפְתֵיהֶם (cf. § 16.2.(b)) may be used ; the use of שִׂפְתֹתֵיהֶם (i.e. plur., not dual) belongs to the later books of the Old Testament.

[14-14] This second clause may be translated : וְאֶת־לִבָּם רָחֲקוּ מִמֶּנִּי *but their heart they have removed* (3 pl. perf. *Piʿel* of רָחַק) *far from me.*

[15] For the form אֲנָשִׁים, abs. plur. of אִישׁ *man*, cf. § 16, Hebrew–English Exer., footnote 1.

[16-16] lit. *in which they have been trained*. Strictly, in terms of grammar, בָּהֵן should be used since the antecedent to which it is related is fem. (מִצְוֹת) ; but בָּהֵן is found very seldom in the Old Testament, the plural בָּם (or בָּהֶם) being found in relation to fem. nouns. Another way of translating the relative clause would be by the use of the ptc. אֲשֶׁר מְלֻמָּדִים בָּם הֵם:.

§ 24.

A.

1. Thou[1] hast made me king instead of David my father. 2. Behold my face is (set) against[2] this people and I will destroy them from off the face of the ground.[3] 3. And God placed the cherubim before the garden of Eden, to guard the way to the tree of life. 4. God set luminaries in the firmament of heaven, [4]to divide day and night[4]. 5. Do not hide thy face from me, for thou art my help ; forsake[5] me not, O God of my salvation. 6. You have dealt treacherously with[6] me continually, but[7] I will not [8]hide my face from you[8]. I will [9]call to remembrance[9] my covenant which I made with your fathers[10] and I will separate you from the nations [11]whither I drove you out[11]. I[12] will gather you into

this land and will make David, my chosen one, king over you. He[12] will seek the good and destroy all evil[13] from the land. 7. He [14]put Joseph in charge of[14] the land and of [15]all his property[15], and he knew nothing that was in Joseph's charge except the food which he ate. 8. Truly[16] it is his purpose[17] to destroy and to cut off nations not a few.

9. אַל־[18]תַּסְתֵּר אֶת־פָּנֶיךָ מֵהָעָם הַזֶּה :

Hide not thy face from this people.

10. [19]וַיַּמְטֵר יהוה עַל־הָעִיר אֵשׁ מִן־הַשָּׁמַיִם [19]וַיַּשְׁמֵד אוֹתָה מֵעַל־פְּנֵי הָאֲדָמָה :

And Yahweh rained fire from heaven upon the city and destroyed it from off the face of the ground.[3]

[1] אַתָּה here is both emphatic and reverential : *Thou* (by whom kings reign and princes decree justice) *hast made me king.* This statement has reference to a divinely chosen and anointed king who is under covenant to be faithful to Yahweh.

[2] The context makes it clear that בְּ here does not mean *upon* (cf. Amos 9.8 AV) or *on* or *beside*, but *against* ; cf. Gen. 16.12 : יָדוֹ בַכֹּל וְיַד כֹּל בּוֹ *his hand is against all and the hand of all is against him.*

[3] אֲדָמָה *ground* or *earth.*

[4-4] lit. *to make a separation between the day and between the night.* Note how, in such a construction, Hebrew repeats the preposition בֵּין.

[5] The impf. of נָטַשׁ *to forsake* is יִטֹּשׁ. When נ occurs at the end of a syllable which is not the final syllable of a word, it commonly becomes assimilated to the following consonant, e.g. 3 s.m. impf. Niph. יִקָּטֵל comes from יִנְקָטֵל (cf. § 22.1) and מִן־מַיִם becomes מִמַּיִם (cf. § 12.3.(a)). In the same way יִנְטֹשׁ becomes יִטֹּשׁ.

[6] *with,* as used here, obviously is not the *with* of accompaniment ; it means : *in your dealings with me.* Its force is substantially the same here as that of *against.*

[7] The Hebrew conjunction וְ is not always to be rendered by *and* ; here *but* is much more suitable.

[8-8] *to hide one's face from a person* means to turn away in displeasure, to cease to have association with him, to break off relations.

[9-9] The Hiphʿil of זָכַר can mean *to call to remembrance, to commemorate, to make mention*. The exact shade of meaning in any particular case has to be determined by the context.

[10] For אָבוֹת as pl. of אָב *father*, cf. § 13.5.(f).

[11-11] Another translation is linguistically possible : *whom I drove out thither*, in which case *whom* would relate to *the nations* mentioned immediately before. But in such a translation *thither* has no meaning in the context to the extent to which it is quoted here. The translation given in the Key has clear meaning and is to be preferred. It associates closely אֲשֶׁר ... שָׁמָּה and understands the object as *you* from the preceding clause.

[12] The narrative sequence indicated by the use of *wāw*-consecutive verbal forms in Hebrew is not to be thought to demand the use of *and* or *but* as a connective in every case in the translation. Here and elsewhere in this sentence 6 none is used in the translation given in the Key.

[13] *Every evil* is a possible translation.

[14-14] lit. *appointed Joseph over. . . .*

[15-15] lit. *all which was to him, all he owned.*

[16] כִּי has a wide range of meaning : (*a*) *for, because* ; (*b*) *that* (conj. ; cf. Greek ὅτι); (*c*) as an asseverative, *surely, truly* ; (*d*) as an adversative, *but*. Whether כִּי here should be translated as *truly* or *but* can be determined only from the context in which the sentence occurs (Isa. 10.7).

[17] lit. *to destroy is in his heart, it is his purpose* (or *his intention*) *to destroy*.

[18] Imperf. Hiph. 2 s.m. is תַּסְתִּיר ; but note the Jussive form תַּסְתֵּר after אַל־ to express a prohibition (cf. § 20.1).

[19] Note the *wāw* consec. imperf. Hiph. forms וַיַּמְטֵר and וַיַּשְׁמֵד, not וַיַּשְׁמִיד and וַיַּמְטִיר (cf. § 24.1.(a).i).

B.

1 יֵשׁ־עֵת¹ לִשְׁמֹר וְעֵת לְהַשְׁלִיךְ׃ 2 אַל־תַּצְדֵּק אֶת־
הָרְשָׁעִים׃ 3 אַסְתִּירָה אֶת־פְּנֵי מִן־הָעָם ²הָרַע הַזֶּה כִּי
הִשְׁחִיתוּ לְפָנַי עַל־הָאָרֶץ׃ 4 כִּי הַמָּטָר יַמְטִיר אֵשׁ מִן־
הַשָּׁמַיִם עַל־הָעִיר ³הָרָעָה הַהִיא וְהִשְׁמִיד אֹתָהּ וְלֹא תִזָּכֵר
עוֹד לְעוֹלָם׃ 5 מָצָא הַנָּבִיא אֶת־הַיֶּלֶד ⁴מִשְׁכָּב עַל־מִטָּתוֹ׃
6 יָרַדְנוּ אֶל־הָעִיר לְהִלָּחֶם ⁵עָלֶיהָ וְלֹא יָכֹלְנוּ לְהַשְׁמִיד
אֹתָהּ׃ 7 אָמַר רְאוּבֵן אַל־תִּשְׁפְּכוּ־דָם הַשְׁלִיכוּ אֹתוֹ אֶל־
הַבּוֹר הַזֶּה אֲשֶׁר בַּמִּדְבָּר׃ אַל־תַּשְׁמִידוּ אִישׁ נָקִי וְאַל־
תַּצְדִּיקוּ אֶת־⁶הָרְשָׁעִים׃ 8 רָאָה אֱלֹהִים אֶת־הָאוֹר אֲשֶׁר
עָשָׂה וְהִנֵּה ⁷טוֹב וַיַּבְדֵּל בֵּין הָאוֹר וּבֵין הַחֹשֶׁךְ׃ 9 אַל־
תַּסְתֵּר אֶת־פָּנֶיךָ מִמֶּנִּי אֱלֹהִים ⁸וְאֶשְׁכְּנָה בְהֵיכָלְךָ ⁹וְהִזְכַּרְתָּ
אֹתִי אֶת־כָּל־טוּבְךָ לִי׃ ¹⁰וְהִלְבַּשְׁתָּ אֹתִי ¹¹בִּגְדֵי ¹²הַצְּדָקָה
לְמַעַן לֹא אַשְׁחִית עוֹד ¹³וְכִבַּדְתִּי אֹתְךָ כָּל־יְמֵי חַיָּי׃

---

¹⁻¹ These two words, independently, are יֵשׁ and עֵת. But, wherever possible, Hebrew avoids the collocation of two accented syllables. Therefore, they are joined together by *maqqeph* to form the one tonal unit : יֵשׁ־עֵת. Now the vowel of יֵשׁ is in a closed syllable pre-tonic and is, in consequence, shortened to *sᵉghôl*.

² In Voc. of § 13 we find פַּר *ox* and שַׂר *prince, officer*. The feminines are respectively פָּרָה *cow* and שָׂרָה *princess*. With the article we find הַפָּר, but הַשַּׂר. In the case of רַע *evil*, which belongs to the same type, הָרַע and

הָרָע are both found, cf. § 9, note i to the Voc., and § 40. In each case, of course, the *qāmeṣ* written to the article is due to the following ר (§ 7.7).

³ Cf. note 2 above.

⁴ מָשְׁכָּב the Hophʿal ptc. of שָׁכַב means *laid*; *lying* would be שׁוֹכֵב, the Qal ptc.

⁵ נִלְחַם *to fight* is most often construed with בְּ *against* in respect of an enemy or of a city or other objective; it can be construed with עִם or אֶת־ (both meaning *with*) in the sense of joining *with* an ally to fight or of fighting *with* (i.e. against) an enemy; it is occasionally found, as here, construed with עַל־ in respect of warring *against* a city.

⁶ Or the sing. הָרָשָׁע which may seem better than the plural as a response to אִישׁ נָקִי in the first part of the verse.

⁷ Gen. 1.31 exemplifies this form of expression; it is possible also to add הוּא: i.e. וְהִנֵּה טוֹב הוּא. Gen. 1.4, on which this sentence is based, has simply כִּי טוֹב.

⁸ Or וְהִשְׁכַּנְתָּ אֹתִי a permissive use of the Hiph.

⁹ Note how זָכַר which is transitive in the Qal, can, as here, take two accusatives in the Hiph., often an accus. of person and an accus. of thing, i.e. *to cause* a person *to remember* something.

¹⁰ לָבַשׁ *to wear*; Hiph. הִלְבִּישׁ *to clothe* (cf. § 24.I.1.(d)); thus Hiph. can take two accusatives (cf. note 9 above).

¹¹ In Isa. 61.10, in which there is a phrase similar to this one, בְּגָדַי is used, not בִּבְגָדַי. That is in accordance with what is said in note 10 above; it is *cause me to wear the garments of righteousness*.

¹² In poetic form בִּגְדֵי צְדָקָה would be used, but בִּגְדֵי הַצְּדָקָה is according to the strict rules of Hebrew grammar.

¹³ Or וָאֲכַבְּדָה. § 24.I.1.(c) states that the *Piʿēl* of כָּבֵד *to be heavy* means *to honour* and the *Hiphʿil* to make heavy or *to bring to honour*. But men cannot bring honour to God or bring God to honour; therefore, the

Pi'el should be used in this sentence, which means *to honour* in the sense of *to give* (or ascribe) *honour to, to glorify.* Sentence 9 here is particularly interesting in showing how a series of imperatives in English is commonly rendered in Hebrew, after the initial imperative, by consec. perf. forms.

§ 25.

A.

1. And now, you inhabitants[1] of Jerusalem and men[1] of Judah, pray[2] judge between me and my vineyard. 2. And they hid the child and his nurse from[3] the queen. 3. Your ways are not my ways. 4. The old prophet took his mantle[4] and struck[5] the waters of the Jordan and divided them. So the two men passed through the midst of the waters on dry ground and afterwards went[6] on their way. 5. If you [7]heed my commands by seeking[7] Yahweh your God with all your heart and all your soul, I, even I, will cause the rain to fall[8] in its day and will give grass to feed[9] your cattle[10]; and you will eat and be satisfied. 6. The girl said to him : " Why do you stay outside ? There is room[11] for you in the house and I will give you water[12] to wash your feet and the feet of the men who are with you."[13] 7. And the youth was fleet-footed[14] and pursued after the prince as far as the king's threshing-floor and struck[5] him down there. 8. Behold my servant in whom I trust, my chosen one in whom I delight.[15] 9. I have set him as[9] king upon the throne of David and to be a light to the nations that they also may trust in me.

10. ‏פְּנֵי יהוה בְּרְשָׁעִים לְהַכְרִית מֵהָאָרֶץ זִכְרָם׃‎

The face[16] of Yahweh is against the wicked, to cut off the memory of them[17] from the earth.

11. ‏כַּסְפְּךָ וּזְהָבְךָ לֹא חָפָצְתִּי׃‎

Your silver and your gold I have not desired.[18]

---

[1] ‏יוֹשֵׁב‎ and ‏אִישׁ‎ are sing. but are to be regarded here as collective singulars, and to be translated as plurals in English (cf. Key § 22B, note 14, first paragraph).

[2] Or *I beg you.*

66   § 25. A.

³ Lit. *from the face of the queen.* פָּנִים is used much oftener in Hebrew than *face* is in English, e.g. Jer. 42.17 none of them shall escape *the evil* (מִפְּנֵי הָרָעָה). So Jer. 44.22 *because of* the evil of your doings מִפְּנֵי רֹעַ מַעַלְלֵיכֶם. Indeed, מִפְּנֵי אֲשֶׁר is used with the meaning *because of the fact that,* or *because.* Note also that *the courtiers who attend upon the king,* his confidential advisers, are described as *those who see his face.*

⁴ Note that אַדֶּרֶת *mantle,* which is composed of ʾad-*dereth* is treated as a segholate noun, so that with pron. suffix it appears as אַדַּרְתִּי, etc. (cf. § 25.4.(a)).

⁵ For יִגֹּף (< יִנְגֹּף), the impf. of נָגַף, cf. Key § 24A, note 5.

⁶ Lit. : *went to their way.* This is the normal mode of expression in Hebrew.

⁷⁻⁷ שָׁמַע אֶל־ is more than *to hear* (which would be with a direct accus.) ; it should be rendered *to hearken to, to heed, to obey.* Note also the idiomatic use of לְבַקֵּשׁ *to seek.*

⁸ lit. *to rain.*

⁹ Hebrew says : *give grass for food* (for your cattle). So in sentence 9 : *I set him for king.*

¹⁰ Note abs. בְּהֵמָה ; cstr. בֶּהֱמַת ; with pron. suffix, בְּהֶמְתִּי, etc. (cf. § 25.4.(a)).

¹¹ The normal rule is that a noun in the constr. state before a following noun in the absolute *immediately* precedes that noun (cf. § 14.4, rule 2). Here is an example of a word intervening between two nouns so related, viz. לְךָ. Strict conformity with rule 2 as quoted would demand יֵשׁ מָקוֹם לְךָ *there is a place for you, there is room for you* ; but the order in the text יֵשׁ־לְךָ מָקוֹם is common. ־יֵשׁ is not the cstr. form of יֵשׁ, but is the form which יֵשׁ assumes before a tone syllable (cf. Key § 24B, note 1) : e.g. יֶשׁ־לִי כֶסֶף *I have some money* : וַיִּשְׁמַע יַעֲקֹב כִּי יֵשׁ־שֶׁבֶר בְּמִצְרַיִם *Jacob heard that there was corn in Egypt* (based on Gen. 42.1) ; הֲיֵשׁ בֵּית־אָבִיךְ מָקוֹם

לָנוּ לָלִין *Is there room in your father's house for us to spend the night* (Gen. 24.23) ; אִם־יֶשׁ אָחִינוּ *If our brother is with us* (Gen. 44.26).

[12] The more common order for the Hebrew here is וְנָתַתִּי לָכֶם מַיִם. Note נָתַתִּי > נָתַתִּי. The change to the plur. לָכֶם is unexpected ; cf. אַתָּה at the end of the sentence.

[13] אֶת־ meaning *with* takes the form אִתְּךָ, אִתִּי, etc., with suffixes (full list of forms in § 40.6.(b)) ; אִתָּךְ is pausal form of אִתְּךָ.

[14] Lit. *light* (or *swift*) *on his feet.*

[15] חָפֵץ is commonly construed with בְּ of persons or things. That construction is used in the first part of the sentence with בָּטַחְתִּי but in the second part חָפַצְתִּי is used alone without בוֹ following. It can be assumed, however, that the effect of the בוֹ in the first part is carried over into the second part.

[16] Cf. note 3 above. *The face of Yahweh* as used here illustrates the fact that such phrases as *the face of Yahweh, the name of Yahweh, the angel of Yahweh* and *the glory of Yahweh* are often used in Hebrew where we might expect the divine name alone. They are manifestations of the Godhead.

[17] *their memory* as a translation is possibly not so clear.

[18] This is one example of the use of the verb חָפֵץ followed by an accusative (cf. note 15 above).

B.

1 נִסְתְּרָה דַרְכִּי מֵאֱלֹהָי: 2 כִּי הִשְׁחִית [1]כָּל־בָּשָׂר אֶת־
דַּרְכּוֹ עַל־הָאָרֶץ: 3 לֹא [2]דְרָכֵינוּ דַּרְכֵיהֶם[2]: 4 [3]וַיִּכְרַע כָּל־
הָעָם עַל־בִּרְכָּיו לִפְנֵי הַמֶּלֶךְ: 5 [4]תְּדַבֶּר־נָא שִׁפְחָתְךָ בְּאָזְנֵי
הַמֶּלֶךְ: 6 מָלַךְ אֱלֹהַי וּמַלְכִּי עַל־צִיּוֹן הַר קָדְשׁוֹ: 7 אֲדַרְתִּי
גְּבֻרָתָה: 8 מַמְלַכְתּוֹ [5]מַמְלֶכֶת עוֹלָם[5]: 9 אַכְרִית אֶת־קַשְׁתָּם

וְאֶת־כָּל־כְּלֵי מִלְחַמְתָּם⁶: 10 בָּטַחְתִּי בְחַסְדְּךָ יִשְׂבַּע לְבָבִי

תְּשׁוּעָתְךָ⁷: 11 כַּסְפְּךָ וּזְהָבְךָ לִי יְלָדֶיךָ וְיַלְדֹתֶיךָ ⁸גַּם־לִי

הֵם⁸: 12 אֲשַׁלֵּם אֶת־נְדָרַי אֵלֶיךָ כִּי אַתָּה מַלְכִּי ⁹וֵאלֹהַי

וְלִמַּדְתִּי אֶת־יְלָדַי וְאֶת־יַלְדוֹתַי לִשְׁמֹר אֶת־מִצְוֹתֶיךָ וּלְהַשְׁלִיךְ

אֶת־כָּל־הַצְּלָמִים אֲשֶׁר קִבְּצוּ: 13 אָמַרְתִּי לְעַבְדִּי נָפְלָה

אַדַּרְתִּי עָלֶיךָ ¹⁰וְהָלַכְתָּ בְדַרְכִּי וְלִמַּדְתָּ אֶת־עֲבָדַי לִזְכֹּר

אֶת־דְּבָרַי לְמַעַן יִקְרְאוּ הַגּוֹיִם בְּשֵׁם יהוה ¹¹לִגְדָלוֹ וּלְחֶסֶד

¹²מְבַקְשָׁיו: 14 שְׁמַע אֶת־תְּפִלָּתִי בַּעֲבוּר חַסְדְּךָ כִּי ¹³אֵין

זִכְרְךָ בַּמָּוֶת¹³:

---

¹ We have already had several examples of the omission of the article in the genitive following כָּל־ when it might have been expected : כָּל־רָע all evil, כָּל־אָדָם all mankind, all men. So here כָּל־בָּשָׂר all flesh. (Cf. Key § 24A, note 13).

²⁻² Lit. not our ways (are) their ways cf. sentence 3 of Heb.–Eng. Exer. above ; but the other order is possible : לֹא דַרְכֵיהֶם דְּרָכֵינוּ.

³ When הָעָם (or, as here, כָּל־הָעָם) is subject, the related verb may be singular or plural. But in a narrative sequence (the people came . . . and attacked . . . and took away . . .) if the first verb is singular, the succeeding ones are commonly plural.

⁴ תְּדַבֵּר is the ordinary form of the 3 sing. fem. impf. Piʻel of the verb דבר. The shortening of the ‥ to ֱ is, with the enclitic ־נָא following, to avoid the collocation of two accented syllables ; the two words are united in one accented unit (§ 9, note 1 following the Exercise).

⁵⁻⁵ A kingdom of eternity. עוֹלָם can mean ancient times : e.g. יְמֵי עוֹלָם days of old ; מֵעוֹלָם from of old, from ancient times ; it can also mean ever,

continuity ; this may refer to a man's lifetime, e.g. עֶבֶד עוֹלָם *a perpetual slave*, or in an unlimited sense, e.g. הָאָרֶץ לְעוֹלָם עֹמֶדֶת *the earth will endure for ever* : חֶרְפַּת עוֹלָם *a perpetual reproach* ; בְּרִית עוֹלָם *an everlasting covenant* ; חָק־עוֹלָם *an everlasting statute* ; לְעוֹלָם and עַד־עוֹלָם *for ever*.

⁶⁻⁶ Lit. *all the weapons of their warfare.* For the form of מִלְחַמְתָּם, cf. § 25.4.(a).

⁷ Normally in such a use as this the verb שָׂבַע takes an accus. of respect after it and not בְּ.

⁸⁻⁸ Hebrew would commonly add הֶם here, and not use גַּם־לִי alone. We can say גַּם־הֶם לִי or גַּם־לִי הֶם.

⁹ For the vocalization, cf. § 11.II.(b).

¹⁰ Probably וְהָלַכְתָּ should be preferred to וְהִתְהַלַּכְתָּ. Better Hebrew would be to read וְאַתָּה for emphasis followed by the verbal form in the impf. ; but the necessary form (תֵּלֵךְ) shows that הָלַךְ belongs to a class of verbs which has still to be dealt with (cf. § 29.2.(2).(b)).

¹¹ לְגָדְלוֹ *for, in respect of, his greatness* is a suitable rendering ; עַל־ also would be suitable, as would עַל־דְּבַר (lit. *because of the matter of, because of*).

¹² מְבַקְשָׁיו *his seekers* ; for the absence of the *daghesh forte* in this *Pi'el* ptc. form, cf. § 6.5.

¹³⁻¹³ In Ps. 6.6 these words appear in the order אֵין בַּמָּוֶת זִכְרֶךָ. This is another example of a word intervening between a noun in the constr. state (אֵין) and its related genitive (זִכְרֶךָ) ; cf. Key, note 11 in A of this Exercise. This order was probably used for rhythmic effect.

§ 26.
A.

1. Haters of good and lovers of evil. 2. Their king dealt kindly with[1] our king, our priests and our prophets. 3. I let my enemy go and he escaped. 4. Thine enemy is dead [2]who sought thy life[2].

5. And the inhabitants of the land will go like blind men[3] and their blood will be shed[4] like dust.[3] 6. David took his staff[3] in his hand, chose him[5] some stones[6] from the wadi and approached the enemy, [7]while the enemy carried a shield before him[7]. When [8]he noticed that[8] David was a stripling,[9] he despised[3] him. 7. " Am I a dog[10] that thou approachest me with sticks ? "[3] 8. David said to him : " Thou approachest me with sword and spear, but I approach thee in the name of Yahweh God of Israel." 9. This was the custom[11] of the priest with the people. [12]Whenever any man offered a sacrifice[12], the priest's servant would approach him with his fork in his hand, put his fork into the vessel,[13] and take for himself all that his fork found[14] in (the midst of) the vessel. 10. The servants[15] found the key and opened the doors of the palace ; and, behold, the king was lying on the ground dead.

11. בְּנִי[16]אָתָּה :   Thou art my son.

12. אַתֶּם[16] בָּנַי :   You are my sons.

13. לֹא אֲדַבֵּר עוֹד בִּשְׁמוֹ :   I will speak no more in his name.

14. וּלְקַחְתֶּם אֶת־[17]מַקֶּלְכֶם בְּיֶדְכֶם[17]:

And you shall take your staves in your hands.

---

[1] The preposition *with* is used only once in the English translation, but in the Hebrew עָם is used with each of the three nouns. This represents a difference of usage in the two languages.

[2-2] הַמְבַקֵּשׁ here is an example of a ptc. used verbally and, so, governing a noun in the accus. (אֶת־נַפְשֶׁךָ). For the omission of the *daghesh forte* from the מְ, cf. § 6.5.

[3] עֹוְרִים from sing. עִוֵּר. Cf. § 6.5 ; so for the omission of the *daghesh forte* in מַקְלוֹ (sing. מַקֵּל) and in וַיְקַלֵּל in sentence 6. Note also the use of the generic article in כַּעֹוְרִים (§ 12.2.(b).i) and in כֶּעָפָר at the end of the sentence.

[4] וְשֻׁפַּךְ is 3 sing. masc. perf. consec. *Puʿal* ; the corresponding part of the *Niphʿal* might equally well have been used (cf. § 22 Exercise, Hebrew–English, sentence 4).

⁵ i.e. *for himself.* Dativus Commodi ; cf. § 12.2.(c).i.

⁶ אֲבָנִים *stones* ; מֵאַבְנֵי הַנַּחַל also might have been used, the מִן being partitive ; cf. § 12.4.(c).

⁷⁻⁷ This is a good example of a circumstantial clause ; note the order of subject followed by ptc. נֹשֵׂא is better translated by *carried* than by *raised.*

⁸⁻⁸ Lit. *And he saw David that he was a stripling and he despised him.* Two points should be noted : (*a*) . . . *saw David that he* . . . is a characteristic Hebrew usage ; English . . . *saw that David* . . . ; (*b*) the two clauses introduced by וַיַּבֵּט and וַיְקַלֵּל are in Hebrew parallel. In English the first clause should be made subordinate, as in the translation given in the Key.

⁹ נַעַר is a young, inexperienced lad ; cf. Jer. 1.6.

¹⁰ Note the emphatic order with הַכֶלֶב at the beginning.

¹¹ מִשְׁפָּט, which often means the *judgment* or *ruling* given by a שׁוֹפֵט, probably derives the meaning *custom* from the circumstance that in a tribal society the traditional, customary forms and practices have often their origin in rulings given by a chief. The oldest form of law is that which is based on long established customs.

¹²⁻¹² The first clause in Hebrew is introductory and in suspense : *Any man offering* (lit. *sacrificing*) *a sacrifice—the priest's servant would approach him,* the *him* being recapitulatory in force.

¹³ Sentence 9 is based on 1 Sam. 2.13–14. The *vessel* is the pot in which the meat of the sacrificial animal was boiled to serve, in part, as the common meal of the worshippers who offered the animal.

¹⁴ Lit. *all that was found by his fork* ; it means all that the fork brought up out of the pot.

¹⁵ Cf. notes 2 and 3 above.

¹⁶ בְּנֵי, אַתָּה are the pausal forms of בְּנֵי, אַתָּה ; cf. § 11, note (b) following Voc. Sentences 11 and 12 illustrate two ways of expression.

¹⁷ Examples of the use of the sing. in Hebrew where English commonly uses the plural (cf. Key § 20A, note 18).

B.

1 זֶה ¹וּבְנֵי וְאֵלֶּה ¹וּבְנֵי בְנִי : 2 לָקַחְנוּ אֶת־²מַקְלֹתֵינוּ בְּיָדֵנוּ²:

3 ³עָשׂוּ אֹיְבֵינוּ ⁴חֶסֶד עִם־בָּנֵינוּ : 4 אֵלֶּה הַחֻקּוֹת וְהַמִּשְׁפָּטִים

אֲשֶׁר תִּשְׁמְרוּ בָאָרֶץ אֲשֶׁר אַתֶּם ⁵עֹבְרִים שָׁמָּה ⁶אַתָּה וּבִנְךָ

וּבֶן־⁷בְּנֶךָ : 5 אַתָּה ⁸צָרַף לְבַב הָאֲנָשִׁים שְׁמֹר אֶת־נַפְשׁוֹת

עֲבָדֶיךָ לְמַעַן יִשְׁכְּנוּ ⁹אֹהֲבֵי שְׁמְךָ בְּאַרְצְךָ בְּשָׁלוֹם : 6 אֲנִי

קָטֹנְתִּי מִכָּל־הַחֶסֶד אֲשֶׁר ¹⁰עָשִׂיתָ אִתִּי כִּי ¹¹בְּמַקְלִי עָבַרְתִּי

אֶת־הַיַּרְדֵּן הַזֶּה וְעַתָּה גָּדַלְתִּי ¹²וָאַשְׁחִית אֶת־כָּל־אֹיְבָי:

7 הֲלֹא נִשְׁבַּעְתָּ־לִּי ¹³לֵאמֹר יִמְלֹךְ בִּנְךָ אַחֲרַי וְיֵשֵׁב עַל־

¹⁴כִּסְאִי וְשָׁפַט אֶת־הָעָם הַזֶּה¹³: וְעַתָּה הָלַךְ אֲדֹנִיָּהוּ מִן־

הַהֵיכָל וַיִּקְרָא אֶת־בְּנֵי הַמֶּלֶךְ ¹⁵וַיַּמְלִיכוּ אֹתוֹ: 8 זֶה דוֹר

¹⁶דֹּרְשֶׁךָ דֹּרְשֵׁי פְּנֵי אֱלֹהֵי יַעֲקֹב:

---

¹ In בְּנִי and in בְּנֵי it seems possible in each case to regard the *daghesh* as *daghesh forte conjunctivum* ; cf. § 6.6 ; but probably each should be regarded as *daghesh lene* for emphasis after an open syllable.

²⁻² It would be preferable to use the sing. מַקְלֵנוּ (for the omission of the *dagh. forte* from the ק, cf. § 6.5) here ; the sing. בְּיָדֵנוּ is idiomatic Hebrew. Another rendering of the sentence is possible and good : לָקַחְנוּ אִישׁ אֶת־ מַקְלוֹ בְּיָדוֹ.

³ The form of the 3 pl. perf. Qal of עָשָׂה is עָשׂוּ (cf. § 32.3.(a)). This sentence 3 was taken over from the corresponding section of the 24th edition of the Grammar and it was not noticed that the call for such a form as עָשׂוּ is premature at this stage in the Grammar. It is true that the

sing. אֹיֵב can be used in a collective sense; cf., for instance, Exod. 15.9:
אָמַר אוֹיֵב אֶרְדֹּף אַשִּׂיג אֲחַלֵּק שָׁלָל *The enemy said:* " *I will pursue, I will overtake, I will divide the spoil,*" where the reference is to the Egyptians. But such a use of אֹיֵב occurs mostly in poetic passages. In succeeding editions of the Grammar the difficulty will be avoided by making the subject sing. (*our enemy* אֹיְבֵנוּ).

[4] Commonly חֶסֶד in this usage with the verb עָשָׂה follows the verb immediately; but there are some cases in which it comes at the end of the clause: cf. וְעָשָׂה עִמְּךָ חֶסֶד *and he will deal with you kindly.*

[5] An example of a ptc. which can be translated as a present *you are crossing* or as a future *you are about to cross.*

[6] In Jud. 8.22 this phrase appears as: גַּם־אַתָּה גַּם־בִּנְךָ גַּם בֶּן־בְּנֶךָ but Deut. 6.2 has *wāw* as in the translation. The latter is much the commoner.

[7] בִּנְךָ pausal form of בִּנְךָ.

[8] צָרַף is used of *testing, smelting* and *refining* metals as well as of testing persons; for testing in the latter sense בָּחַן is more common (cf. Jer. 17.10; 20.12).

[9] For the ptc. אֹהֵב, cf. § 19.5. The composite *shᵉwa* in אֹהֲבֵי is owing to the guttural ה (cf. the corresponding form of קָטַל: קֹטְלֵי).

[10] The 2 sing. masc. perf. Qal of עָשָׂה (cf. § 32.3.(b).ii). This form is introduced prematurely here, and in succeeding editions of the Grammar *Yahweh has* will be introduced into the sentence in place of *thou hast*. As an alternative to אַתָּ in this clause עָמִי may be used.

[11] Cf. note 2 above.

[12] Notice the 3 sing. masc. imperf. consec. Hiph. is וַיַּקְטֵל but 1 sing. com. is וָאַקְטִיל; cf. § 24.I.1; *Hiphʿil* (a).i.

[13-13] Hebrew usage would undoubtedly express the terms of the promise quoted here in direct speech. When this is done, note the changes

in the pronom. suffixes. After יִמְלֹךְ, בִּנְךָ or בְּנֶךָ may be used; in 1 Kings 1.17, on which this sentence is based, בְּנֵךְ is used since it is Solomon's mother, Bathsheba, who is being addressed.

[14] כִּסֵּא has to be noted. The form with 1 sing. pron. suffix. is כִּסְאִי (for the omission of the *daghesh forte*, cf. § 6.5); but the form in use with the 2 sing. masc. suffixes is כִּסְאֲךָ, in which the *shᵉwa* written to the ס must be silent in view of the vocal *shᵉwa* immediately following (cf. § 3.6). The plur. is כִּסְאוֹת.

[15] Or וְהֵם הִמְלִיכוּ because of the change of subject.

[16] To seek God is usually דָּרַשׁ in Hebrew; but it is notable that in Ps. 24.6, on which this sentence is based, מְבַקְשֵׁי is used in place of דֹּרְשֵׁי.

§ 27.

A.

Thou (m.) hast kept me. I have kept thee (m.). And he will keep him. To keep thee.[1] And to keep her. Keep (thou) me, *or* to keep me (cstr. infin. Qal). And he kept me. And it wore me as a garment.[2] Thou (m.) wilt keep them. That I may keep her.[3] He will keep him. She will keep thee.[4] They judged me. They judged them. When thou judgest.[5] Judge (thou (m.)) me *or* to judge me. Thou (m.) hast remembered them. I will remember her.[6] And he remembered her. They will remember me. When he mentioned.[7] Make (thou (m.)) me remember. They stole thee (m.). And he will gather thee (m.). He gathered them (m.). And I shall gather them *or* And thou (f.) wilt gather them. And those that gather him (or it). When I gather. I shall gather thee (fem.). He will gather thee (m.).

[1] Cf. § 27.8.(a).ii. As is said in this para., קָטְלְךָ is more common than קָטְלֶךָ as the form of the infin. cstr. with 2 sing. masc. suffix; but when ל is prefixed, as here, לִשְׁמֹר (liš-mōr) takes with 2 sing. masc. suffix the form לִשְׁמָרְךָ (*liš-mo-rᵉkhā*).

[2] לָבַשׁ means *to be clothed, to wear*; the *Hiph'il* הִלְבִּישׁ means *to clothe*.
Job 29.14, where the form used here is to be found, reads: צֶדֶק לָבַשְׁתִּי
וַיִּלְבָּשֵׁנִי *I put on* (became clothed in) *righteousness and it wore me*, i.e.
became incarnate in me; for Hiph., cf. Gen. 41.42: וַיַּלְבֵּשׁ אֹתוֹ בִּגְדֵי שֵׁשׁ
and he put on him (or *clothed himself in*) *garments of fine linen*.

[3] The pron. suffix used here is the 3 sing. fem. with *nûn energicum*
(cf. § 27.6).

[4] This is said of חָכְמָה *wisdom* in Prov. 4.6. The suffix is 2 sing. masc.
with *nûn energicum*: יְךָ > אֶךָ, the נ becoming assimilated to the ךָ, so
that the *daghesh* in the second is *forte* while that in the first is *lênê*.

[5] Cf. § 27.8.(b).

[6] 3 sing. fem. suffix with *nûn energicum*. The following word shows
the ordinary form of the same suffix.

[7] *Hiph'il* of זָכַר means *to call to remembrance, to make mention, to
celebrate*.

B.

1. Thou[1] hast requited me good,[2] whereas I requited thee
evil.[2] 2. They honoured[3] me with their lips.[4] 3. Keep the words of
Yahweh, write them on the tablets[5] of thy heart. 4. Seek peace
and pursue it. 5. Lead[6] me in the path of thy commands, for in
it I delight. 6. Seek Yahweh while he may be found.[7] 7. The old
man said to him: " Stand before me that I may adjure[8] thee to
seek a wife for my son in the land of his kindred."[9] 8. Yahweh the
God of Israel who took me from the land of my kindred, (he) will
send his angel[10] to keep thee in the way. 9. Yahweh has sent
thee to gather the broken-hearted[11] and he will keep thee in all
the places to which he has sent thee. 10. Do not forget me, O God
of my salvation; remember me for thy love's sake. 11. Teach me
the way of thy statutes and I will magnify thee all the days of
my life. 12. Blessed is the man whom thou hast chosen, [12]that he
may dwell in thy courts[12]; he will trust[13] in thee and honour thee
with all his heart.

F

13. הָרַג מֹשֶׁה אֶת־הַמִּצְרִי וַיִּטְמְנֵהוּ בַחוֹל׃

Moses slew the Egyptian and hid him in the sand.

14. יהוה יִשְׁמָרְךָ מִכָּל־רָע יִשְׁמֹר אֶת־נַפְשֶׁךָ׃

Yahweh will keep thee from all evil ; he will keep thy soul.[14]

¹ The use of אַתָּה in the first clause and אֲנִי in the second sharpens the contrast between David and Saul to whom, in the original passage, the reference is made (cf. 1 Sam. 24.18).

² Cf. § 13.5.(g).

³ Or *honour*.

⁴ שִׂפְתֵיהֶם is the dual of שָׂפָה with 3 plur. masc. suffix. In such a case as this Hebrew often uses the sing. (here שְׂפָתָם).

⁵ The assumption is probably sound that the figure of speech used here is expressed by *the tablets of the heart* in the case of an individual person and not *the tablet of the heart*. On that assumption we have here an idiomatic use of the sing. in Hebrew where the English idiom prefers the plur.

⁶ Lit. *Cause me to walk.*

⁷ This is an example of the *Niphʿal tolerativum* ; cf. § 22.3.

⁸ נִשְׁבַּע means *to swear*. The *Hiphʿil* means *to cause to swear, to put (a person) on oath, to adjure*.

⁹ מוֹלֶדֶת, in view of ־לֶדֶת, is treated as a *segholate* noun, so that, with pron. suffixes, it takes the form מוֹלַדְתִּי, etc. (cf. § 25.4.(a)).

¹⁰ Or *messenger*.

¹¹ Or נִשְׁבְּרֵי לֵב without the article, cf. Key § 15C, note 10–10 and D, note 6.

¹²⁻¹² Or *for he will dwell in thy courts*. The preceding verbal form בְּחָרְתּוֹ is to be explained in this way : בְּחָרְתּוֹ < בְּחָרְתָהוּ (owing to the elision of the weak ה) < בְּחָרְתּוֹ.

¹³ Or *and that he may trust.*

¹⁴ Not *soul* as distinct from body. Often נֶפֶשׁ simply means the self, so that we may say here *thee* or *thy life* in place of *thy soul.*

C.

1 ¹קִבַּצְתִּיךָ : 2 ²אֲקַבְּצֶךָ ³מִמְּקֹמוֹת הָאָרֶץ הָרְחֹקִים³:

3 וּשְׁמַרְתַּנִי בְּדַרְכֶּךָ : 4 שָׁמְרֵהוּ : 5 לִפְנֵי שָׁמְרָה אֶת־הָאִישׁ :

6 בְּיוֹם פָּקְדִי אֶת־יִשְׂרָאֵל ⁴אַשְׁמִיד אֶת־מִזְבְּחוֹת ⁵בֵּיתְאֵל :

7 שָׁפְטֵנִי ⁶כְּצִדְקָתִי : 8 ⁷אַל־תִּקְבְּרֵנִי ⁸בְּמִצְרַיִם וְשָׁכַבְתִּי עִם־

⁹אֲבוֹתַי וּקְבַרְתַּנִי בִּקְבֻרָתָם : 9 ¹⁰מָה־אָדָם כִּי ¹¹תִזְכְּרֶהוּ

¹²וּבֶן־אָדָם כִּי ¹¹תִפְקְדֶהוּ : 10 אָמַר לְהַזְכִּירוֹ לִפְנֵי כֹהֲנֵי

הַהֵיכָל : 11 הַזְכִּירֵנִי אֶת־חַסְדְּךָ ¹³וּפְקַדְתַּנִי בְּצִדְקָתְךָ לְמַעַן

אַגְדִּילְךָ וְסָפַרְתִּי אֶת־טוּבְךָ לְבָנַי : 12 אֶת־מְכַבְּדַי אֲכַבֵּד

וְאֶת־שֹׁכְחַי אַשְׁלִיךְ : 13 ¹⁴בַּקְּשׁוּנִי בְּכָל־לְבַבְכֶם וּשְׁמַרְתִּיכֶם

¹⁵מִיַּד אֹיְבֵיכֶם : בִּטְחוּ בִי ¹⁶וְשָׁלַחְתִּי לָכֶם מָטָר ¹⁷לְאַדְמַתְכֶם

וּשְׂמְחָה לְנַפְשֹׁתֵיכֶם :

---

¹ So with 2 sing. masc. verbal suffix ; or, with corresponding fem.
suffix קִבַּצְתִּיךְ.

² Or, with *nûn energicum,* אֲקַבְּצֶנָּה.

³⁻³ Note in this phrase מְקֹמוֹת (or רְחֹקוֹת from sing. מָקוֹם, and רְחֹקִים
since מָקוֹם, commonly masc., is sometimes fem.) from sing. רָחוֹק (cf.
§ 2.7.(d)). There are two other Hebrew words which may be used to translate
distant places. First, יַרְכָּה *side* is used in the dual, יַרְכָּתַיִם *sides* ; so
Jer. 31.8 : הִנְנִי מֵבִיא אוֹתָם מֵאֶרֶץ צָפוֹן וְקִבַּצְתִּים מִיַּרְכְּתֵי אָרֶץ. *Behold I
will bring them from the land of the north and gather them from distant lands.*
Second, כָּנָף *wing* is used meaning *extremity, far corner* ; cf. Isa. 11.12b :
וּנְפֻצוֹת יְהוּדָה יְקַבֵּץ מֵאַרְבַּע כַּנְפוֹת הָאָרֶץ : *and he will gather the dispersed
of Judah from the four corners of the earth.*

⁴ But note that וְהִשְׁמַדְתִּי can also be used. Such a use of the *wāw* consec. form וְהִשְׁמַדְתִּי shows that such a form can be used after a *temporal clause or phrase*; e.g. Gen. 3.5 : בְּיוֹם אֲכָלְכֶם וְנִפְקְחוּ עֵינֵיכֶם *in the day when you eat* (lit. of your eating) *your eyes will be opened*; Exod. 16.6 : עֶרֶב וִידַעְתֶּם *in the evening you will know*; 1 Kings 13.31 : בְּמוֹתִי וּקְבַרְתֶּם אֹתִי *when I die, you shall bury me*. . . .

⁵ בֵּיתְאֵל is always written with *methegh* in this way, but it is sometimes written in the form בֵּית־אֵל, where the *methegh* may be interpreted as emphasizing a long vowel in a closed syllable which is linked by *maqqēph* with the following tone syllable.

⁶ Or כְּצִדְקִי (from צֶדֶק).

⁷ Or אַל־נָא תִקְבְּרֵנִי with the נָא־ of entreaty introduced. In this case there is no *daghesh lênê* in the initial ת of the verbal form following the open syllable נָא־.

⁸ The form of the dual ending in מִצְרַיִם might seem to mean a reference to the two Egypts, upper and lower (and that in מַיִם to the waters above and below the firmament (Gen. 1.7)). But the ending should be regarded as a plur. rather than a dual.

⁹ The noun אָב *father* has now been used several times; observe the plur. in וֹת—(§ 13.5.(f)).

¹⁰ אָדָם *humanity*, not אִישׁ. The form in the original (Ps. 8.5) is אֱנוֹשׁ, a poetic form, meaning *mankind*.

¹¹ Ps. 8.5 introduces *nûn energicum* in both these verbal forms : תִּפְקְדֶנּוּ and תִּזְכְּרֶנּוּ.

¹² Not *a son of man* in our genealogical use of the word *son*. A *son of man* is simply *a human being*, without any restriction as to age.

¹³ An example of the common Hebrew practice of not using a second imperative in such a case as this (unless the first is קוּם לֵךְ, or another, more or less auxiliary imperative), but a *wāw* consec. perf. form.

¹⁴ Or דְּרָשׁוּנִי ; for the *dagh. forte* in בֻּקְשׁוּנִי, cf. Key § 23B, note 1.
דָּרַשׁ is used commonly in the sense *to seek God, to resort to* God. But, while
בָּקֵשׁ has commonly the general sense of *to seek, to search for*, it is sometimes
found with the same force as דָּרַשׁ ; e.g. Ps. 27.8 : אֶת־פָּנֶיךָ יהוה אֲבַקֵּשׁ
thy face, Yahweh, will I seek; Amos 5.4f. דְּרָשׁוּנִי וִחְיוּ וְאַל־תִּדְרְשׁוּ בֵּית־אֵל
seek me and live, but do not resort to Bethel; Zeph. 2.3 בַּקְּשׁוּ אֶת־
יהוה בַּקְּשׁוּ צֶדֶק בַּקְּשׁוּ עֲנָוָה *Seek Yahweh, seek righteousness, seek
humility*; and note the following verses in which the two verbs occur
together; Ps. 24.6 (So LXX) זֶה דּוֹר דֹּרְשָׁיו מְבַקְשֵׁי פְנֵי אֱלֹהֶי יַעֲקֹב *this is
the generation of those who seek him, who seek the face of the God of Jacob*;
Jer. 29.13 : וּבִקַּשְׁתֶּם אֹתִי וּמְצָאתֶם כִּי תִדְרְשֻׁנִי בְּכָל־לְבַבְכֶם *You
shall seek me and find me when you seek me with all your heart.*

¹⁵ *power*, as it is used here, is commonly translated into Hebrew by
יָד, the *hand* being a symbol of power, as *horn* or *horns* is of strength. Very
seldom in such a case is גְּבוּרָה, חַיִל, כֹּחַ or other such word for *power* or
strength used.

¹⁶ Or וְהִמְטַרְתִּי (§ 25 Exercise Heb.–Eng., sentence 5).

¹⁷ Or עַל־אַדְמַתְכֶם.

§ 28.

קרא *'Ayin* guttural¹ and *lāmedh 'aleph*. אכל *Pē 'aleph*.²
שלח *Lāmedh* guttural. שחט *'Ayin* guttural. שאף *'Ayin* guttural.
בין *'Ayin yôdh*. ילד *Pē yôdh*.³ ישע *Pē yôdh*³ and *lāmedh* guttural.
רום *'Ayin wāw*. ברך *'Ayin* guttural. עבר *Pē* guttural.
שאל *'Ayin* guttural. נחה *'Ayin* guttural and *lāmedh hē*.⁴ נחם
'Ayin guttural.⁵ נגף *Pē nûn*. רעע Double *'Ayin*. קלל Double
'Ayin. בוא *'Ayin wāw*.⁶ סבב Double *'Ayin*. קרע *'Ayin* guttural¹
and *lāmedh* guttural. ירא *Pē yôdh*,³ *'ayin* guttural and *lāmedh
'aleph*. ירה *Pē yôdh*,³ *'ayin* guttural and *lāmedh hē*.

¹ For classification of these verbs a medial ר usually counts as a guttural (cf. § 36.1.(c)).

² Pē guttural is not a sufficient definition ; there is a class of Pē 'aleph verbs, a sub-class of Pē gutturals, to which אכל belongs (§ 37).

³ The student can describe this verb in the meantime only as Pē yôdh, but the majority of the verbs of this type are really Pē wāw. There is no distinction between the two kinds in the perf. Qal (cf. § 29).

⁴ נחה is obviously a verb whose first radical is nûn but we do not class it as Pē nûn because the nûn does not undergo assimilation as happens with those which are classified as Pē nûn (§ 34.1.(d)).

⁵ Cf. § 34.1.(d).

⁶ While this verb has א as its final radical, it is not commonly described as a lāmedh 'aleph, this term being reserved for disyllabic verbs such as מָצָא (§ 38).

§ 29.

A.

רֵד sing. masc. imperative Qal of ירד.

רְדָה sing. masc. imperative (emphatic form) Qal of ירד.

לָרֶדֶת infin. construct Qal of ירד with לְ.

דַּע sing. masc. imperative Qal of ידע.

דַּעַת infin. construct Qal of ידע.

נֵלְכָה 1 plur. cohortative Qal of הלך.

אִינַק 1 sing. imperf. Qal of ינק.

תִּירָא 2 sing. masc. or 3 sing. fem. imperf. Qal of ירא.

הַנּוֹרָא masc. sing. participle Niph. of ירא with the article.

The one who is feared, or *to be feared, the terrible.*

אִוָּרֵשׁ 1 sing. imperf. Niph. of ירשׁ, *I shall be dispossessed.*

וַיּוֹרֶשׁ 3 sing. masc. imperf. Hiph. of יָרֵשׁ with *wāw* consecutive.

The Hiph. הוֹרִישׁ can mean (*a*) *to cause* (a man) *to possess*.

(*b*) *to cause* (another man) *to possess*, so *to dispossess* (the possessor).

וָאֵישָׁנָה Not *wāw* and the 1 sing. cohort. Qal of יָשֵׁן (which is וְאֵישָׁנָה), but the 1 sing. consec. impf. Qal (with the ending הָ), a form which is found in the later books of the Old Testament.

תּוּשַׁב 2 sing. masc. or 3 sing. fem. imperf. Hoph. of יָשַׁב.

בְּהוֹרִידִי infin. construct Hiph. of יָרַד with בְּ and 1 sing. suffix.

תֵּרַדְנָה 2 or 3 plur. fem. imperf. Qal of יָרַד.

וַיִּרְדָּהוּ 3 plur. masc. imperf. Hiph. of יָרַד with *wāw* consec. and 3 sing. masc. suffix.

הוּרַד 3 sing. masc. perf. Hoph. of יָרַד.

מַצִּיג masc. sing. participle Hiph. of יָצַג.

וַנֵּדָעֵם 1 plur. imperf. Qal of יָדַע with *wāw* consec. and 3 plur. masc. suffix.

יִירָשׁוּם 3 plur. masc. imperf. Qal of יָרֵשׁ with 3 plur. masc. suffix.

B.

1. And Abram went down[1] to Egypt with his wife, and the king of Egypt did not know that she was his wife ; and he married her and treated Abram[2] well for her sake. Then Yahweh afflicted him with great plagues and he recognized[3] that she was his wife. 2. Yahweh said to Abram : " I am Yahweh who brought thee out from Ur of the Chaldees to give thee[4] this land for a possession."[5] And he said : " O Lord Yahweh,[6] how am I to know that I will possess it ? "[7] 3. Then Jacob's sons said to him[8] : " The man kept asking[9] us about[10] ourselves and our relatives,[11] saying : ' Is your

father still[12] alive ?   Have you[13] a brother ? '   We told him[14]
according to[15] the tenor of these words. [How] were we to know[16]
that he would say : ' Bring your brother down '."[17]   4. The
everlasting God[18] Yahweh, the creator of heaven and earth, does
not grow weary or exhausted.   Youths may[19] grow weary and
exhausted and young men may[19] stumble to their fall[20] ; but
those who trust in Yahweh will go on[21] unweariedly. 5. And now,
if I have found favour in thy sight, pray [22]let me know[22] thy ways
[23]and I shall know thee,[23] in order that I may find favour in thy
sight.   6. So David went out and succeeded[24] in everything to
which Saul sent him and it pleased[25] all the people and all the
servants of Saul also.

7. וְזָכַרְתָּ֫ אֶת־כָּל־הַדֶּ֫רֶךְ אֲשֶׁר [26]הוֹלִיכְךָ֫ יהוה אֱלֹהֶ֫יךָ [27]זֶ֫ה
[28]אַרְבָּעִים שָׁנָה בַּמִּדְבָּר לְדַ֫עַת אֶת־אֲשֶׁר בִּלְבָבְךָ [29]הֲתִשְׁמֹר
מִצְוֺתָיו אִם־לֹא:

And thou shalt remember all the way Yahweh thy God has led
thee now for forty years in the wilderness, to discover what was
in thy heart, whether thou wouldst keep his commands or not.

[1] In an impf. consec. form such as וַיֵּ֫רֶד, with the final syllable closed
and the penultimate syllable open, the accent is retracted to the penultimate
syllable, with a consequent shortening of the vowel in the final syllable.

[2] Note how for emphasis the object *Abram* precedes the verb הֵיטִיב.
It is to be noted that הֵיטִיב does not take a direct accus. of person, but is
construed with לְ, i.e. *do good to someone*. There is also the usage of הֵיטִיב
in § 29.4 which should be noted.

[3] וַיֵּ֫דַע is not suitably rendered here by *and he knew*. The meaning
rather is *and so he learned*, or *recognized the fact*, or *concluded*.

[4] *To give* is לָתֵת תֵּת (> תֶּנֶת) being the cstr. infin. of נָתַן). But since
the following לְךָ is counted as virtually a monosyllable, לָתֵת and לְךָ, to
avoid the collocation of two tone-syllables, are joined together in one tonal
unit, so that the vowel of תֵּת is shortened to *s*eghôl, being in a closed pre-tonic
syllable.

⁵ לְרִשְׁתָּהּ. Infin. cstr. of יָרַשׁ is רֶשֶׁת ; רִשְׁתָּהּ is the infin. cstr. with the 3 sing. fem. pron. suffix ; cf. § 29.2.(2).(b).iii.

⁶ For the normal vocalization and reading of יהוה, cf. § 15, final para. When יהוה is preceded by אֲדֹנָי, it is read as אֱלֹהִים and is vocalized יֱהֹוִה. This was done to avoid the repeated reading of אֲדֹנָי.

⁷ אִירָשֶׁנָּה is composed of אִירַשׁ, 1 sing. com. impf. Qal of יָרַשׁ, with the 3 sing. fem. pron. suffix written with *nûn energicum*. Note that the *pathaḥ* of the verbal form becomes *qāmeṣ* before the tone ; impfs. in *a* with verbal suffixes are vocalized on the analogy of First Declension nouns (cf. § 27.3.(a)).

⁸ אֵלָיו in such a clause as this is placed commonly, but not invariably, immediately after the verb. If לוֹ had been used instead of אֵלָיו, it would have been so placed.

⁹ The use of the adverbial infin. שָׁאוֹל with the finite form שָׁאַל probably indicates a strengthening of the verbal idea, and *kept asking* or *asked explicitly* seems to fit the need. The implication may be that the information was not freely given by Jacob's sons but Joseph had to elicit it piecemeal.

¹⁰ לְ here means *with reference to, in regard to*. The person to whom a question is directly addressed is put in the accus. ; e.g. שָׁאַל אֶת־הָאִישׁ *he asked the man. . . .*

¹¹ *relatives* seems a more suitable rendering than the customary *kindred*. The noun מוֹלֶדֶת, with pron. suffix מוֹלַדְתִּי, etc., cf. § 25.4.

¹² For the vocalization of the interrogative particle, cf. § 46.1.

¹³ הֲיֵשׁ לָכֶם lit. *is there to you* ? *have you* ? But where יֵשׁ occurs before the tone, as in יֶשׁ־לִי *I have*, יֶשׁ־לָנוּ *we have*, the vowel is shortened, since it is now in a closed pre-tonic syllable.

¹⁴ וַנַּגֶּד is the 1 plur. com. impf. consec. Hiph. of נגד, the נ becoming assimilated to the following ג in the way which is common with this class

of verb ; cf. § 24.I.1.(a).i ; § 34. The *ṣērê* here is shortened to *sᵉghôl* because it is united with the following לוֹ in one tonal unit. The tone is on לוֹ, so that the vowel of the closed pre-tonic syllable of וַנַּגֶּד has to be shortened.

¹⁵ עַל־פִּי can have various meanings : (*a*) lit. *according to the mouth of*, so *according to the word of* (cf. Gen. 45.21 ; Exod. 17.1) ; (*b*) but פֶּה (of which פִּי is the cstr. form) can mean *portion, measure* ; e.g. אִישׁ כְּפִי אָכְלוֹ *each man in proportion to his eating.* So here " *according to the measure of these words* " which means in this sentence " *in terms such as we are using now* ".

¹⁶ הֲיָדוֹעַ נֵדַע can be rendered in several ways : *Were we to know ? How were we to know ? Could we possibly know ?*

¹⁷ הוֹרִדוּ is the plur. masc. imper. Hiph. of יָרַד. It is not written הוֹרִידוּ to avoid two vocalic consonants in contiguous syllables ; cf. § 2.7.(d).

¹⁸ For the meaning of אֱלֹהֵי עוֹלָם, cf. Key § 25B, note 5–5.

¹⁹ *may* or *shall*. Probably *may* is to be preferred.

²⁰ כָּשַׁל, *Qal* and *Niphal*, means *to stumble*, or *to fall* (presumably as the result of stumbling). It seems suitable, therefore, to express the possible effect of the use of the adverbial infin. here by the translation given, rather than by *surely stumble.*

²¹ Sentence 4 is based on Isa. 40.28–31. In verse 31 יֵלֵכוּ is suitably translated as *will walk*, following upon *mount up on wing as eagles* and *run* earlier in the verse. Possibly *go on* or *continue* is more suitable in the shortened form of these verses which is used in sentence 4.

²²⁻²² The Hiph. imper. הוֹדִעֵנִי can be rendered as causative or permissive ; *cause me to know* or *let me know* ; cf. § 24.I.1.(b).i,ii.

²³⁻²³ Or *that I may know thee*. This is quite often the meaning of an impf. or cohortative like this preceded by simple *wāw*. For some examples, cf. § 43.II.5.(b).

[24] The *Hiph'il* הִשְׂכִּיל means *to prosper, to succeed* or *to act prudently or wisely.*

[25] Lit. *it was good in the eyes of*; and *it pleased* according to Hebrew usage, rather than *he pleased.*

[26] 3 sing. masc. perf. Hiph. of הָלַךְ with the 2 sing. masc. suffix. *he caused you to go, he led you* or *has led you.*

[27] זֶה is here proclitic. זֶה is often used as an enclitic; e.g. מִי־זֶה *who?* לָמָּה־זֶּה *why?* But it can be used as a proclitic, particularly with temporal phrases as here; cf. also זֶה־פַעֲמַיִם *two times.* It does not vary in number according to the noun with which it is in relation.

[28] In the meantime note that the Hebrew for *forty,* אַרְבָּעִים, is obviously a plural form, but שָׁנָה *year* is a singular. The Hebrew way of using numbers will be dealt with in § 45.

[29] For the interrogative הַ (הֲ), cf. note 12 above.

C.

1 וַתֵּלֶךְ הַתֵּבָה עַל־פְּנֵי הַמָּיִם: 2 הוֹדִיעֵנִי אֶת־דְּרָכֶיךָ:

3 וַיֹּאמְרוּ אֵלֶיהָ הֲתֵלְכִי עִם־הָאִישׁ הַזֶּה וַתֹּאמֶר אֵלֵךְ:

4 וַיֹּאמֶר הוֹצִיאוּ כָל־אִישׁ מִן־הַבַּיִת [1]וְלֹא עָמַד אִישׁ עִמּוֹ

[2]בְּהִתְוַדַּע אֶל־[3]אֶחָיו: 5 וַיִּפְתַּח הָאִישׁ אֶת־[4]דַּלְתוֹת הַבַּיִת

וַיֵּצֵא לָלֶכֶת לְדַרְכּוֹ: 6 וַתֹּאמֶר־לָהּ בַּת־פַּרְעֹה [5]קְחִי אֶת־

הַיֶּלֶד הַזֶּה [6]וְהֵינִיקִהוּ לִי [5]וַתִּקַּח אֶת־הַיֶּלֶד וַתְּנִיקֵהוּ: 7 הִנֵּה

שָׁמַעְתִּי כִּי [7]יֶשׁ־שֶׁבֶר בְּמִצְרַיִם רְדוּ שָׁמָּה [8]וּשְׁבַרְתֶּם־לָנוּ

מְעַט־[9]אֹכֶל: 8 וַיֹּאמֶר לוֹ יהוה אַל־תֵּרֵד מִצְרָיְמָה [10]שֵׁב

בָּאָרֶץ אֲשֶׁר [11]אֹמַר אֵלֶיךָ: 9 וַיִּירָא וַיֹּאמַר מַה־נּוֹרָא הַמָּקוֹם

הַזֶּה: 10 ¹²קִלְלַנִי הָאִישׁ הַהוּא ¹³קְלָלָה נִמְרֶצֶת¹³ בְּיוֹם ¹⁴לֶכְתִּי
אֶל־הַיַּרְדֵּן וָאֹמַר ¹⁵בִּלְבָבִי ¹⁶לְהָרְגוֹ בֶּחָרֶב: 11 וְעַתָּה אַל־
נָא תִשְׁכָּחֵהוּ כִּי ¹⁷אַתָּה אִישׁ חָכָם¹⁷ וְיָדַעְתָּ¹⁸ לִגְמֻלוֹ וְהוֹרַדְתָּ
אֶת־שֵׂיבָתוֹ ¹⁹בַדָּם ²⁰שְׁאוֹלָה:

1-1 This form of translation records the historical fact that no man stood after the command to withdraw had been given. But another translation is also possible : וְאֵין אִישׁ עוֹמֵד עִמּוֹ, which describes the *circumstance* that no man remained standing where he was.

2 This is the cstr. infin. *Hithpaʿel* (הִתְוַדֵּע) with the 3 sing. masc. pron. suffix and the preposition בְּ.

3 Cf. § 29, footnote 3 to the Heb.–Eng. Exercise and § 42.

4 דַּלְתֵי, cstr. dual of דֶּלֶת, would also be possible. The dual of רֶגֶל is רַגְלַיִם (cstr. רַגְלֵי *ragh-lê*), of בֶּרֶךְ, בִּרְכַּיִם (cstr. בִּרְכֵּי), of קֶרֶן, קַרְנַיִם (cstr. קַרְנֵי *qar-nê*) ; in each case the dual is built on the monosyllabic base of the word. But it is not so in the case of the dual of דֶּלֶת ; the forms found in use are דְּלָתַיִם, cstr. דַּלְתֵי. But the plural דְּלָתוֹת and especially the cstr. plural דַּלְתוֹת are more frequently used than the dual (דַּלְתֵי and דְּלָתַיִם). Strictly דְּלָתַיִם means *two doors* which close a single entrance. Thus the use of the plural to designate the (double?) doors at several entrances to a building can easily be understood.

5 תְּקַח here is 3 sing. fem. impf. Qal of לָקַח (יַקַּח < יִלְקַח < יַקַּח by the assimilation of the ל to the following ק) and קְחִי is fem. of קַח, m.s. imper. of לָקַח (cf. § 34.3.(b)).

6 This is the sing. fem. imper. *Hiphʿil* of יָנַק in *scriptio plena* ; a *wāw* consecutive perf. form would also be in order, which in this case would be וְהֵינַקְתִּיו or וְהֵינִקְתִּיהוּ (cf. Gram., p. 268, column on extreme right).

⁷ Notice how the long vowel of the יֵשׁ is reduced to יֶשׁ‑ before the tone in the first vowel of שֶׁבְרָ.

⁸ Or וְשִׁבְרוּ.

⁹ Or מַאֲכָל or אָכְלָה.

¹⁰ Or, as in Gen. 26.2, שְׁכֹן. שְׁבָה, the emphatic imper., would also be possible, but שֵׁב is somewhat more frequently used.

¹¹ Or אֲנִי אֹמֵר.

¹² Cf. § 6.5. קַל means *light* or *swift*; קִלֵּל can mean *to make light*, but normally means *to make light of, to belittle*, and (more strongly, as here) *to curse*.

¹³⁻¹³ גְּדוֹלָה or כְּבֵדָה may be used here, or עֲצוּמָה. Note the use of the cognate accusative קְלָלָה, which is preferable to the use of בִּקְלָלָה.

¹⁴ For this form, cf. § 29.2.(2).(b).iii.

¹⁵ Or בְּלִבִּי (from לֵב).

¹⁶ הָרְגוֹ is the infin. cstr. of הָרַג with the 3 sing. masc. pron. suffix; cf. § 27.8.(a).i (final line).

¹⁷⁻¹⁷ Or אִישׁ חָכָם אַתָּה.

¹⁸ Note that יָדַע can mean *to know, to care for* (the result of knowledge and sympathy) and *to know how* (to do anything); יוֹדֵעַ לִכְתֹּב *one who knows how to write, a skilled writer*; יוֹדֵעַ סֵפֶר lit. *skilled in a book, learned*; לֹא יָדַעְתִּי דַבֵּר *I do not know how to speak* (Jer. 1.6).

¹⁹ Or בְּדָם.

²⁰ Or לִשְׁאוֹלָה. 1 Kings 2.9, on which this sentence is based, has simply שְׁאוֹל.

§ 30.
A.

נָס 3 sing. masc. perf. Qal or sing. masc. ptc. Qal of נוּס.

סָרָה 3 sing. fem. perf. Qal (סָרָה) or fem. sing. ptc. Qal

סוּר (סָרָה) of.

שָׁבָה fem. sing. ptc. Qal of שׁוּב.

וּבָאָה 3 sing. fem. perf. Qal of בּוֹא with *wāw* consec.
(cf. § 20.4.(b)) or fem. sing. ptc. Qal with the
conj. *wāw*.

וְסָרוּ 3 plur. perf. Qal of סוּר with *wāw* consec.

אָרוּם 1 sing. imperf. Qal of רוּם.

תָּשׁוּבִי 2 sing. fem. imperf. Qal of שׁוּב.

תְּשׁוּבֶינָה 2 or 3 fem. plur. imperf. Qal of שׁוּב[1].

יָרֹם 3 sing. masc. jussive Qal of רוּם.

אָמוּתָה 1 sing. cohortative Qal of מוּת (cf. § 20.2).

וַיָּמָת 3 sing. masc. imperf. Qal of מוּת with *wāw* consec.

לָסוּר infin. constr. Qal of סוּר with לְ.

תִּכּוֹן 2 sing. masc. or 3 sing. fem. imperf. Niphʿal of כּוּן.

הֲרִימֹותָ 2 sing. masc. perf. Hiphʿil of רוּם.

וַהֲשִׁיבֹתִי 1 sing. perf. Hiphʿil of שׁוּב with *wāw* consec.[2]

יָאִיר 3 sing. masc. imperf. Hiphʿil of אוֹר.

וְיָרֵם 3 sing. masc. jussive Hiphʿil of רוּם with simple *wāw*.

[1] Note carefully that, while, תָּשׁוּבִי has a pretonic *qāmeṣ* in the open syllable before the tone, in the form תְּשׁוּבֶינָה the *qāmeṣ* which follows the תּ in the singular form has to be reduced to vocal shᵉwa since it is now removed from the position immediately before the tone.

[2] הֲשַׁבְתִּי is a type found as the 1 sing. perf. Hiphʿil form of this class of verbs. Note that the corresponding form derived from the root יָשַׁב is הוֹשַׁבְתִּי.

B.

1. He will raise up [1]the poor from the dust[1] and cause them to inherit [1]the throne of princes[1]. 2. [2]Know for certain[2] that, if you put me to death,[3] [4]you will bring innocent blood[4] on yourselves.

3. But the dove did not find a resting-place for the sole of her foot, and returned[5] to Noah into the ark ; and he put[5] out his hand and took[5] her and brought[5] her to him into the ark. 4. O Yahweh my God, pray restore[6] the life of this boy. 5. Then the king called to David and spoke to him thus[7] : " You are honourable[8] and [9]it seems right to me[9] [10]that you should share with me[10] in the war ; no wrong[11] has been found in you from the day you came[12] to me until this day." 6. And Yahweh said to him : " Take now thy son[13] whom thou lovest and go to a distant country and offer him[14] as[15] a burnt-offering on one of the hills there." So he [16]took his way[16], he and his son, in the morning to the place of which Yahweh had told him. On the third day Abraham lifted up his eyes and [17]saw the place in the distance[17]. And he said to his [18]young men[18] : " You[19] wait in this place, my son and I will go on our way and return to you." So Abraham and his son came to the place, and he laid his son upon the altar. [20]But when Abraham raised[21] his hand to kill him, the angel of Yahweh[20] called to him from heaven and said[22] : " Abraham, raise not thy hand against the boy, for now I know that thou fearest God."

‎7. הִנֵּה אָנֹכִי מֵת וְהָיָה אֱלֹהִים [10]עִמָּכֶם וְהֵשִׁיב אֶתְכֶם אֶל־
אֶרֶץ אֲבוֹתֵיכֶם׃

Behold, I am dying[23] ; but God will be with you and bring you back to the land of your fathers.[24]

‎8. אִם־שָׁכֹחַ תִּשְׁכַּח אֶת־יהוה אֱלֹהֶיךָ וְהָלַכְתָּ אַחֲרֵי אֱלֹהִים
אֲחֵרִים וַעֲבַדְתָּם הַעִדֹתִי בְךָ הַיּוֹם כִּי מוֹת תָּמוּת׃

If thou shalt at all[25] forget Yahweh thy God and walk after other gods and serve them, I [26]testify against[26] thee this day that thou shalt certainly[25] die.

[1-1] In poetic form in Hebrew, as here, the article is often omitted when the noun is definite ; we could write ‎מֵהֶעָפָר הָאֶבְיוֹנִים . . . כְּסֵא הַשָּׂרִים . . .

[2-2] The meaning is not conveyed by the translation : *You will certainly know*, i.e. *you will be left in no doubt.* ‎תֵּדַע is to be taken as a jussive (of the same form as the imperf.) and rendered : *You must indeed know*, i.e. *you must be clearly aware*. Taken in this way, the sentence asserts that the

people addressed are aware now of the nature and implication of their conduct.

3 מְמִתִים is the plur. of מֵמִית, the Hiph. ptc. of מוּת. In participial clauses the subject usually precedes the ptc., but commonly when they are introduced by כִּי or אִם, the ptc. precedes the subject.

4-4 דָם נָקִי, the object is placed here before the subject and the ptc. for emphasis. Note also the use of a resumptive כִּי at the beginning of this clause, because of the conditional clause which intervenes immediately after the first כִּי.

5 Four consec. impf. verbal forms in sequence should be noted in sentence 3. וַתָּשָׁב is not to be read as wat-tā-šābh but as wat-tā-šobh. The 3 s.f. impf. Qal of שׁוּב is תָּשׁוּב. But in a consec. impf. form in which the final syllable is closed and the penultimate syllable is open, the tone is retracted from the final to the penultimate syllable, with a consequential shortening of the vowel of the final one.

וַיִּקָּחֶהָ requires a note. The Voc. of § 29 gives יִקַּח as the impf. Qal of לָקַח. Such an impf. in a, when written with verbal suffixes, follows the analogy of First Declension nouns. Therefore, its form with the 3 s.f. suffix is יִקָּחֶהָ (cf. § 27.3.(a)).

וַיָּבֵא 3 sing. masc. impf. Hiph. of בּוֹא to come. Hiph. means to cause to come, to bring, to bring in. The final vowel is not shortened in וַיָּבֵא (cf. § 30.2.(b)), because the final 'aleph has no consonantal value, leaving the final syllable open (§ 7.6.(b).ii).

6 Lit. let the life (soul) of this boy return. תָּשָׁב is the form of the 3 sing. fem. jussive Qal of שׁוּב (תָּשֹׁב) with its final vowel shortened because it is closely associated with the following נָא in one accentual or tonal unit. But note that the qāmeṣ of the penultimate syllable of תָּשָׁב remains long and must, therefore, be assumed to have a secondary accent, marked by methegh.

⁷ לֵאמֹר *saying* ; but to render it always in this way in English translation is to disregard English idiom.

⁸ Lit. *upright, straight, honest.*

⁹⁻⁹ Lit. *it is good in my eyes, it seems good to me, I consider it right.*

¹⁰⁻¹⁰ Lit. *your going out and your coming in with me.* It is also possible
to translate the full clause as : *You are honourable and your association
with me in the war has seemed good to me,* i.e. *I have been well satisfied with
your association . . . war.* But the translation given in the Key is the one
which suits the context of 1 Sam. 29.6, on which the whole sentence
constituting this verse is based. For the form אֹתִי and אֶתְכֶם in verse 7,
cf. Key § 25A, note 13 and § 40.6.(b) in the Grammar. The phrase *going out
and coming in* is found fairly frequently in Hebrew. A good example is in
Ps. 121.8 ; יהוה יִשְׁמָר־צֵאתְךָ וּבוֹאֶךָ מֵעַתָּה וְעַד־עוֹלָם *Yahweh will
preserve thy going out and thy coming in from now and for ever,* i.e. *will
preserve thee in all thine undertakings* (cf. 2 Kg. 19.27).

¹¹ Lit. *evil* ; but *wrong* or *fault* seems a better translation.

¹² Lit. *the day of your coming.* Here the infin cstr. has a gerundial (or
nominal) use.

¹³ For the form of בִּנְךָ from בֵּן *son,* cf. § 26.2.(e).

¹⁴ הַקְרִיבֵהוּ is the sing. masc. imper. Hiph. of קָרַב with the 3 sing.
masc. suffix. Notice the series of imperatives here.

קַח . . . וָלֵךְ . . . וְהַקְרִיבֵהוּ. Such a series of imperatives is not frequent
in Hebrew prose; commonly the third would be expressed by a consec.
perf. form (here וְהִקְרַבְתּוֹ or וְהִקְרַבְתָּהוּ).

¹⁵ Hebrew idiomatically *for* (לְ).

¹⁶⁻¹⁶ Hebrew idiom here is normal : *he went to his way.* The corresponding phrase later in this passage is to be rendered by *my son and I will
go on our way* or *will make our journey.*

¹⁷⁻¹⁷ Lit. *he looked towards the place from afar,* i.e. when he was still at
a distance from it.

¹⁸⁻¹⁸ Or *servants.*

G

[19] לָכֶם must be interpreted here as a *Dativus Commodi* (cf. § 12.2.(c).i), but the use of an emphatic personal pronoun may express it in English here.

[20–20] It is, of course, possible to translate this part of the narrative in another way : *And Abraham raised his hand to kill him. Then the angel of Yahweh. . . .* The rendering given in the key is more graphic. Notice how the Hebrew narrative has simply a series of imperf. consec. verbs and does not make any clause subsidiary.

[21] Lit. *sent, put forth.*

[22] יֹּאמֶר is the pausal form of יֹאמֶר ; cf. § 29, footnote 2 to the Heb.– Eng. Exercise.

[23] Or futural rendering of the ptc. : *I am about to die.*

[24] For the form אֲבוֹתֵיכֶם, cf. §§ 13.5.(f) and 16.2.(b).

[25] At the beginning and the end of sentence 8, the adverb. infin. strengthens the verbal form with which it is associated.

[26–26] *Scriptio defectiva* for הַעִידֹתִי. We should expect הֶ, not הַ, at the beginning, but the full *paṭaḥ* is always found in the Hiph. perf. of עוּד. As for the rendering of the use of the Hiph. of עוּד here, *I solemnly warn thee* or *I give my solemn word to thee* expresses the force of it.

C.

וַיָּנוּסוּ ¹דֶרֶךְ הַמִּדְבָּר : 2 אַל־תָּסוּרוּ ²מֵאַחֲרֵי יהוה וַעֲבַדְתֶּם

אֹתוֹ בְּכָל־לְבַבְכֶם : 3 קוּמִי אוֹרִי כִּי בָא אוֹרֵךְ : 4 וְלֹא

לָקַח מִיָּדוֹ ³אֶת־אֲשֶׁר הֵבִיא : 5 שׁוּב אָשׁוּב אֵלֶיךָ : 6 וַיָּקָם

בַּבֹּקֶר וַיֵּלֶךְ עִם־⁴שָׂרֵי מוֹאָב : 7 וַיִּקְרָא לָאִישׁ וַיֹּאמֶר אֵלָיו

⁵הֲבֵאתָ עָלַי וְעַל־מַמְלַכְתִּי ⁶חֲטָא גָדוֹל : 8 ⁷וַתֵּצֵא הָאִשָּׁה

⁷וַתָּבֹא אֶל־שַׂר ⁸צְבָא הַמֶּלֶךְ וַתֹּאמֶר ⁹סוּרָה אֲדֹנִי ⁹סוּרָה

אֵלַי אַל־תִּירָא ¹⁰וַיָּסַר אֵלֶיהָ ¹¹הָאֹהֱלָה : 9 יָדַעְתִּי אֶת־

¹²שִׁבְתְּךָ וְאֶת־צֵאתְךָ וְאֶת־בֹּאֶךָ : 10 הִתְהַלֵּךְ עַם־יִשְׂרָאֵל
בְּכָל־הַחֲטָאִים אֲשֶׁר עָשָׂה הַמֶּלֶךְ : לֹא סָרוּ מֵהֶם עַד־אֲשֶׁר
הֵסִיר יְהוָה אֶת־יִשְׂרָאֵל מִלְּפָנָיו : 11 הַגּוֹיִם אֲשֶׁר הוֹלַכְתֶּם
אֹתָם וַתּוֹשִׁיבוּ בְּעָרֵי הָאָרֶץ לֹא יָדְעוּ אֶת־תּוֹרַת אֱלֹהֵי
הָאָרֶץ :

¹ דֶּרֶךְ, without a preposition, occasionally means, as here, *in the direction of*, practically = *towards*: cf. 1 Kings 8.44 וְהִתְפַּלְלוּ דֶּרֶךְ הָעִיר " and they shall pray (Hithpa. of פלל : note absence of dagh. forte from first ל ; § 6.5) *towards* the city " ; 8.48 דֶּרֶךְ אַרְצָם " *towards* their land " ; 18.43 הַבֶּט דֶּרֶךְ־יָם " look (s.m. Hiph. imperat. of נבט) *towards* the sea ".

² An example of a compound preposition, being composed of אַחֲרֵי and מִן, lit. *from after*, i.e. *from following*.

³ Cf. § 10.4.(c). אֲשֶׁר here is not a simple particle of relation, but a correlative, meaning here *that which, what*.

⁴ שַׂר *officer, official*, etc. ; pl. שָׂרִים, cstr. pl. שָׂרֵי (not שָׂרֵי) ; cf. Voc. of § 13 and § 40.2.(a),3 ; and Table of nouns on p. 309.

⁵ Or הֲבִיאֹתָ ; but such a form is seldom found in an *'Ayin Wāw* verb which is also a *Lāmedh 'Aleph*.

⁶ For חֲטָא, cf. § 25.1, final sentence.

⁷ In וַתָּבֹא and וַתֵּצֵא, the final syllable in each case being open because the א has no consonantal value in this position, the vowel of that syllable is not shortened but remains long (§ 30.1.(b).iii).

⁸ Notice the *qāmeṣ* in the final syllable of this form (צָבָא, cstr. צְבָא ; cf. דָּבָר, cstr. דְּבַר) owing to the final א which is quiescent.

⁹ סוּרָה, the emphatic form of the sing. masc. imper. Qal of סוּר, is much more effective here than the brief mandatory סוּר which is the ordinary form of the imper.

[10] Note the final vowel *paṭhaḥ* which is due to the influence of the final consonant *reš* (cf. וַיָּקָם from קוּם, and וַיָּמָת from מוּת ; and § 7.3.(b)).

[11] Or אֶל־הָאֹהֶל. For the form הָאֹהֱלָה which is composed of הָאֹהֶל with *he locale* attached, cf. § 14.5.

[12] Or בּוֹאֲכֶם, שִׁבְתְּכֶם and צֵאתְכֶם.

§ 31.

A.

1. My eyes are on all their ways, they are not hidden from me[1]; and their iniquity is not concealed[2] out of my sight.[3] 2. The wealth[4] of (the) nations shall come[5] to thee.[6] 3. You have saved[7] our lives from death. 4. I do not delight[8] in the death of him who dies. 5. So they rose early[9] in the morning and returned and came back home ; and the man knew his wife and Yahweh remembered her. 6. And now [10]send, bring into safety[10] all thou hast in the field, and the hail will not descend on them so that they die. 7. Behold now, thy servant has found favour with thee, and thou hast shown great love to me[11]; but I cannot escape[12] to the hill-country[13] lest the evil cleave to me and I die. 8. Now hast thou[14] taken the silver, and taken with it gardens, and olive-trees and vineyards, flocks and herds, men-servants and women-servants ?

9. וַיִּשְׁמְעוּ אֶת־קוֹל יהוה מִתְהַלֵּךְ בְּתוֹךְ עֵץ הַגַּן [15]לְרוּחַ הַיּוֹם
[16]וַיִּסְתֵּר הָאָדָם וְאִשְׁתּוֹ מִפָּנָיו :

When they heard the voice of Yahweh as he walked in the midst of the trees of the garden in the cool of the day, the man and his wife hid themselves from his presence.

10. [17]וְלִמַּדְתֶּם אֶת־דְּבָרַי אֶת־בְּנֵיכֶם [18]לְדַבֵּר [19]בָּם בְּשִׁבְתְּךָ
[20]בְּבֵיתֶךָ [21]וּבְלֶכְתְּךָ בַדֶּרֶךְ [22]וּבְשָׁכְבְּךָ וּבְקוּמֶךָ :

And you shall teach my words to your children, speaking of them when thou sittest in thy house, when thou walkest by the way, when thou liest down, and when thou risest up.

[1] Lit. *from my presence.*

[2] There are several Hebrew verbs which mean *to conceal.* הִסְתִּיר (passive in use, Niph.) means *to hide, to conceal* in the ordinary senses of these verbs ; צָפַן is used likewise, but sometimes means *to reserve, to treasure up* ; טָמַן is *to hide* in the sense of *to bury out of sight* (מַטְמוֹן, *buried treasure*) ; כִּסָּה (of a type of verbs still to be dealt with : cf. § 32) means *to cover, to conceal, to overwhelm* ; הֶחְבִּיא *to hide* is not found so frequently ; its Niph. means *to hide oneself, to withdraw.*

[3] Lit. *from before my eyes.*

[4] חַיִל has a very wide range of meaning—*strength, army* ; *efficiency, capacity, ability* ; *wealth.* The capacity may be physical, e.g. Jud. 3.29 אִישׁ חַיִל *a man of valour* ; or intellectual and moral, e.g. Exod. 18.21,25 אַנְשֵׁי־חַיִל *men of ability and worth* ; Prov. 31.10 אֵשֶׁת חַיִל *a woman of worth* or *a virtuous woman.*

[5] A collective noun may be followed (as here) or preceded by a plur. (but in this case the plur. גּוֹיִם may have exercised an influence on the verb). Both are illustrated in 2 Kings 25.5 וַיִּרְדְּפוּ חֵיל־כַּשְׂדִּים אַחַר הַמֶּלֶךְ *and the army of the Chaldeans pursued after the king* ; וְכָל־חֵילוֹ נָפֹצוּ *and all his army was scattered* (3 pl. pf. Niph. of פּוּץ, in Qal and Niph. *to be scattered* ; in Hiph.—הֵפִיץ *to scatter*).

[6] This may be Dativus Commodi—*for thine advantage* (cf. § 12.2.(c).i) or *to* in the sense of *into* (or *unto*)—or there may be a blend of both ideas. In 1 Sam. 9.12 occurs בָּא לָעִיר *he has come into the city* ; but the usual prepos. after בּוֹא is אֶל־. לְ is sometimes used with vbs. of motion, such as שׁוּב, בּוֹא, הָלַךְ, but it is not so common as אֶל־.

[7] הִצַּלְתֶּם is 2 pl.m. of הִצִּיל (< הִנְצִיל ; root נצל) ; cf. הִבִּיט in Voc. § 26.

[8] So Ezek. 18.32. But in 33.11 occurs the strange אִם אֶחְפֹּץ with the same meaning, only more emphatic. This form occurs chiefly after an oath, expressed or implied. The full form is found in 1 Sam. 3.17 " God

do so unto thee and more also, *if* (אִם) thou hide anything from me ".

But the formula of imprecation is very frequently omitted : e.g. 2 Sam.

11.11 אִם־אֶעֱשֶׂה אֶת־הַדָּבָר הַזֶּה (may God bring all manner of evil

upon me) *if I do this thing* = *I will certainly not do this thing.*

Similarly a very strong affirmation may be introduced by אִם לֹא ; cf.

1 Kings 20.25 אִם לֹא נֶחֱזַק מֵהֶם *surely we shall be stronger than they* —

(cursed be we) *if we be not stronger.* (For מִן to express the comparative,

see § 44.1).

It is possible, however, to explain this אִם as an interrogative particle

(cf. 1 Kings 1.27, Amos 3.6) following an oath. Note the use of an interroga-

tive following an oath in ordinary colloquial English—*By heaven, do*

you think I shall do that ? when the answer *No* is clearly expected.

So 1 Kings 20.25, *Are we not stronger than they ?*

⁹ הִשְׁכִּים is a denominative verb from שְׁכֶם *shoulder.* הִשְׁכִּים means

to load (the baggage animals), *to shoulder packs*, as men did when they struck

camp in the morning to resume their journey.

¹⁰⁻¹⁰ הָעֵז is sing. masc. imper. Hiph. of עוז. הָעֵז שְׁלַח *send, bring*

into safety practically means *take measures to bring to safety.*

¹¹ Lit. *thou hast made great thy love with me.*

¹² לְהִמָּלֵט is infin. cstr. Niph. of מלט (not found in the Qal), with לְ.

¹³ For the use of *he locale* as here, cf. § 14.5.

¹⁴ The interrogative הֲ, when it occurs before a guttural, is often pointed

with *pathaḥ* (cf. § 46.1.(c)).

¹⁵ Lit. *towards the wind of the day*, i.e. *at the time of the evening breeze,*

in the cool of the evening.

¹⁶ Notice the Hebrew *singular.* In the case of a compound subject, as

here, when the pred. is first, it perhaps oftenest agrees in gend. and numb.

with the element of the subj. which is next to it ; but it may be in plur.

When the subj. has once been mentioned, the following vbs. are in the plur. ;

cf. Gen. 31.14 וַתַּעַן רָחֵל וְלֵאָה וַתֹּאמַרְנָה *and Rachel and Leah answered and said* (תַּעַן, 3 sing. fem. apocopated impf. Qal of עָנָה; § 33.1.(a).iii);

Num. 12.1f וַתְּדַבֵּר מִרְיָם וְאַהֲרֹן ... וַיֹּאמְרוּ *and Miriam and Aaron spoke and said.* Note that the plur. vb. in the last illustration is *masc.,* while in the former (referring to *two women*) it is fem. For the form אֲשָׁתּוֹ in sentence 9 of this Exercise, cf. Voc. § 29 and § 42.

¹⁷ *To learn* (לָמַד Qal) followed by an accus.; *to teach* (לִמַּד Pi.), by two accus., accus. of person and of thing.

¹⁸ Inf. cstr. with לְ has something like the force of a gerund in the ablative—*dicendo*; *by speaking.*

¹⁹ בְּ *about,* occasionally used with vbs. of *speaking, thinking,* etc. But עַל־ is commoner; e.g. Jud. 9.3: וַיְדַבְּרוּ אֲחֵי־אִמּוֹ עָלָיו *and his mother's brethren spoke about him.*

²⁰ בַּיִת cstr. בֵּית, with 1 sing. suffix בֵּיתִי; like זַיִת in the sing.

²¹ Cf. § 29.2.(2).(b).iii.

²² Cf. § 27.8.(a).ii.

B.

1 ¹הִנֵּה זָקַנְתִּי לֹא יָדַעְתִּי אֶת־יוֹם מוֹתִי: 2 בַּיָּמִים הָהֵם ²אֵין מֶלֶךְ בְּיִשְׂרָאֵל ³יַעֲשֶׂה ⁴אִישׁ אֶת־הַיָּשָׁר בְּעֵינָיו: 3 וַיַּקְרֵב אֶת־אֵיל הָעוֹלָה: 4 וַיִּרְאוּ הָאֲנָשִׁים לָשׁוּב אֶל־⁵בָּתֵּיהֶם: 5 ⁶יִהְיֶה ⁷כְּבוֹדוֹ כַּזַּיִת ⁸וְרֵיחוֹ כַּלְּבָנוֹן: ⁹יָשׁוּבוּ ⁹וְשָׁכְנוּ בְאַרְצָם וּפָרְחוּ כְיֵין לְבָנוֹן⁹: 6 ¹⁰שָׁמָה אֶת־¹¹בִּגְדוֹ אֶצְלָהּ ¹²עַד־שׁוּב אֲדֹנָיו¹³ אֶל־בֵּיתוֹ¹⁴: 7 בִּימֵי הַנָּבִיא הַזָּקֵן נָטְעוּ הָעָם כְּרָמִים וְלֹא קִבְּצוּ אֶת־יֵינָם וַיִּזְרְעוּ בַשָּׂדֶה וְלֹא אָכְלוּ אֶת־אָכְלָם בְּשָׁלוֹם:

[1] In Gen. 27.2 הִנֵּה־נָא *behold, I pray*. When a request follows such a sentence as this (as in Gen. 27.3) נָא־ is sometimes added to הִנֵּה to crave or induce favourable consideration of the fact to which attention is called by הִנֵּה, and נָא־ is often repeated with the request; cf. here שָׂא־נָא כֵלֶיךָ *take* (s.m. imperat. of נָשָׂא), *I pray thee, thy weapons* (Gen. 27.3). So Gen. 12.11,13 הִנֵּה־נָא יָדַעְתִּי כִּי אִשָּׁה יְפַת־מַרְאֶה אָתְּ׃ אִמְרִי־נָא אֲחֹתִי אָתְּ *Behold now, I know that thou art a beautiful woman* (fair in appearance): *say, I pray thee, thou art my sister*.

[2] The particle אַיִן is strictly a noun meaning *non-existence*, the negative of יֵשׁ *existence*. Its normal place is, therefore, before the word which it denies, and in the *construct* state; cf. Gen. 20.11 אֵין־יִרְאַת אֱלֹהִים בַּמָּקוֹם הַזֶּה *there is* (non-existence of =) *no fear of God in this place*. The word denied may stand for emphasis before אַיִן, in which case the negative is properly in the *absolute* in apposition; e.g. Gen. 2.5 וְאָדָם אַיִן לַעֲבֹד *and man there was not* (i.e. there was no man) *to till*. . . .

[3] The use of יַ עֲ שֶׂ ה exemplified here is described by some grammarians as the frequentative use (cf. § 43.II.2.(b)); but others render it simply as a historic past.

[4] Or כָּל־אִישׁ.

[5] For this form, cf. § 31.5 and § 42. The purpose of the *methegh* in בָּתִּים is to ensure the pronunciation *bâ-tîm* and to guard against the pronunciation *bot-tîm*.

[6] Or וְהָיָה; for יִהְיֶה, cf. § 33.2.(c).

[7] Or הוֹדוֹ.

[8-8] In Hosea 14.7 the pointing is כַּלְּבָנוֹן, but in 14.8 it is without the article, and in place of וְרֵיחוֹ there is read לוֹ וְרֵיחַ לוֹ *and it will have a smell*.

[9-9] וְיֵשְׁבוּ or וְשָׁבוּ may be used. The second part of Hos. 14.8 reads thus: וְיִפְרְחוּ כַגֶּפֶן זִכְרוֹ כְּיֵין לְבָנוֹן׃ *they shall flourish like a vine and*

their renown will be like (the renown of) *the wine of Lebanon*. In the 26th and later editions of the Grammar *vine of Lebanon* will be read in place of *wine of Lebanon*.

[10] Or וַתָּשֶׂם (cf. § 30.2.(b)) or וַתָּנַח. For the latter, cf. Voc. of § 30, which states that נוּחַ *to rest* has two forms in the Hiph'il. וַתָּנַח comes from pf. הֵנִיחַ, impf. יָנִיחַ, fem. תָּנִיחַ, juss. and *wāw* consec. תָּנַח and וַתָּנַח.

[11] Note בְּגְדוֹ without the dagh. lene in the דּ which would be normal for בֶּגֶד, a second declension noun of the type מֶלֶךְ. The omission of the dagh. lene may be due to the effect of the velar ג in the middle of the stem. The *ḥireq* in place of the common *pathaḥ* in the first syllable (cf. דִּרְכּוֹ, מַלְכּוֹ, etc.) has parallels (צֶדֶק, צִדְקוֹ ; בֶּרֶךְ, dual בִּרְכַּיִם).

[12] Or עַד־אֲשֶׁר יָשׁוּב (cf. § 27.8.(b) and (c)).

[13] אָדוֹן (cstr. אֲדוֹן) takes suffixes of the plural form except in the case of the first person sing. (cf. Key § 39B, note 31). The meaning of the word is *lord* or *master* with regard to men.

[14] Or הַבַּיְתָה (cf. § 14.5).

§ 32.

A.

1. Command the priests who carry the ark of Yahweh [1]that they come up out of the Jordan[1]. 2. I will not again[2] destroy every living thing as I have done. 3. The[3] stone which the builders rejected has become the head[4] of the[3] corner. 4. Lift up[5] thine eyes and look ; for all the land which thou seest, [6]I will give to thee[6]. And I will make thy posterity as the dust of the earth, so that,[7] if a man can number the dust of the earth, thy posterity also may be numbered. 5. Then Pharaoh said : " Go from[8] me ; be careful[9] how you behave ; do not see my face again,[10] for in the day thou seest my face thou shalt die. 6. O that I had[11] water to drink. 7. Should thy people go out to war against their enemies, and call (for help) to the city which thou hast chosen and the house which I have built, then thou

wilt hear their prayer. 8. It will happen that, when you increase in numbers and flourish[12] in the land in those days, you will no more remember the ark of the covenant of Yahweh. 9. The servant of the man of God rose early and went out and, behold, an army surrounded[13] the city, with horses[14] and chariots.[14] So the lad said to the prophet : " Master,[15] what are we to do ? " And his master said to him : " Have no fear, for there are many on our side."[16] Then the prophet [17]said this prayer[17] : " Open his eyes, I beseech thee, that he may see."[18] [19]And he saw[19] the mountain full of horses [20]and chariots of fire[20] around the prophet. The prophet prayed again : " Strike down this enemy." And he struck them down according to the word of the prophet.

10. וַאֲנִי [21]הִנְנִי מַמְטִיר עַל־הָאָרֶץ אַרְבָּעִים [22]יוֹם וְאַרְבָּעִים לַיְלָה וּמָחִיתִי אֶת־כָּל־אֲשֶׁר עָשִׂיתִי מֵעַל־פְּנֵי הָאֲדָמָה׃

And I, for my part, will cause it to rain upon the earth forty days and forty nights and I will blot out everything that I have made from off the face of the ground.

11. נַעַר הָיִיתִי [23]גַּם זָקַנְתִּי וְלֹא רָאִיתִי צַדִּיק [24]נֶעֱזָב [25]וְזַרְעוֹ [26]מְבַקֶּשׁ־לָחֶם׃

I have been young and now I am old ; yet I have not seen the righteous forsaken nor his children begging bread.

[1-1] Note the simple *wāw* with the jussive—a construction common after an imperative (§ 20.5.(a)), lit. " and let them come up." It is " greatly used to express *design* or *purpose* ; or, according to our way of thought, some-times *effect* " (Davidson, *Syntax*, § 65)—and natural, therefore, after a vb. signifying " command " : cf. Ex. 27.20 תְּצַוֶּה אֶת־בְּנֵי יִשְׂרָאֵל וְיִקְחוּ שֶׁמֶן *thou shalt command the Israelites that they fetch oil* (lit. *and let them fetch* ; יִקְחוּ is 3 pl. m. of יִקַּח, the impf. Qal of לָקַח ; for the elision of the dagh. forte in יִקְחוּ, cf. § 6.5). But the inf. (with לְ) may also be used after צוה (Pi) : e.g. Gen. 50.2 וַיְצַו יוֹסֵף אֶת־עֲבָדָיו לַחֲנֹט אֶת־אָבִיו (for this form, cf. § 33.1.(d)), " and Joseph commanded his servants *to embalm* his father."

² Lit. " *I will not add* (1 s. impf. Hiph. of יסף) *any further to the striking down* " (inf. cstr. Hiph. of נכה) : for the idiom, see § 29.4. אָסַף *to gather* or *gather away* has as impf. Qal יֶאֱסֹף and יֹסֵף (written defectively without א) ; 1 s.c. of the latter would be אֹסֵף. The form here, אֹסֵף, is 1 s.c. impf. Hiph. of יסף.

³ Note the omission of the article in the Hebrew here ; this usage occurs in poetic form (cf. Key §§ 15D, note 6 and 24B, note 12).

⁴ For this use of לְ after הָיָה, cf. Key § 19B, note 4.

⁵ Note שָׂא as the imper. masc. sing. of נָשָׂא ; similarly קַח is the corresponding imper. of לָקַח (cf. § 30, Exercise Heb.–Eng. ; sentence 6 and note). An alternative to the use of שָׂא here would be הָרֵם (2 sing. masc. Hiph. imper. of רוּם ; cf. § 30).

⁶⁻⁶ לְךָ, as emphatic, is placed before the verbal form. אֶתְּנֶנָּה is composed of אֶתֵּן (1 sing. impf. Qal of נָתַן) with *nûn energicum* and the 3 sing. fem. suffix (cf. § 27.6).

⁷ To say that אֲשֶׁר here means *so that* is wrong. It expresses relative relation ; its antecedent is זַרְעֶךָ and the clause which it introduces is the final three words of the sentence, of which זַרְעֶךָ is simply recapitulatory. Thus, literally, with a change in order to make the relation clear : *I will make thy posterity as the dust of the earth which* (i.e. *thy posterity*) *also may be numbered if a man can number the dust of the earth.* That is obviously clumsy and makes the word *also* come in inconveniently ; this clumsiness is at once relieved by using the translation with the introductory *so that.*

⁸ מֵעָלַי, a vivid phrase, *from beside me*, i.e. *from my presence* or *from upon me*, i.e. *from* being a burden *upon me*, a trouble to me.

⁹ Lit. *look to thyself.* The ordinary form of imper. Niph. of שָׁמַר is הִשָּׁמֶר ; but the following לְךָ, which is a *Dativus Commodi* (cf. § 12.2.(c).i), is united with הִשָּׁמֶר to form the one tonal or accentual unit, לְךָ being

treated as virtually monosyllabic. Hence the final vowel of הִשָּׁמֵר is
shortened to *seghôl* in the closed, pre-tonic syllable.

[10] Lit. *do not add* (juss. Hiph. of יסף) *to see my face*, i.e. *do not come
before me again.* See note 2 above.

[11] Lit. *who will give me water to drink*? שָׁתָה means *to drink*; the
causative use *to water* (animals), *to give water to drink, to let* (someone) *drink*
is not provided by the Hiph. of שָׁתָה which is not found, but by הִשְׁקָה
which itself is not found in the Qal. This sentence illustrates one way of
expressing a wish (i.e. an optative) in Hebrew (cf. § 46.3.(b)). A wish also
may be expressed in Hebrew by the jussive or cohortative: e.g. 1 Sam. 1.23
יָקֵם יהוה אֶת־דְּבָרוֹ *may Yahweh establish* (Hiph. of קוּם) *his word.* It may
also be expressed interrogatively, as in the above sentence, by מִי—*Who
will give me water to drink*? Ps. 4.7 מִי־יַרְאֵנוּ טוֹב *who will cause us to see*
(i.e. *show us*, 3 s.m. impf. Hiph. of ראה with 1 pl. suff.) *good* (i.e. prosperity)? = O that we might see some prosperity. More idiomatic still is the
use of מִי־יִתֵּן *who will give*? Cf. Deut. 28.67 מִי־יִתֵּן עֶרֶב *would that it were
evening*; 2 Sam. 19.1 מִי־יִתֵּן מוּתִי אֲנִי תַחְתֶּיךָ *would that I had died in thy
stead* (lit. who will grant my dying, me (§ 40.8) instead of thee); for תַּחַת
see § 36.4.(a).i.

[12] Lit. *are fruitful*, but, with reference to a people as here, we must
say *flourish* or *prosper.*

[13] Lit. *surrounding* (ptc.), or *investing, besieging.*

[14-14] סוּס and רֶכֶב should be construed as collective singulars and
translated *with* (not *and*) *horses and chariots* since this is a more particular
description of the army.

[15] Lit. *my master, my lord.* This use of *my* in vocatives is characteristic
of Hebrew. For example, cf. Gen. 22.7i; וַיֹּאמֶר יִצְחָק אֶל־אַבְרָהָם אָבִיו
וַיֹּאמֶר אָבִי וַיֹּאמֶר הִנֶּנִּי בְנִי וַיֹּאמֶר הִנֵּה הָאֵשׁ וְהָעֵצִים וְאַיֵּה הַשֶּׂה לְעֹלָה:
וַיֹּאמֶר אַבְרָהָם אֱלֹהִים יִרְאֶה־לּוֹ הַשֶּׂה לְעֹלָה בְּנִי: *Isaac said to Abraham
his father: " Father". And he said: " Here I am, my son." Then Isaac said:*

" Here are the fire and the firewood but where is the sheep for the burnt-offering?"
Abraham replied : " God will see to the sheep for the burnt-offering, my son."
Gen. 27.18 : וַיָּבֹא אֶל־אָבִיו וַיֹּאמֶר אָבִי וַיֹּאמֶר הִנֶּנִּי מִי אַתָּה בְּנִי
He came to his father and said : " Father ". And he replied : " Here I am,
Who art thou, my son ? " (i.e. *Which of my sons art thou ?* The father was
blind).

[16] Lit. *with us.*

[17-17] Lit. *prayed saying.*

[18] Or *and let him see.*

[19-19] Lit. *and behold.*

[20-20] *Horses and chariots* would be in Hebrew סוּסִים וָרֶכֶב with רֶכֶב
used as a collective sing. ; the *wāw* has pre-tonic *qāmeṣ* (cf. § 11.II.(e)).
But here רֶכֶב is in the constr. before אֵשׁ, so that רֶכֶב אֵשׁ is one tonal
unit, with the tone on אֵשׁ.

[21] For this form, cf. § 40.6.(b).

[22] For the sing. after *forty,* see § 45.1.(e).

[23] Lit. *I have also grown old.* The first two phrases in the sentence
constitute a Hebrew way of saying : *" In all my long experience."*

[24] For the vocalization of נֶעֱזָב, cf. § 7.2 and 5.(a).

[25] Lit. *his seed, his posterity.*

[26] Notice the shortening of the *ṣērê* of מְבַקֵּשׁ to *seghôl* before the
penultimate tone-syllable in לֶחֶם.

B.

1 הִנֵּה שִׁפְחָתֵךְ בְּיָדֵךְ עֲשִׂי־לָהּ אֶת־הַטּוֹב בְּעֵינָיִךְ :
2 יַיֵּחָדְלוּ לִבְנֹת אֶת־הָעִיר : 3 לֹא יָכֹלְתִּי לַעֲשׂוֹת דָּבָר
עַד־אֲשֶׁר תָּבוֹא שָׁמָּה : 4 וַיִּרְבּוּ הַמַּיִם מְאֹד וַיְכֻסּוּ רָאשֵׁי
הֶהָרִים : 5 צִוִּיתִיךְ לְבִלְתִּי אֲכֹל מִן־הָעֵץ אֲשֶׁר בְּתוֹךְ הַגַּן
פֶּן־תָּמוּת : 6 כִּי אַתָּה יהוה צְבָאוֹת אֱלֹהֵי יִשְׂרָאֵל גָּלִיתָ

אֶת־אֹזֶן עַבְדְּךָ לֵאמֹר: בֵּית אֶבְנֶה־¹⁰לָךְ: 7 הִנֵּה עָשִׂיתִי

חֶסֶד עִמּוֹ ¹¹וָאַפְרֵהוּ וָאַרְבֵּהוּ ¹²מְאֹד מְאֹד: בָּנִים וּבָנוֹת

יוֹלִיד וּנְתַתִּיו ¹³לְגוֹי גָּדוֹל: 8 שָׁם יָשַׁבְנוּ ¹⁴וְגַם בָּכִינוּ בְּזָכְרֵנוּ

אֶת־צִיּוֹן כִּי ¹⁵שְׁאֵלוּנוּ אֹיְבֵינוּ שִׁיר ¹⁶לֵאמֹר שִׁירוּ לָנוּ שִׁיר

צִיּוֹן: אֵיךְ נָשִׁיר אֶת־שִׁיר יהוה בְּאֶרֶץ ¹⁷נָכְרִיָּה: 9 וַיֹּאמְרוּ

הָאֲנָשִׁים ¹⁸הִנֵּה נִבְנֶה־¹⁹לָּנוּ עִיר ²⁰אֲשֶׁר רֹאשָׁהּ בַּשָּׁמַיִם

²¹וְנַזְכִּירָה אֶת־שְׁמֵנוּ פֶּן־²²נָפוּץ עַל־פְּנֵי הָאָרֶץ: וַיֵּרֶד יהוה

לִרְאוֹת אֶת־הָעִיר אֲשֶׁר בָּנוּ: 10 וַיִּבֶן הַמֶּלֶךְ אֶת־שְׁכֶם בָּהָר

וַיֵּשֶׁב בָּהּ וַיֹּאמֶר בִּלְבָבוֹ תָּשׁוּב הַמַּמְלָכָה לְבֵית דָּוִד: אִם

²³יַעֲלוּ הָעָם הַזֶּה ²⁴לִזְבֹּחַ בְּבֵית יהוה בִּירוּשָׁלַ͏ִם יָשׁוּב לְבָבָם

אֶל־רְחַבְעָם ²⁵וְאֹתִי יַהַרְגוּ:

---

¹ יַחְדְּלוּ, with *paṭaḥ* in the first syllable, is the form found for the 3 plur. masc. impf. Qal, although the sing. is יֶחְדַּל. Other examples of such vocalic modification will be found later in the Grammar (cf. § 35.2.(c)).

² Or אוֹכַל.

³ In עֲשׂוֹת, the infin. cstr. Qal of עָשָׂה, the simple vocal shewa of the normal form (גְּלוֹת) becomes a composite shewa because of the guttural (cf. § 7.1.(a),(b)).

⁴ דָּבָר, which is often used in the sense of *word*, can also mean *matter*, *affair* and, as here, *anything*. Cf. Gen. 18.14 הֲיִפָּלֵא מֵיהוה דָּבָר is *anything too wonderful* (Niph.) *for Yahweh* (for מִן to express comparison, *more wonderful than*, see § 44.1) ; cf. Deut. 17.8. Consequently *nothing* may be rendered by לֹא ... דָּבָר : cf. Deut. 2.7. לֹא חָסַרְתָּ דָּבָר *thou hast lacked nothing* ; 2 Sam. 17.19 לֹא נוֹדַע דָּבָר *nothing was known* (Niph.). *Anything*

may also be מְאוּמָה : cf. Num. 22.38 הֲיָכוֹל אוּכַל דַּבֵּר מְאוּמָה *have I any power at all* (abs. inf. and impf. Qal of יָכֹל, cf. § 41.2.(4)) *to speak* (notice absence of לְ after אוּכַל) *anything ?* מְאוּמָה is usually found in *negative* sentences, so לֹא . . . מְאוּמָה is another way of expressing *nothing*, cf. Gen. 30.31 לֹא־תִתֶּן־לִי מְאוּמָה *thou shalt give me nothing* ; Gen. 39.9 לֹא־חָשַׂךְ מִמֶּנִּי מְאוּמָה *he withheld nothing from me.*

[5] Or עַד־בּוֹאֲךָ.

[6] כסה is used only 3 times in Qal (twice in act. ptc. and once in pass. ptc.) and twice in Niph. The regular part is the Pi. of which the Pu. (as above) is passive. For omission of the dagh. forte in י, see § 6.5.

[7] Cf. § 31.5.

[8] So (not אֱכֹל) after לְבִלְתִּי, in Deut. 12.23, and—quite naturally—in Gen. 3.11 אֲכָל־מִמֶּנּוּ, where the vowel is further from the tone (§ 7.1.(b)). Nearly always the inf. cstr. and imperat. of Pē 'Aleph vbs. take ֱ (§7.1.(b)), but in a very few cases ֲ : cf. Num. 26.10 בַּאֲכֹל הָאֵשׁ *when the fire devoured.*

[9] גָּלָה *to uncover, to open* is a very suitable verb for use here ; פָּתַח is possible.

[10] לָךְ is pausal form of לְךָ (cf. § 12.1.(f)). For the *daghesh,* cf. § 6.6.

[11] פָּרָה *to be fruitful* is a more suitable verb to use here than פָּרַח *to blossom, to flourish.*

[12] מְאֹד may be used alone or duplicated as here ; בִּמְאֹד מְאֹד is also found.

[13] Note this idiomatic use of לְ in Hebrew ; it has already occurred several times in the Exercises.

[14] The use of וְגַם is very effective here ; otherwise use וַנִּבְכֶּה.

[15] Note the ṣērê here after the 'aleph. It is ṣērê and the short related vowels which are used in parts of the perf. Qal of the verb שָׁאַל with suffixes ; cf. וּשְׁאֵלְךָ *and he will ask you* ; שְׁאֵלְתִּיו *I asked him* ; and in the 2 plur. masc. perf. without suffix שְׁאֶלְתֶּם.

¹⁶ לֵאמֹר is inserted here ; it may be dispensed with.

¹⁷ נָכְרִי, fem. נָכְרִיָּה ; cf. § 13.5.(a). The root נכר means *to be strange,*
to be unknown ; cf. Prov. 26.24 בִּשְׂפָתָיו יִנָּכֵר שׂוֹנֵא *by the words he uses an*
enemy makes himself a stranger (i.e. *disguises himself*) ; 1 Kings 14.5
וַיְהִי כְבֹאָהּ וְהִיא מִתְנַכֵּרָה *What happened was that, when she came, she*
disguised herself (i.e. *made herself unrecognizable*). But נכר has a derived
sense : *to become known, to be discerned* ; this meaning is seen notably in
the Hiph. הִכִּיר (< הִנְכִּיר) *to distinguish, to recognize.*

¹⁸ Hebrew would probably introduce הִנֵּה or קוּמוּ or some such introductory word before נִבְנֶה.

¹⁹ For the *daghesh,* cf. § 6.6.

²⁰ For אֲשֶׁר רֹאשָׁהּ בַּשָּׁמַיִם we may read the words as a circumstantial
clause introduced by the conjunction וְ ; וְרֹאשָׁהּ בַּשָּׁמַיִם.

²¹ It is possible to read, as an alternative here, וְהִזְכַּרְנוּ.

²² Or the Niph. form נָפוֹץ, although no impf. Niph. forms of פוץ are
actually found in the Old Testament.

²³ עָלָה, impf. יַ. עֲלֶה. For this vocalization as affected by the guttural
ע, cf. § 7.3.(a),5.(a).

²⁴ For the *pathaḥ* furtive, cf. § 7.4.

²⁵ וְאֹתִי is read for emphasis ; otherwise, read וַהֲרָגְנִי.

§ 33.
A.

1. Walk before me and be loyal[1] and I will establish my
covenant to be thy God.[2] 2. And Noah planted[3] a vineyard and
drank of[4] the wine and became drunk ; and he uncovered
himself[5] within his tent. 3. And the king developed a disease[6]
in his feet ; [7]yet, ill as he was,[7] he did not seek Yahweh. 4. Then
a quarrel broke out between the herdsmen[8] of Abram's cattle and
the herdsmen of Lot's cattle ; but they said to one another :
" Pray let there[9] be no quarrelling between thee and me."[10]

5. And Yahweh appeared[11] to Abram, and Abram built an altar there to Yahweh who had appeared[12] to him. 6. Let the name of Yahweh be blessed.[13] 7. And he said to him : " Show me[14] thy glory." And he said to the man : " Thou canst not see my face, for man cannot see me and live." 8. " And now if thy servant[15] has found favour in thine eyes, make me to know[16] thy ways and I will know thee[17] so that I may find favour again in thine eyes ; and let me see[18] thy glory that I may perceive that this people is precious to thee." And he said : " My presence will go[19] with you and I will give thee rest."[20] And he said to him : " If thy presence does not go with us, do not bring us up[21] from here." 9. And the people cried to Yahweh and he heard their voice and [22]saw their suffering[22] and healed them. 10. And they kept calling[23] to one another : " Holy is the God of Israel ; righteous and upright is he in all his acts."

11. וַיִּרְאוּ הַשֹּׁמְרִים אִישׁ יוֹצֵא מִן־הָעִיר וַיֹּאמְרוּ לוֹ [24]הַרְאֵנוּ־

נָא אֶת־מְבוֹא הָעִיר וְעָשִׂינוּ עִמְּךָ חֶסֶד : [25]וַיַּרְאֵם אֶת־מְבוֹא

הָעִיר [26]וַיַּכּוּ אֶת־הָעִיר [27]לְפִי חֶרֶב וְאֶת־הָאִישׁ שִׁלֵּחוּ :

Then the watchmen saw a man coming out of the city and said to him : " Pray show us the entrance to the city and we will deal kindly with thee." And he showed them the entrance to the city and they destroyed the city with the sword ; but the man they let go.

[1] Note וְהָיָה < וֶהֱיֵה < וֶהְיֵה, cf. § 33.2.(a),(b). תָּמִים means *whole, complete* ; in the sentence *loyal* probably conveys the meaning better than any other word, implying, as it does, *without divided loyalty, wholly true.*

[2] Note the Hebrew idiom ; lit. *to be to thee for* (or *as*) *God.*

[3] In the impf. Qal of נָטַע *to plant*, the נ is assimilated to the following ט, and the *ḥôlem* of the regular impf. form (יִקְטֹל) is modified to *pathaḥ* owing to the final guttural (cf. § 7.3.(a),4 ; § 36.2.(a).ii).

[4] מִן partitive ; cf. § 12.4.(c).

H

⁵ 3 sing. masc. *wāw* consec. impf. Hithpaʿel, apoc. form, of גָּלָה ;
cf. § 33.1.(d).

⁶ וַיֶּחַל is 3 sing. masc. impf. consec. Qal of חָלָה. The ordinary impf.
form is יֶחֱלֶה (cf. § 7.5.(a)) ; when, in the apocopated form, the vocalic
ending ה is elided, the preceding composite shewa is in a closed syllable
and must become a full vowel. That is, the process is יֶחֱלֶה > יֶחַל > יַחַל.

^{7–7} גַּם and וְגַם sometimes have a kind of adversative force : e.g.
הֹבִישׁוּ כִּי תוֹעֵבָה עָשׂוּ גַּם־בּוֹשׁ לֹא־יֵבוֹשׁוּ גַּם־הַכְלִים גַּם־הַכְלִים לֹא יָדָעוּ Jer. 6.15.
(בּוֹשׁ *to be ashamed* ; impf. Qal יֵבוֹשׁ (§ 30) ; Hiph. הֵבִישׁ. But a secondary
form הֹבִישׁ is found (from root יבשׁ) and is exemplified in the first word of
this sentence). הַכְלִים is the cstr. infin. Hiph. of כלם.

Were they ashamed when they acted abominably ? Not at all, they had no
sense of shame ; they did not know how to be ashamed.

But more often they introduce an additional element or lead to a
climax : e.g. Deut. 23.4 : לֹא יָבֹא עַמּוֹנִי וּמוֹאָבִי בִּקְהַל יהוה גַּם דּוֹר עֲשִׂירִי
לֹא־יָבֹא לָהֶם בִּקְהַל יהוה עַד־עוֹלָם :

No Ammonite or Moabite shall enter the assembly of Yahweh ; even to the
tenth generation none of them shall enter the assembly of Yahweh for ever.
גַּם לֹא־שָׁמַעְתָּ גַּם לֹא יָדַעְתָּ גַּם מֵאָז לֹא־פִּתְּחָה אָזְנֶךָ : Isa. 48.8 :

Hast thou not heard ? Hast thou not known ? Has not thine ear been
open to it from of old ?

The use of גַּם in sentence 3 here is of this second type and, in conjunction
with the following preposition בְּ, allows two ways of translating the whole
clause : (*a*) *yet, ill though he was, he did not seek Yahweh* ; (*b*) *yet even in his*
illness he did not seek Yahweh.

⁸ רֹעֵי is the cstr. plur. of רֹעֶה, act. part. Qal of רָעָה *to shepherd* ;
cf. § 33.3, the form קָנָה.

⁹ 3 sing. fem. jussive Qal of הָיָה ; cf. § 33.2.(d).

[10] Note the difference between Hebrew and English usage in the order of these personal pronouns.

[11] וַיַּרְא is the 3 sing. masc. apoc. *wāw* consec. impf. Niph. of רָאָה, the vowel after the *yôdh* being the long *ṣērê* because the following *rêš* cannot take dagh. forte (cf. יְקַטֵּל and § 7.7).

[12] הַנִּרְאֶה masc. sing. ptc. Niph. of רָאָה with the article. The ptc. as such has no time reference ; *who had appeared* is the translation required here.

[13] יְבָרֵךְ might have been used instead of יְהִי מְבֹרָךְ, but it would not necessarily be construed as a jussive, being the same form as the imperf. (Puʿal). The regular Puʿal forms are, of course, יְקַטַּל and מְקֻטָּל ; for the lengthening of the short ֻ to *ḥôlem*, cf. note 11 above. For יְהִי, cf. § 33.2.(d).

[14] הַרְאֵנִי is composed of הַרְאֵה, sing. masc. imper. Hiph. of רָאָה, and the 1 sing. suffix ; cf. § 32.2.(d) and 5.

[15] *If thy servant has found* is a polite form of speech in Hebrew for *If I have found.*

[16] הוֹדִעֵנִי is the sing. masc. imper. Hiph. of יָדַע with the 1 sing. suffix. The corresponding Hiph. form of יָשַׁב (cf. § 29) is הוֹשֵׁב ; but in יָדַע, owing to the final guttural, it is הוֹדַע. But when an affirmative or verbal suffix is added to this form, the characteristic long ִי vowel of the Hiph. re-appears, as in הוֹדִעֵנִי here, written defectively for הוֹדִיעֵנִי ; cf. § 2.7.(d).

[17] Or *that I may know thee.*

[18] See note 14 above.

[19] Note that פָּנִים is often construed with a plural verb.

[20] נוּחַ *to rest* has two forms in the Hiph. ; cf. § 30. Voc. : הֵנִיחַ, הֵנִיחַ. The one used here, הֵנִיחַ, means *to give rest to* and usually takes after it the accus. of the person. The form might have been written as הֲנִיחֹתִי, but not normally as הֲנִיחוֹתִי ; cf. § 2.7.(d).

[21] תַּעֲלֵנוּ is composed of the 2 sing. masc. juss. Hiph. with the 1 plur. suffix ; cf. § 33.1.(c),(d).

[22–22] For וַיִּרָא, cf. § 33.1.(d), at the foot of the list of forms. עֳנִי *suffering* is of the same type as חֳלִי ; cf. § 33.3, paradigm of second declension nouns.

[23] וְקָרְאוּ may thus be rendered as an iterative impf. ; cf. § 20.4.(b).i, and § 43.II.2.

[24] For the form of הֶרְאָנוּ, cf. note 14 above ; here the suffix is 1 plur.

[25] The Hiph. impf. of רֹאָה is יַרְאֶה, of which the apoc. form is, as in the Qal, יַרְא (cf. § 33.1.(d), at the foot of the list of forms) ; the form here is the 3 sing. masc. impf. consec. Hiph. with the 3 plur. masc. suffix.

[26] The root נכה is not used in the Qal. In the Hiph. the נ is assimilated to the following consonant and the form is הִכָּה, of which the impf. is יַכֶּה, plur. יַכּוּ.

[27] פִּי is the cstr. form of פֶּה *mouth.* לְפִי חֶרֶב *according to the mouth of the sword,* i.e. *as the sword devours, utterly, without quarter.*

B.

וַיַּעַשׂ נֹחַ כְּכָל־אֲשֶׁר ¹צִוָּהוּ יהוה: 2 ²וַיְצַו אֶת־הַכֹּהֲנִים
לֵאמֹר עֲלוּ מִן־הַיַּרְדֵּן וַיַּעֲלוּ: 3 וַיֹּאמֶר שַׂר הַצָּבָא ³אֲשֶׁר
⁴יַכֶּה אֶת־הָעִיר הַזֹּאת וּלְכָדָהּ ⁵וְנָתַתִּי לוֹ אֶת־⁶בִּתִּי לְאִשָּׁה:
4 ⁷הַט אֶת־שָׁמֶיךָ ⁸וְיָרַדְתָּ ⁹וְיָרַדְתָּ: 5 וַתֹּאמֶר לִי ⁹שְׁתֵה ¹⁰וְהִשְׁקִיתִי גַם
אֶת־גְּמַלֶּיךָ¹⁰ : ¹¹וָאֶשְׁתְּ ¹²וַתַּשְׁקְ אֶת־גְּמַלַּי ¹³וַתַּעַשׂ עִמִּי חֶסֶד
מְאֹד : 6 ¹³וַתַּהַר הָאִשָּׁה וַתֵּלֶד בֵּן ¹⁴וַתֵּרֶא ¹⁵אֹתוֹ כִּי יֶלֶד טוֹב
הוּא וַתִּקַּח לוֹ תֵּבָה וַתִּצְפְּנֵהוּ: וַתֵּרֶא בַּת־הַמֶּלֶךְ אֶת־הַתֵּבָה
וַתִּשְׁלַח שִׁפְחָה ¹⁶לְקַחְתָּהּ ¹⁷וַתִּפְתָּחֶהָ וַתֵּרֶא אֶת־הַיֶּלֶד וְהִנֵּה

בְּכֹה הוּא וַתְּשְׁלַח ¹⁸וַתִּקְרָא מֵינֶקֶת וַתְּצַוֶּהָ לִשְׁמֹר אֶת־הַיָּלֶד:

7 וַיָּשָׁב הַמֶּלֶךְ אֶל־הָעִיר לְהִתְרַפֵּא מֵחֳלָיו וּמִן־הַמַּכּוֹת אֲשֶׁר

¹⁹הִכֻּהוּ הָאֲרַמִּים בְּהִלָּחֲמוֹ עַל־חֵיל אֲרָם:

¹ The 3 sing. masc. verbal suffix to a perfect form is commonly וֹ
(cf. שְׁמָרוֹ he watched him), but ל״ה verbs take הוּ——; hence צִוָּהוּ here,
he commanded him.

² צִוָּה to command is not used in the Qal. The 3 sing. masc. impf.
Pi‘el is יְצַוֶּה. The apocopated form is arrived at by the elision of the vocalic
ending הֶ ; that leaves the form יְצַוּ. But a word cannot end in a doubled
letter (cf. §§ 4.3 and 6.3.(c)) ; therefore, the form written is יְצַו.

³ אֲשֶׁר, as used here, is a correlative, i.e. he who, or whoever.

⁴ See note A,26 above. The impf. Hiph. of the root נכה is יַכֶּה, pl. יַכּוּ.

⁵ אֶתֵּן would be possible Hebrew here, but the consec. perf. is a more
idiomatic usage.

⁶ בֵּן son, fem. בַּת > בְּנַת ; my daughter בִּתִּי (< בְּנִתִּי).

⁷ Qal נָטָה; Hiph. הִטָּה > הִנְטָה (so נָכָה; Hiph. הִכָּה to strike). The
impf. of הִטָּה is יַטֶּה, imper. הַטֵּה, apoc. form הַט (cf. Pi‘el imper. גַּלֵּה,
apoc. form גַּל; cf. § 33.1.(d)).

⁸ Actually Psalm 144.5 has וְתֵרֵד that thou mayest come down or and
come down (juss.).

⁹ This may be expressed somewhat more gracefully by גַּם אַתָּה שָׁתָה.

¹⁰⁻¹⁰ An alternative order of expression would be וְגַם אֶת־גְּמַלֶּיךָ אַשְׁקֶה.
Note the dagh. forte in גְּמַלִּים, pl. of גָּמָל ; cf. קָטָן small, pl. קְטַנִּים.

¹¹ For this form, cf. § 33.1.(a).iv. The explanation of the form is אֶשְׁתֶּה >
by apocopation אֶשְׁתְּ > by lengthening of the vowel אֵשְׁתְּ.

¹² For this form, cf. § 33.1.(b).i.

[13] עָשָׂה *to do, to make* has impf. הֵעָשֶׂה ; apoc. form. יַעַשׂ; cf., in § 33.1.(d), the forms of עָלָה, which also explain וַתַּהַר (from the root הָרָה) at the beginning of sentence 6.

[14] For this form, cf. § 33.1.(a).iii and (d). Note particularly the 3 s.m. impf. Qal form וַיֵּרָא and the 3 s.f. וַתֵּרֶא.

[15] It is common usage in Hebrew to add this anticipatory accus. ; i.e. *when she saw him that he was a fine child.*

[16] לָקַח, impf. יִקַּח (< יִלְקַח), imper. קַח (cf. Voc. § 29). Infin. constr. קַחַת (cf. דַּעַת from יָדַע *to know* ; § 29.2.(2).(b).iii), with suffix קַחְתִּי, etc. Instead of לְקָחְתָּהּ we may use וַתִּקָּחֶהָ *and she fetched it.*

[17] This verb and the following one are parallel in the Hebrew. That is common Hebrew usage. In English we make the first verb subsidiary ; *when she opened it, she saw.*

[18] Note the *qāmeṣ* in the final syllable. A final guttural in such a verbal form demands an *a* vowel, commonly *paṯaḥ* ; cf. שָׁלַח *to send*, impf. יִשְׁלַח. Final א being without consonantal value, the final syllable of יִקְרָא is open ; hence the long vowel *qāmeṣ*. Cf. § 7.6.(b).ii.

[19] הִכָּהוּ is composed of the 3 sing. masc. suffix and הִכּוּ, plur. of הִכָּה ; see note 7 above.

§ 34.

A.

Give (*sing. masc. imper. Qal* of נָתַן). Take (*pl. masc. imper. Qal* of לָקַח). Fall (*sing. masc. imper. Qal* of נָפַל).[1] Be thou struck down (*sing. masc. imper. Niph.* of נָגַף) *or* to be struck down (*infin. cstr. Niph.* of נגף). I will cause to fall (1 *sing. impf. Hiph.* of נָפַל). Thou hast delivered (2 *sing. masc. perf. Hiph.* of נצל). Delivering (*sing. masc. ptc. Hiph.* of נצל). And they were delivered (3 *pl. masc. impf. consec. Niph.* of נצל). Give (*sing. masc. emphatic imper. Qal* of נָתַן).[2] Thou shalt deliver them *or* she will deliver them (2 *sing. masc.* or 3 *sing. fem. impf. Hiph.* of נצל with the 3 *pl. masc. suffix*). Ye shall touch (2 *pl. masc. impf. Qal* of נגע). Struck down (*sing. masc. ptc. Niph.* of נגף) *or* he was struck down (3 *s.m. perf. Niph.* of נגף, *pausal form*). It was told (3 *sing. masc. pf. Hoph.* of נגד). Tell (*pl. masc. imper. Hiph.* of נגד). Look *or* let her look (2 *sing. masc.* or 3 *sing. fem. juss. Hiph.* of נבט). To fall (*cstr. infin. of* נפל *with* ל). To approach (*cstr. infin. of* נגש *with* ל *written with pre-tonic qāmeṣ*).

¹ Or infin. cstr. Qal.

² Cf. § 34.3(a).

B.

1. Save me from blood-guiltiness,¹ my Saviour God, and my tongue will tell² of thy righteousness. 2. Shouldst³ thou vow⁴ a vow to Yahweh, do not forget to fulfil it.⁵ 3. His enemies feared⁶ to approach him. 4. Look⁷ heavenwards⁸ and number the stars. 5. Yahweh said to Abram : " Walk through⁹ the land, in¹⁰ its length and breadth,¹¹ for to thee¹² I will give it."¹³ And Abram fell on his face. 6. Jacob had a dream ¹⁴in which he saw¹⁴ a ladder set¹⁵ on the earth⁸ while the top of it reached¹⁶ the heavens.⁸ 7. We have been delivered¹⁷ into the hands¹⁸ of the kings of the lands. 8. And Moses brought¹⁹ Israel out from there and they went into the wilderness. But the Israelites quarrelled with Moses and said to him : " Would that²⁰ we had died by the hand of Yahweh in the land of Egypt, for thou hast brought us²¹ out into this wilderness to destroy all Israel with hunger." 9. I²² have trusted in thee, O Yahweh ; I have said : " Thou art my God " ; deliver me²³ from the hands²⁴ of my enemies and save me from the power of my persecutors. Make thy face shine²⁵ upon thy servant and make me rejoice in thy love.²⁶ 10. Then he brought him out and said : " Pray look heavenwards and count the stars if thou canst count them." Then he said to him : " So shall thy people be. I am Yahweh who brought thee out from a distant land to give thee this land ²⁷as thy possession."²⁷ Then the man said to him : " How am I to know that I will possess it ?"²⁷ And

Yahweh said : " [28]Thou canst know for certain[28] that thy people will be sojourners in a land which is not theirs and they will be subject[29] to the people there. But the nation to which they will be subject I shall judge and thereafter they will go out with great possessions." 11. It was told the king of Egypt that the people had fled ; and the heart of Pharaoh and his servants [30]was turned against the people,[30] and they said : " What is this that we have done ? For we have let Israel go free of their subjection to us."[31] And Yahweh hardened the heart of Pharaoh the king of Egypt and he pursued after the Israelites ; but the Israelites went out with a high hand.[32]

12. וַיֹּאמֶר בְּכֶסֶף אֶת־כַּרְמְךָ [33]תְּנָה־לִּי הַמֶּלֶךְ לוֹ וַיֹּאמֶר
לֹא אֶתֵּן לְךָ אֶת־כַּרְמִי :

And the king said to him : " Give me thy vineyard at a price." But he said : " I will not give thee my vineyard."

[1] דָּם *blood* has plur. דָּמִים which can mean *acts of bloodshed* or *blood-guiltiness* ; cf. Key § 17B, note 2.

[2] תַּגִּיד is 3 sing. fem. impf. Hiph. of נגד. Nouns indicating parts of the body are feminine except the masc. רֹאשׁ, אַף, פֶּה, and לֵב. Cf. § 13.5.(d).

[3] The value of כִּי here can be rendered in several ways. In addition to the translation given above, we may translate it as : *When thou vowest* or *If thou vowest.*

[4] תָּדוּר is an incorrect *scriptio plena*. The final vowel is tone-long and not pure long ; the form, therefore, should be תָּדֹר. Cf. § 2.7.(b).

[5] The infin. cstr. *Piʿel* is שַׁלֵּם. When used with pronominal suffixes, it is treated as a noun of the 3rd declension (cf. § 26). Cf. also § 27.3.(b) and 8.(a).

[6] If an infin. follows a use of יָרֵא to fear, לְ or מִן may be used with it, the מִן being a kind of מִן separative, i.e. *to fear away from* [doing some-thing] ; e.g. יָרְאָה לֵאמֹר אִישִׁי *she was afraid to say :* " *My husband* " ; יָרֵא מֵהַבִּיט אֶל־הָאֱלֹהִים *he was afraid to look towards God.*

⁷ Or *Scan the heavens.* The imper. of הַבִּיט *to look* is הַבֵּט (נבט√) ; but הַבֶּט־נָא is one tonal unit ; therefore, the vowel of the pre-tonic syllable has its *ṣērê* shortened to *s⁽ghôl*.

⁸ For the use of *He Locale* cf. § 14.5.

⁹ Cf. § 23.3.(b).iv.

¹⁰ Lit. *according to its length and its breadth.* This use of the prep. לְ is fairly common ; e.g. אִישׁ לִלְשֹׁנוֹ *each according to his tongue* (i.e. in his own language) ; לְבֵית אֲבוֹתָם *according to their fathers' houses.*

¹¹ In רֹחַב *breadth* the vowel *pathaḥ* is due to the final guttural ; but it is a second declension noun of the same class as אֹרֶךְ *length.*

¹² Note the emphatic order.

¹³ אֶתְּנֶנָּה is composed of נה (3 sing. fem. suffix), נ (*nûn energicum*) and אֶתֵּן (1 sing. impf. Qal of נָתַן), written with *athnaḥ.*

¹⁴⁻¹⁴ Literally *and behold.*

¹⁵ Ptc. Hoph. of נצב. For the ֻ, cf. § 24.2.

¹⁶ Ptc. Hiph. of נגע.

¹⁷ 1 plur. perf. Niph. of נָתַן ; נִתַּנּוּ < נִנְתַּנּוּ.

¹⁸ Hebrew characteristically uses the sing. *hand.*

¹⁹ Lit. *caused to go.*

²⁰ Cf. the note at the foot of the Voc. in this section.

²¹ In הוֹצֵאת (cf. § 29.2.(2).(b).ii and § 38.1.(b).i), the basic form is הוֹצֵאתָ. But א at the end of a syllable is commonly quiescent ; that makes the syllable צא open and would give the form הוֹצָאתָ. But in the Hiph. of verbs of this type (ל״א) the form which is found is with a *ṣērê*, הוֹצֵאתָ.

²² Pronoun emphatically expressed.

²³ The Hiph. imper. sing. masc. is הַצֵּל (נצל√) ; but when a suffix is added, the long *î* vowel which is characteristic of the Hiph. is found. Hence the form with the 1 sing. suff. is as here.

²⁴ Cf. note 18 above.

[25] The emphatic sing. masc. imper. Hiph. of אוֹר.

[26] חֶסֶד is used of a close personal relation or association. No one word will serve as the translation for all occasions ; *loyalty, love, devotion* are, on the whole, preferable to *mercy* or *kindness*.

[27-27] Literally, *to possess it.* The infin. cstr. Qal of יָרַשׁ is רֶשֶׁת (with suffixes, רִשְׁתִּי (etc.), not רַשְׁתִּי ; cf. § 29.2.(2).(b).iii). אִירָשֶׁנָּה is composed of נָה (3 sing. fem. suffix) נ (*nûn energicum*) and אִירַשׁ (with the *pathaḥ* lengthened to *qāmeṣ* before the tone, which is marked by *sillûq* ; cf. note following Exer. § 11).

[28-28] יָדֹעַ תֵּדַע is not easily translated. *Thou shalt surely know* is not an expression used in current English and has uncertain meaning. *Thou shalt indeed learn* is possible, or *Thou canst know for certain* (here and now). The meaning in the latter case is almost *Be assured of this.*

[29] Literally, *shall serve them,* in the sense of *shall be subject to them.*

[30-30] Or *was perturbed because of the people.* This is at least a possible rendering ; cf. Hosea 11.8 נֶהְפַּךְ עָלַי לִבִּי *my heart within me is perturbed.* And עַל־ meaning *because of, on account of* is well known : cf. Gen. 20.3 הִנְּךָ מֵת עַל־הָאִשָּׁה אֲשֶׁר־לָקַחְתָּ *behold, thou wilt die because of the woman whom thou hast married* ; Gen. 42.21 אֲשֵׁמִים אֲנַחְנוּ עַל־אָחִינוּ אֲשֶׁר רָאִינוּ צָרַת נַפְשׁוֹ בְּהִתְחַנְנוֹ אֵלֵינוּ וְלֹא שָׁמָעְנוּ (√ אשם means *to be guilty* ; אָשֵׁם, used here, means *guilty* ; אָשָׁם *guilt.* צָרָה *distress, sorrow* is from √ צרר (cf. § 40). הִתְחַנֵּן is Hithpaʿel infin. cstr. of חָנַן *to be gracious* (חֵן *grace*), the Hithpaʿel means *to ask for grace, to plead for mercy, to entreat*) *we are guilty concerning our brother for we saw his anguish of soul when he pled with (or entreated) us, and did not listen to him.*

[31] Literally *away from* (מִן) *being subject to us.* עָבְדֵנוּ is the infin. cstr. Qal of עָבַד with the 1 plur. suffix.

[32] Means *with mighty hand, with power.*

[33] תְּנָה is emphatic sing. masc. imper. of נָתַן (cf. § 34.3.(a)) ; the daghesh in the following word לִי is *dagh. forte conjunctivum* (cf. § 6.6.).

C.

1 תְּנוּ: 2 לֹא אֶתֵּן אֶת־כַּסְפִּי וְאֶת־זְהָבִי: 3 אַל־תַּגִּידוּ [1]בְגַת: 4 אַל־²תַּבִּיטִי אַחֲרַיִךְ פֶּן־יִגְּפֵךְ אֱלֹהִים: 5 הַצִּילֵנִי כִּי אַתָּה יְשׁוּעָתִי³: 6 ⁴יִתְּנוּ כָּבוֹד לַיהוה עַל⁴־חַסְדּוֹ: 7 ⁵בִּתַּתִּי אֶת־הָאִשָּׁה לָאִישׁ לְאִשָּׁה: 8 אַצִּילֵךְ ⁶וּלְשׁוֹנֵךְ תַּגִּיד אֶת־צִדְקָתִי: 9 הַשִּׂיאָה הַנָּחָשׁ וַתִּקַּח מִן־הָעֵץ וַתִּתֵּן לָאִשָּׁה: 10 ⁷יֵרְאוּ לָגֶשֶׁת⁷ פֶּן־יִגְּפוּ לִפְנֵי אֹיְבֵיהֶם: 11 וַיִּפֹּל יוֹסֵף עַל־פְּנֵי ⁸אָבִיו וַיֵּבְךְ עָלָיו וַיֹּאמֶר לְפַרְעֹה אִם־מָצָא ⁹עַבְדְּךָ חֵן בְּעֵינֶיךָ שְׁמַע אֶל־תְּפִלָּתִי: הִשְׁבִּיעַנִי ¹⁰אָבִי כִּי אֶקְבְּרֵהוּ בַּקֶּבֶר אֲשֶׁר קָנָה בְּאֶרֶץ כְּנַעַן וְעַתָּה אֶעֱלֶה־¹¹נָּא מִמִּצְרַיִם ¹²לְמַעַן אֶקְבֹּר¹² אֶת־אָבִי ¹³וְשַׁבְתִּי עוֹד: 12 לֹא ¹⁴יִעֲמֹד אִישׁ לִפְנֵיכֶם¹⁴ כָּל־יְמֵי חַיֵּיכֶם וַאֲנִי אֶהְיֶה אִתְּכֶם וְלֹא ¹⁵אֶשְׁכָּחֲכֶם ¹⁶וְהִנְחַלְתֶּם אֶת־הָעָם הַזֶּה אֶת־הָאָרֶץ הַזֹּאת אֲשֶׁר נִשְׁבַּעְתִּי ¹⁷לַאֲבֹתֵיכֶם לָתֵת לָהֶם:

[1] גַת in pause does not become גָּת. The reason often given for this is that the form גִּתִּי *a man of Gath*, a Gittite, is from an original גִּנְתִּי, in which the נ becomes assimilated to the following ת (cf. § 40.4.5). That may explain the retention of *pathah* in pause ; but אַף, which with suffixes takes the form אַפִּי (< אַנְפִּי), has, nevertheless, אָף as its pausal form.

[2] Sing. masc. juss. Hiph. of נבט is תַּבֵּט ; but when the afformative of the 2 sing. fem. juss. form is added, the long $î$ characteristic of the Hiph. is used ; so תַּבִּיטִי ; cf. B, note 23 above.

[3] Or יְשׁוּעָתִי אַתָּה.

[4-4] עַל here means *on the grounds of*, or *because of*; cf. note 30 in B above and אֶת־שִׁמְךָ עַל־חַסְדְּךָ אוֹדֶה *I will give thanks to thy name because of thy love.* For יִתְּנוּ כָבוֹד we may read יְכַבְּדוּ followed by the direct accus. אֶת־יהוה. For אוֹדֶה (√ידה), cf. *Pē Wāw* Verbs (§ 29), *Lāmedh Hē* Verbs (§ 32) and § 41.1.(6).

[5] Cf. § 34.3.(a) and § 27.8.(b).

[6] וְהִגִּידָה לְשׁוֹנְךָ could also be given as the translation, but placing the subject first emphasizes the transition from the subject of the first clause to that of the second.

[7-7] מִגֶּשֶׁת or לָגֶשֶׁת ; cf. B, note 6 above. For וַיִּירְאוּ, יִרְאוּ may be read.

[8] For the form of אָבִיו, cf. § 29 Heb.–Eng. Exercise, footnote 3.

[9] This is a characteristically Hebrew mode of expression. מָצָאתִי may be used, but note, in the vocalization of it, the *qāmeṣ* following the צ (cf. קָטַלְתִּי) which is due to the fact that the א is quiescent at the end of the syllable צא, which thus is open ; cf. § 7.6.(b).ii.

[10] For the form אָבִי, cf. note 8 above.

[11] For the *dagh. forte conjunctivum* in נָּא־, cf. § 6.6.

[12-12] Or וְאֶקְבְּרָה in which the simple *wāw* and the cohortative expresses purpose ; cf. § 20.5.(a).

[13] Or וְאָשׁוּבָה, which expresses purpose, while וְשַׁבְתִּי expresses sequence or consequence. Gen. 50.5 has וְאָשׁוּבָה.

[14-14] An alternative translation is given in Deut. 11.25 : לֹא יִתְיַצֵּב אִישׁ בִּפְנֵיכֶם.

[15] שָׁכַח, impf. יִשְׁכַּח ; with light suffix יִשְׁכָּחֵנִי, etc.; with heavy suffix

יִשְׁכָּחֲכֶם ; cf. Grammar, pp. 268, 294.

[16] נָחַל to *possess* or *inherit* ; Hiph. הִנְחִיל takes two accusatives, of person and thing.

[17] Note that plur. of אָב *father* is אָבוֹת.

§ 35.

A.

1. And he left all his property[1] in the charge of Joseph.
2. Behold the two kings[2] did not stand before him. How then
shall we[3] stand ? 3. And God remembered Noah and made a
great wind sweep[4] over the earth. 4. And he and I[5] dreamed a
dream in the one night. 5. Be strong and resolute[6], for thou shalt
[7]cause this people to inherit the land[7] which I swore to give[8] to
their fathers.[9] 6. And Abraham trusted[10] in Yahweh and he
counted it to him as[11] righteousness. 7. Give us[12] this land and
do not make us cross the river. 8. Yahweh has sent me to bind
up the broken-hearted.[13] 9. If thine enemy[14] be hungry, give him
bread to eat.[15] 10. Who made thee a judge[16] over us ? Dost thou
[17]intend to kill me,[17] as thou didst kill the Egyptian ?[18] 11. When[19]
Aram saw that they had been defeated by[20] Israel, they assembled
together[21] and the king of Aram sent and brought out the men
of military age[22] from all the land. When that was reported[23]
to David, he gathered all Israel and crossed the Jordan ; and
Aram took up battle-order to fight with David. But Aram fled[24]
before Israel and David slew of Aram forty thousand men.
Thereafter Aram served[25] them a long time.[26] 12. Hear my prayer,
Yahweh, for in thee I have trusted[27] ; thy face, my God, will
I seek. Hide not thy face from me,[28] for thou art my God ; leave
me not nor forsake me, my Saviour God. 13. When the people
cried out to Pharaoh because of the famine, Joseph released[29] all
the food which he had gathered in the cities, for Joseph had
stored corn as the sand of the sea and he had ceased to keep
account of it. All[30] the lands came to Egypt to buy corn,[31] and
Joseph sold[32] it to them ; the famine was severe in all the lands.

14. ‏וְאַתֶּם אַל־תַּעֲמֹדוּ רִדְפוּ אַחֲרֵי אֹיְבֵיכֶם כִּי נְתָנָם יהוה[33]
אֱלֹהֵיכֶם[34] בְּיֶדְכֶם‏:

And you, do not stand still ; pursue after your enemies, for
Yahweh your God has delivered them into your hands.

[1] Lit. *all which was to him, all that he had.*

[2] Lit. *the two of the kings*, ‏שְׁנַיִם‏ cstr. ‏שְׁנֵי‏ being a noun. Cf. Key § 15C,
note 4 ; and § 45.1.(b).i in the Grammar.

[3] The emphatic ‏אֲנַחְנוּ‏ is placed at the end of the sentence.

[4] Lit. *pass* or *cross.*

[5] Note the Hebrew form of expression *And we dreamed . . . I and he.*

[6] Note the *ḥaṭeph paṭhaḥ* in ‏חֲזַק‏ and the *ḥaṭeph sᵉghôl* in ‏אֱמָץ‏ ;
cf. §§ 7.1.(b) and 35.1.(a),2.(d).

[7-7] Cf. Key § 34C, note 16.

[8] For ‏תֵּת‏, infin. cstr. of ‏נָתַן‏, cf. § 34.3.(a). Note that while *to give to us*
is ‏לָתֶת־לָנוּ‏ because ‏לָנוּ‏ is accented on the penult, in ‏לָתֵת לָהֶם‏ the *ṣerê* of
‏לָתֵת‏ remains unchanged because ‏לָהֶם‏ is accented on the ultimate.
Cf. Key § 34B, note 7.

[9] Cf. Key § 34C, note 17. Observe the Hebrew order : *which I swore to
their fathers to give them.*

[10] The original (Gen. 15.6) has ‏וְהֶאֱמִין‏ which may have the frequentative value of the impf., meaning that Abraham repeatedly trusted in
Yahweh, or may refer to a continuing attitude.

[11] Another mode of expression of this in Hebrew would be ‏לִצְדָקָה‏.

[12] Cf. Key § 34B, note 33.

[13] Cf. Key § 22C, note 1–1. The use of ‏לְ‏ before ‏וְשִׁבְרֵי לֵב‏ after the
cstr. infin. instead of a direct object is a usage found in the later books of
the Old Testament and common in Aramaic.

[14] ‏שָׂנֵא‏ *to hate* has ptc. of the form ‏שֹׂנֵא‏ ; cf. § 19.5. The meaning of
‏שֹׂנֵא‏ is commonly *enemy*, not *hater.*

[15] Not *cause him to eat bread,* but rather the permissive use of the Hiph. *let him eat bread,* i.e. give him some to eat (cf. § 24.I.1.(b).ii).

[16] Note characteristic Hebrew use of לְ. Contrast note 11 above.

[17–17] Lit. *say.* That might mean *to threaten* or (understanding בְּלִבְּךָ) *to intend, to propose.* Note that the form לְהָרְגֵנִי is to be pronounced *lᵉho-rᵉghē-nî.* The cstr. infin. of הָרַג is הֲרֹג.

[18] יִ֯ is the so-called gentilic ending; e.g. מִצְרִי *Egyptian,* עִבְרִי *Hebrew,* מוֹאָבִי *Moabite,* כְּנַעֲנִי (cf. Voc. of § 36) *Canaanite.*

[19] Sentence 11 gives a good example of a series of impf. consec. verbal forms in a narrative passage in which English style (as shown in the translation) demands that some of the clauses should be made dependent or or subsidiary.

[20] Lit. *before.*

[21] אָסַף *to gather* (trans.) means in the *Niph. to gather together* (intrans.), *to assemble.*

[22] Lit. *the men of war.* That is not an idiomatic English usage; *militia* is too technical and specific a term; *soldiery* may serve; *men of military age* is probably the best translation.

[23] Lit. *When it was told.*

[24] Note how *Aram* as subject is construed with a pl. verb in וַיַּעַרְכוּ and with a sing. in וַיָּנָס here. Such fluidity of usage is not uncommon in Hebrew.

[25] *Served* prob. does not mean in this instance *served as slaves* (עֲבָדִים), but *was subject to.*

[26] Lit. *many days.*

[27] Or *I trust;* cf. § 19.2.(c).

[28] For the form, cf. § 12.3.(d).

[29] Lit. *opened.*

[30] The connective is better left unexpressed in this instance.

[31] שֶׁבֶר is corn which has been threshed and is ready for sale (cf. שָׁבַר *to break*); grinding corn was a domestic chore. דָּגָן is the word used for

growing grain, corn in the field. From שֶׁבֶר there comes the denominative

verb שָׁבַר to buy (corn, grain) and Hiph. הִשְׁבִּיר to cause to buy, to sell.

[32] Impf. Hiph. יַשְׁבִּיר ; wāw consec. impf. form וַיַּשְׁבֵּר ; for the meaning
see note 31 above.

[33] Emphatic personal pronoun at the beginning of the sentence.

[34] Note the *seghôl* following the *yôdh* ; cf. § 26 Heb.–Eng. Exercise,
footnote 3.

B.

Up to this point *'athnah* and *sillûq* have been used only in the
Hebrew sentences to be translated into English. Now students
may wish to attempt to use these accents in their own Eng.–
Hebrew Exercises. For that reason they will be used in the Key
from now on in suitable sentences in the Hebrew rendering of the
Eng.–Heb. Exercises.

1 וַיַּרְא אַבְרָהָם אַיִל נֶאֱחַז ¹בְּקַרְנָיו : 2 אַל־תַּעַבְרוּ אֶת־
הַנָּהָר פֶּן־תִּנָּגְפוּ לִפְנֵי אֹיְבֵיכֶם : 3 לֹא־תַעֲבֹד אַרְצֵנוּ כִּי
יָעַמְדוּ אֹיְבֵינוּ ²בְּקִרְבָּהּ : 4 ³אֶעְבְּרָה־נָּא אֶת־הַנָּהָר לְמַעַן
⁵אַנְחִיל אֶת־הָעָם הַזֶּה אֶת־הָאָרֶץ אֲשֶׁר נִשְׁבַּע יהוה
⁶לַאֲבוֹתָם לָתֵת לָהֶם : 5 אֱהַב חָכְמָה אַל־⁷תַּעַזְבֶנָּה : 6 לֹא־
תַעַזְבוּ אֶת־אָהֳלֵי יִשְׂרָאֵל לַעֲבֹד אֱלֹהִים אֲחֵרִים וְלָשֶׁבֶת
בְּקֶרֶב עַם ⁸אֲשֶׁר לֹא יָדְעוּ אֹתִי : 7 ⁹בָּטַח אַבְרָם בֵּאלֹהִים
¹⁰וַיַּחְשָׁב לוֹ לִצְדָקָה¹⁰ : 8 ¹¹נָס יַעֲקֹב מֵאֲרָם וַיָּשֶׂם אֶת־פָּנָיו
לַעֲבֹר אֶת־הַנָּהָר וְלָבוֹא אֶל־¹²אַרְצוֹ וַיֵּגַד לְלָבָן כִּי נָס הוּא
¹³וַיֶּאֱסֹף אֶת־עֲבָדָיו וַיִּרְדֹּף אַחֲרֵי יַעֲקֹב : 9 וַיַּעַזְבוּ בְּנֵי
יִשְׂרָאֵל אֶת־יהוה אֱלֹהֵיהֶם אֲשֶׁר הוֹצִיאָם מֵאֶרֶץ מִצְרַיִם
וַיֵּלְכוּ אַחֲרֵי אֱלֹהִים אֲחֵרִים לְעָבְדָם : וַיִּקְצֹף יהוה עַל־
יִשְׂרָאֵל וַיִּמְכְּרֵם בְּיַד אֹיְבֵיהֶם וְלֹא יָכְלוּ לַעֲמֹד עוֹד
לִפְנֵיהֶם : וַיֹּאמֶר ¹⁴הָעָם הַזֶּה עָבַר אֶת־בְּרִיתִי¹⁴ ¹⁵וְאֲנִי לֹא
אֶזְכְּרֵם עוֹד : 10 וַיַּעַבְדוּ הָעָם אֶת־אֱלֹהֵיהֶם כָּל־יְמֵי יְהוֹשֻׁעַ
וְכָל־יְמֵי הַזְּקֵנִים אֲשֶׁר ¹⁶הֶאֱרִיכוּ יָמִים אַחֲרֵי יְהוֹשֻׁעַ :
11 וַיַּעֲבֹר אֶת־¹⁷יְלָדָיו בָּאֵשׁ :

¹ קַרְנָיו, i.e. the dual קַרְנַיִם with 3 sing. masc. suffix. The plur. קְרָנוֹת is used of the horns of an altar and as a symbol of strength. Ps. 75.11 has the dual and plur. used as such a symbol : וְכָל־קַרְנֵי רְשָׁעִים אֲגַדֵּעַ

תְּרוֹמַמְנָה קַרְנוֹת צַדִּיק : *All the horns of the wicked I will cut down* (גדע Qal and Pi‘el *to cut off, to cut down*) but *the horns of the righteous will be exalted* (cf. § 30.4). Note how Hebrew style can use a plural in the first half of a verse (רְשָׁעִים) and the contrasting noun in the second half in the sing. (צַדִּיק).

² Or בְּתוֹכָה.

³ The impf. of עָבַר is יַעֲבֹר, 1 sing. אֶעֱבֹר, of which we would expect the cohortative form to be אֶעֱבְרָה ; but the form in use is, as in the text, אֶעְבְּרָה ; for the 1 plur. cohortative the form in use is נַעְבְּרָה. Students should not of course at this stage attempt to memorize such variants from normal forms.

⁴ The daghesh is *dagh. forte conjunctivum* : cf. § 6.6.

⁵ Cf. Key § 34C, note 16.

⁶ The plur. of אָב *father* with the 3 plur. masc. suffix is more often אֲבוֹתָם (with the form of suffix used with sing. nouns) than אֲבֹתֵיהֶם.

⁷ Or תַּעַזְבֶהָ. The form in the text has *nûn energicum*, which is often used in pause.

⁸ It should be noted that, in the relative clause which closes sentence 6, the relative אֲשֶׁר may be omitted. This is quite a common usage in Hebrew when the antecedent is indefinite, as it is here (עַם).

⁹ Sentence 6 of the Heb.–Eng. Exercise in this section is substantially the same as this sentence ; note הֶאֱמִין in the one and בָּטַח in the other, צְדָקָה in the one and לִצְדָקָה in the other. These are possible alternatives.

¹⁰⁻¹⁰ לִצְדָקָה, a common Hebrew usage in such a sentence, commoner than צְדָקָה alone. In later editions of the Grammar the second half of this

I

sentence will read : *and God did not leave him to his enemies* : וְלֹא עֲזָבוֹ
אֱלֹהִים בְּיַד אֹיְבָיו :

[11] Or וַיָּנַס ; cf. sentence 11 of Heb.–Eng. Exercise in this section.

[12] Or אֶרֶץ מוֹלַדְתּוֹ *the land of his kindred.*

[13] אסף is listed in the Voc. of § 35 as having its Qal impf. in *ō* ; but the
initial א gives the vocalization יֶאֱסֹף and not as in יַעֲמֹד (cf. § 35.2.(d)).
An alternative verb here would be יְקַבֵּץ.

[14–14] Note the emphatic order in this clause with the subject placed first.

[15] אֲנִי used for emphasis, but וְלֹא אֶזְכְּרֵם is possible.

[16] הֶאֱרִיכוּ יָמִים *they prolonged days*, a Hebrew idiom for *they survived* ;
so *to prolong days after* a person is *to outlive* him.

[17] Or בָּנָיו.

§ 36.

A.

Cleanse (thou) me (*sing. masc. imper. Pi.* with 1 *sing.* suffix).
Taste (*plur. masc. imper. Qal*). Bless (*plur. masc. imper. Pi.*).
He will serve (3 *sing. masc. impf. Pi.*). Cry out (*sing. fem. imper.
Qal*). And they fought (3 *plur. masc. consec. impf. Niph.*). He
will cleanse (3 *sing. masc. impf. Pi.*). I shall wash (1 *sing. impf.
Qal*). I shall wash thee (1 *sing. impf. Qal* with 2 *sing. fem.* suffix).
Crying out (*sing. masc. ptc. Pi.*).

I shall hear. Let me hear. When it was heard. (*Infin. cstr.
Niph. with* בְּ). Cause it to be heard *or* Let her cause it to be
heard (2 *sing. masc.* or 3 *sing. fem. juss. Hiph.*). To send. Send
(*sing. masc. imper. Qal*). He will forget him. Thou (fem.) hast
forgotten.

B.

1. Pray let a little[1] water be fetched, and wash your feet ; then
have a rest[2] under the tree. And let me fetch[3] a bit of bread
[4]to put fresh vigour into your hearts[4] ; after that you may pass
on your way.[5] 2. Yahweh drove out[6] the man and [7]sent him out[7]
of the garden to till the ground from which he had been taken.[8]

3. Then the Israelites cried out to Yahweh and said : " We have forsaken our God and served the Baals."[9] 4. And I shall[10] bless thee and make thy name great ; I shall[10] bless [11]those who bless thee[11] and all the families of the earth will [12]bless themselves by thee.[12] 5. Taste and see that Yahweh is good ; blessed[13] is the man who trusts in him. 6. Remember me, Yahweh, according to thy love[14] ; according to thy [15]many mercies[15] blot out my transgressions. Wash me[16] from all my iniquities and cleanse me from my sins. 7. When the man heard the words of his father,[17] he [18]cried out[18] and said to his father : " Bless me, me also,[19] father." But he said : " Thy brother[17] came deceitfully[20] and got thy blessing." Then the man said to his father : " Hast thou only one blessing, father ?[21] Give me also thy blessing."[22] 8. See, I am sending an angel ahead of thee to look after thee on the journey ; pay heed to him and obey his voice. 9. And Yahweh planted a garden and made to sprout out of the ground every tree attractive in appearance[23] and good for food. 10. Then Jacob took his wives and his children, and himself crossed the ford ; there-after he took them and [24]got them across[24] the ford ; and he put across also all his belongings. Then a man fought with Jacob and the man said : " Let me go for the dawn has risen." But he said : " I will not [25]let thee go unless thou bless me." [25] Then the angel said : " Thy name shall no more be called Jacob, but Israel." And he blessed him there.

11. וַיַּשְׁבִּיעֵנִי לֵאמֹר לֹא־תִקַּח אִשָּׁה לִבְנִי מִבְּנוֹת הַכְּנַעֲנִי אֲשֶׁר אָנֹכִי יֹשֵׁב בְּאַרְצוֹ׃

And he adjured me, saying : " You must not take a wife for my son from the daughters of the Canaanites in whose land I dwell."

12. הַשְׁמִיעֵנִי בַבֹּקֶר חַסְדֶּךָ כִּי־בְךָ בָטָחְתִּי׃

Make me to hear thy love in the morning, for in thee do I trust.[26]

13. בָּרְכִי נַפְשִׁי אֶת־יהוה וְאַל־[27]תִּשְׁכְּחִי כָּל־גְּמוּלָיו׃

Bless Yahweh, O my soul, and forget not all his acts of love.[28]

---

[1] מְעַט *a little* is a noun ; here it is in the cstr. before מַיִם, i.e. *a little of water*. The constr. form is the same as the absol. ; in pause the form is מָעַט (cf. Isa. 10.7). The plur. מְעַטִים is very seldom found.

[2] Lit. *lean, support yourselves.* So the noun מִשְׁעֶנֶת (with suffix, מִשְׁעַנְתִּי) is a thing on which a man leans, *a staff.*

[3] Cohortative; וְלָקְחָתִּי would mean *and I will fetch.*

[4-4] Lit. *and support your hearts* (Heb. *heart*). The meaning would be conveyed more accurately by such a translation as *and revive your strength* or *and renew your vigour.*

[5] תַּעֲבֹרוּ is the pausal form of תַּעֲבְרוּ ; cf. § 11, note following Exercise, para. (c).

[6] Since in יְגָרֵשׁ (3 sing. masc. impf. Pi'el) the final syllable is closed and the penultimate open, the impf. consec. form is וַיְגָרֶשׁ, the tone being retracted to the penult. (the dagh. forte in the *yôdh* is elided because it is followed by vocal she wa, § 6.5) ; cf. § 20.4.(d). Similarly וַיִּלָּחֶם in verse 10 below.

[7-7] The *Pi'el* שִׁלַּח can mean *send away* or *let go* ; cf. verse 10 below.

[8] In form לֻקַּח could be construed as perf. Pu'al of לָקַח but is probably to be regarded as a passive Qal ; cf. § 34.3.(d). It is fittingly translated here as a pluperfect.

[9] The *Baals* or *the Baalîm* (cf. cherubim, seraphim).

[10] Note the simple *wāw* before this impf. form. The translation may be given as in the Key or *that I may bless. . . .*

[11-11] Masc. plur. *Pi'el* ptc. of ברך with 2 sing. masc. suffix ; lit. *thy blessers.*

[12-12] Alternatively *will be blessed in thee.* This translation would mean that all the families of the earth would enjoy the benefits of the blessing and share in it ; the translation in the Key means that they would use his name in blessing others ; e.g. *May God bless you* (or *us*) *as he blessed Abraham.*

[13] This is the only part of the verb ברך used in the Qal ; the *Pu'al* ptc. מְבֹרָךְ also is used for *blessed.*

¹⁴ חֶסֶד is difficult to translate satisfactorily ; *love* and *devotion* often suit ; *kindness* and *mercy* are weak.

¹⁵⁻¹⁵ Lit. *According to the multitude of thy mercies.* The English language lacks a noun related to the adjective *many* ; *bounty, abundance,* and other nouns are sometimes used. Probably *many mercies* or simply *great mercy* should be accepted as adequate and suitable.

¹⁶ כִּבֶּס has a *sᵉghôl* in the final syllable of its 3 sing. masc. perf. *Piʿel,* cf. § 23.1.(a).i. כִּבֶּס is commonly used of washing clothes, etc. ; רָחַץ is used of washing hands, feet, etc.

¹⁷ For the forms of אָב and אָח with suffixes, cf. § 29, note 3 to the Heb.–Eng. Exercise.

¹⁸⁻¹⁸ Lit. *he cried a great cry.*

¹⁹ Not גַּם־אֹתִי. For the pausal form אָנִי, cf. § 40.8 and Gen. 27.38.

²⁰ Note that בְּמִרְמָה *with deceit* has the effect of an English adverb ; cf. בֶּאֱמֶת *loyally, faithfully* ; בְּצֶדֶק *righteously, victoriously.* Hebrew makes much less use of adverbs than English ; see also § 36.3.

²¹ Heb. characteristically : *my father.* Note how the interrogative particle הַ takes full *pathaḥ* before the following vocal shᵉwa.

²² Lit. *Bless me, me also.* Cf. note 19 above.

²³ Lit. *desirable in respect of appearance,* i.e. pleasant and attractive to look at. For the meaning *desirable,* cf. נִכְבָּד *honourable,* נוֹרָא *terrible* (cf. §§ 29.2.(1).(b) and 7.6.(b).ii).

²⁴⁻²⁴ *And made them cross* (or *pass over*) ; 3 sing. masc. impf. consec. Hiph. of עָבַר.

²⁵⁻²⁵ For the meaning of שָׁלַח, cf. note 7–7 above. The following כִּי אִם is used, after a negative, for *unless* or *except.* The final pf. form would be expressed by a fut. pf. in a language with a well developed structure of tense-forms, i.e. *unless thou shalt have blessed me.*

²⁶ Or *have I trusted.*

²⁷ Both these fem. sing. forms are fem. in agreement with נַפְשִׁי which is a vocative.

²⁸ Cf. note 14 above. *Lovingkindnesses* is not found in current English usage ; *acts of love* may sound stilted ; *all his love and devotion* would express the meaning in free translation.

C.

1 לֹא תִשְׁכַּח הַשִּׁירָה הַזֹּאת ¹לְעוֹלָם: 2 בְּיוֹם ²הִמָּשְׁחוֹ:
3 ³תֶּאֱהַב אֶת־יהוה אֱלֹהֶיךָ וְאֹתוֹ תַעֲבֹד: 4 וַיִּזְעֲקוּ ⁴אֵלַי
אֲבֹתֵיכֶם וַיֹּאמְרוּ נֹאבַד מֵחֲמַס אֹיְבֵינוּ: 5 יִתֵּן לָכֶם יהוה
בָּעֶרֶב בָּשָׂר לֶאֱכֹל וְלֶחֶם בַּבֹּקֶר לִשְׂבֹּעַ: 6 הֲשְׁמִיעֲךָ אֶת־
דְּבָרָיו ⁵מִתּוֹךְ הָאֵשׁ: 7 ⁶יֹאמְרוּ אֹהֲבֵי יְשׁוּעָתֶךָ יִגְדַּל אֱלֹהִים:
8 שָׁמֹעַ תִּשְׁמְעוּ בְּקוֹל מַלְאָכִי ⁷בְּשָׁלְחִי אֹתוֹ אֲלֵיכֶם: 9 וַיֹּאמֶר
שְׁמוּאֵל דַּבֵּר יהוה ⁸כִּי שֹׁמֵעַ עַבְדֶּךָ: 10 וַיִּשְׁכְּחוּ אֶת־יהוה
וַיִּמְכְּרֵם בְּיַד אֹיְבֵיהֶם וַיִּלָּחֲמוּ ⁹בָּם: 11 ¹⁰וַיִּקְחוּ ¹¹לָהֶם נָשִׁים
מִכָּל־אֲשֶׁר בָּחָרוּ: 12 אִם אָבִיא אֶת־הַחֶרֶב עַל־אָרֶץ וְלָקְחוּ
עַם הָאָרֶץ אִישׁ ¹²אֶחָד ¹³וְנָתְנוּ אֹתוֹ לְשֹׁמֵר לָהֶם: וְרָאָה
¹⁴הוּא אֶת־הַחֶרֶב בָּאָה עַל־הָאָרֶץ וְתָקַע בַּשּׁוֹפָר ¹⁵לְהַזְהִיר
אֶת־הָעָם: אִם יִשְׁמַע אִישׁ אֶת־קוֹל הַשּׁוֹפָר וְלֹא ¹⁶יִשִׂים לוֹ
אֶת־לְבָבוֹ¹⁶ וּבָאָה הַחֶרֶב וְלָקָחָה אֹתוֹ דָּמוֹ יִהְיֶה בְרֹאשׁוֹ:

¹ *Never* may be rendered by לֹא ... לְעוֹלָם; Joel 2.26f לֹא־יֵבֹשׁוּ
עַמִּי לְעוֹלָם *my people shall never be ashamed* (impf.—note the *plur.*—of
בּוֹשׁ, § 30.1.(b).i). עַד־עוֹלָם is found in 2 Sam. 12.10 לֹא־תָסוּר חֶרֶב
מִבֵּיתְךָ עַד־עוֹלָם *the sword shall never depart* (impf. Qal of סוּר, § 30.1.(b).i)
from thy house.

² This is the simplest translation and it is both clear and adequate. But
every time the phrase *his being anointed* occurs, it always appears in the
form הַמָּשַׁח אֹתוֹ (3 times after בְּיוֹם, Lev. 6.13, Num. 7.10,84, and once
after אַחֲרֵי, Num. 7.88). This—to us—curious construction is explained

thus. The passive (i.e. Niph., Pu., Hoph.) may be used impersonally (3 s.m.) while retaining the direct accus. which would follow an active form of the verb : cf. Gen. 27.42 וַיֻּגַּד לְרִבְקָה אֶת־דִּבְרֵי עֵשָׂו *and there were told* (i.e. one told) *to Rebekah the words of Esau* ; Exod. 21.28 לֹא יֵאָכֵל אֶת־בְּשָׂרוֹ *its flesh shall not be eaten* ; 1 Kings 2.21 יֻתַּן אֶת־אֲבִישַׁג *let Abishag be given* (for יִתֵּן, cf. § 34.3.(d)). Naturally this construction can also be used (as in the sentence translated above) in the inf. cstr. ; cf. Gen 21.8 בְּיוֹם הִגָּמֵל אֶת־יִצְחָק *on the day when Isaac was weaned* (lit. of Isaac's weaning).

³ For this form from the verb אָהֵב, cf. § 35.2.(d).

⁴ In sentences like this, where the vb. is accompanied by a prepositional phrase, a good working rule, which, however, is by no means invariable, is to put that phrase immediately after the vb., if the preposition has a pronominal suffix, but to put the subject immediately after the vb., if the preposition is followed by a noun. E.g. Gen. 24.6 וַיֹּאמֶר אֵלָיו אַבְרָהָם (cf. Gen. 16.9,10,11 וַיֹּאמֶר לָהּ מַלְאַךְ יהוה; also cf. 24.5) but 24.2 וַיֹּאמֶר אַבְרָהָם אֶל־עַבְדּוֹ. Cf. Key §§ 26B, note 4 and 29B, note 8. Later in this sentence נָמוּת may be read as an alternative to נֹאבַד, for which see § 37.1.(a),(b).

⁵ מִתּוֹךְ *out of the midst of* is to be preferred here to מִן.

⁶ יֹאמְרוּ here renders *let them say* ; it can also have the meaning *they shall say*, so that, if we were to translate this sentence, as it is in Hebrew, into English, there would be at least two ways of doing it. The context in which the sentence occurs will commonly enable us to choose between the two renderings.

⁷ For this form, cf. § 27.8. For a sentence of the same type, cf. Exod. 3.12 בְּהוֹצִיאֲךָ אֶת־הָעָם מִמִּצְרַיִם תַּעַבְדוּן אֶת־הָאֱלֹהִים עַל הָהָר הַזֶּה *when thou bringest forth* (i.e. shalt have brought forth : Hiph. inf. cstr. of יָצָא, § 29.2.1.(a)) *the people from Egypt, ye shall serve God upon this mountain.*

[8] The subject, as a rule, precedes the ptc. in a circumstantial clause, but after כִּי the pred. generally precedes the subj., whether the former is adj. or ptc.: cf. Gen. 12.10 כִּי־כָבֵד הָרָעָב *for the famine was severe*; Gen. 3.5 כִּי יֹדֵעַ אֱלֹהִים *for God knows*.

[9] בָם or בָּם; both forms are found in a position like this after a word with a vocalic ending. Remember that the short form בָּם is commonly used, not בָּהֶם (contrast לָהֶם); cf. § 12.1.(f). After the verb נִלְחַם *to fight*, *against* is usually rendered by בְּ of the enemy, but sometimes עִם, and by עַל־ of a city, but sometimes בְּ.

[10] The usual verb *to capture* is לָכַד. The meaning of וַיִּקְחוּ here is that *they took* the women *as wives*; לָקַח can thus mean *to marry*. The 3 sing. masc. impf. consec. Qal is וַיִּקַּח; note the elision of the dagh. forte from the ק when vocal sheʷwa follows it; cf. § 6.5.

[11] Hebrew characteristically inserts לָהֶם here, *for themselves (Dativus Commodi)*; cf. § 12.2.(c).i.

[12] Probably אֶחָד *one* should be inserted, but it is not necessary.

[13] It is not possible to use עָשָׂה *to do, to make* here. Obviously the English does not mean that they *fashioned* or *constructed* him into a watch-man, but *appointed* or *set* him as such. The appropriate Hebrew verb is נָתַן. Note the idiomatic use of the preposition in לְשֹׁמֵר; for צָפָה, שָׁמַר may be used.

[14] Possibly Hebrew usage would introduce הוּא here owing to the change of subject. Instead of וְרָאָה here, וְאִם יִרְאֶה would be possible. A little later in the verse stands בָּאָה, sing. fem. of the Qal ptc. of בּוֹא. This בָּאָה is accented on the final syllable. But בָּאָה, 3 sing. fem. perf. Qal of בּוֹא, is accented on the penult.

[15] לְהַזְהִיר *to warn* is very suitable here, but לְהַגִּיד לָעָם is possible.

[16-16] Lit. *and does not set his mind to it*, i.e. *does not pay heed to it.* Two other ways of rendering the English clause here may be mentioned: וְלֹא יִשְׁמַע בּוֹ, since, while שָׁמַע, followed by an accus., means simply *to hear*, שָׁמַע בְּ or שָׁמַע אֶל־ means *to listen to, to pay heed,* and sometimes *to obey* ; or we may use וְלֹא יִזָּהֵר *and he is not warned,* which corresponds to the use earlier in the sentence of לְהַזְהִיר.

§ 37.

A.

1. And Yahweh said to the man : " From every tree of the garden thou mayest[1] freely eat." 2. If you are willing[2] and obedient,[3] you will eat[4] the good of the land. 3. Take for thyself of[5] every food which is eaten,[6] and it shall be food for them and for thee. 4. O Yahweh, let us not perish, we entreat thee,[7] for[8] the life of this man, and do not lay upon us innocent blood. 5. Go up[9] to my father posthaste and say[10] to him : " Thus saith thy son Joseph : ' God has made me master[11] in Egypt. Come down to me and do not delay[12] ; and make your home[13] in this land and be near me.' And tell my father all that you have seen, and all my renown[14] in Egypt, and [15]bring my father down here quickly."[15] 6. Then Judah said : " What shall we say to my lord ? What are we to tell him,[16] and how are we to plead innocence ?[17] [18]Behold, we are my lord's slaves."[18] But he said : " God forbid[19] that I should do this. The man in whose possession the spoil is found shall be my slave but you[20] will return unharmed[21] to your own land." 7. Then they called to God and said[22] : " Who knows whether God will have mercy again[23] and we shall not perish ?" 8. Beware lest thou forget the day on which thou didst stand before the Lord thy God in Horeb, when Yahweh said to me : " Gather me[24] the people."

9. וַתִּקַּח הָאִשָּׁה מִפְּרִי הָעֵץ וַתֹּאכַל וַתִּתֵּן גַּם לְאִישָׁהּ [25]וַיֹּאכַל :

And the woman took of the fruit of the tree and ate, and she gave also to her husband and he ate.

10. [26]הֶאֱכַלְתָּם לֶחֶם בַּמִּדְבָּר :

Thou gavest them bread to eat in the wilderness.

[1] This is an example of the potential use of the impf. ; cf. §§ 17.5.(d) and 43.II.5.(b) ; and Syntax §§ 42–43.

[2] אָבָה is both *Pē ʾĀleph* and *Lāmedh Hē* ; impf. Qal is יֹאבֶה, the first syllable יֹ being characteristic of the *Pē ʾĀleph* verbs dealt with in this section and the final syllable בֶה having the vocalization of *Lāmedh Hē* verbs ; cf. § 32.2.(b).

[3] The verb שָׁמַע here means more than *to hear* (cf. Key § 36C, note 16).

[4] The apodosis—" you will eat "—might equally well have been introduced by *wāw* consec. with the pf. (וַאֲכַלְתֶּם) instead of the simple impf. תֹּאכֵלוּ (pausal form of תֹּאכְלוּ, § 11, note (c) following Exercise ; § 37.2.(b)). Cf. Gen. 44.9 אֲשֶׁר יִמָּצֵא אִתּוֹ וָמֵת *with whomsoever it be found, he shall die.* This form of apodosis (*wāw* cons. with pf.) is very common after a protasis introduced by כִּי or אִם ; e.g. Deut. 22.2 אִם־לֹא קָרוֹב אָחִיךָ אֵלֶיךָ וַאֲסַפְתּוֹ " if thy brother be not near thee, *then thou shalt bring it* . . ." where תַּאַסְפֵהוּ (from תֶּאֱסֹף ; cf. § 35.2.(d)) would have been possible. An excellent illustration of the practical equivalence of these constructions occurs in 2 Kings 7.4 : אִם־יְחַיֻּנוּ נִחְיֶה וְאִם יְמִיתֻנוּ וָמָתְנוּ *if they spare us, we shall live, and if they kill us, we shall (but) die.* (יְחַיֻּנוּ 3 pl. masc. Pi. impf. of חָיָה with 1 plur. suffix, § 23.1.(b).ii ; יְמִיתֻנוּ 3 pl. masc. Hiph. impf. of מוּת with 1 pl. suffix, § 30.2.(a), 7).

[5] I.e. *every kind of food.*

[6] I.e. which is commonly eaten ; cf. § 17.5.(a) and § 43.II.2.(a).

[7] The enclitic ־נָא *pray* may be translated here suitably by *we entreat thee.*

[8] בְּ in this case gives the cause or occasion of an event : *because of the (loss of) life of this man* ; cf. Gen. 18.28 הֲתַשְׁחִית בַּחֲמִשָּׁה *Wilt thou destroy* (the whole city) *because of five ?* Deut. 24.16 אִישׁ בְּחֶטְאוֹ *each man on account of his own sin.*

⁹ עָלָה is *Pē Guttural* and *Lāmedh Hē*; so its 3 sing. masc. impf. Qal

is יַעֲלֶה (cf. יַעֲמֹד, § 35.2.(d) and יִגְלֶה, § 32.2.(b)); imper. עֲלֵה, plur.

עֲלוּ (cf. § 32.2.(d) and 3.(a)).

¹⁰ Note how Hebrew uses here the consec. perf. This is normal in prose; Hebrew does not use a series of imperatives as English does.

¹¹ Or *a master, an officer of state.*

¹² Lit. *do not stand.* The verb עָמַד has quite a wide semantic range : *to stand ; to stand up, to rise,* e.g. Neh. 8.5 וּכְפִתְחוֹ עָמְדוּ כָל־הָעָם *and when he opened* [the book] *all the people stood up ; to stand still,* e.g. Josh. 10.13 וַיִּדֹּם הַשֶּׁמֶשׁ וְיָרֵחַ עָמָד *and the sun was motionless and the moon stood still ; to stop,* e.g. 2 Kings 4.6 וַתֹּאמֶר אֶל־בְּנָהּ הַגִּישָׁה אֵלַי עוֹד כֶּלִי וַיֹּאמֶר אֵלֶיהָ אֵין עוֹד כֶּלִי וַיַּעֲמֹד הַשָּׁמֶן: *and she said to her son :* " *Fetch me one vessel more.*" *But he said to her :* " *There is not a vessel left.*" *Thereat the oil stopped* [flowing] ; *to delay ; to remain standing, to continue, to endure, to survive :* e.g. Amos 2.15 וְתֹפֵשׂ הַקֶּשֶׁת לֹא יַעֲמֹד וְקַל בְּרַגְלָיו לֹא יְמַלֵּט *the bowman shall not stand his ground and the swift-footed will not escape.*

¹³ Lit. *and you shall dwell ;* but the translation in English should use an imper.

¹⁴ Or *glory* or *splendour.*

¹⁵⁻¹⁵ Lit. *and hasten and bring down my father here ;* cf. § 36.3. וְהוֹרַדְתֶּם and לְהוֹרִיד can both be used after וּמִהַרְתֶּם.

¹⁶ Lit. *What are we to speak ?*

¹⁷ Or *How are we to clear ourselves ?* or *How are we to vindicate ourselves ?* Lit. *How are we to justify ourselves ?* i.e. How are we to show ourselves as צַדִּיקִים, *innocent men ?* Note the *qāmeṣ* in the final syllable of נִצְטַדָּק in pause.

¹⁸⁻¹⁸ The men see their predicament. In these words they pass sentence on themselves : slavery now confronts them as the penalty of their crime. In the form לַאדֹנִי note the elision of the ֲ of אֲדֹנִי ; cf. בַּאדֹנִי, וַאדֹנִי.

[19] √ חלל means *to pollute, to profane.* חֲלִילָה is used in what may be termed prohibitive oaths in which a man binds himself not to do some specific act. The meaning of חָלִילָה־לִּי מֵעֲשׂוֹת זֹאת is: *A curse be on me if I do this* or *God forbid that I should do this.*

[20] Note the emphatic use of הוּא . . . וְאַתֶּם.

[21] לְשָׁלוֹם *to peace, in peace, peacefully.* But the root idea of שָׁלוֹם is *wholeness, completeness,* so that *unharmed* or *without loss* conveys the meaning better.

[22] Pausal form for וַיֹּאמְרוּ; cf. § 37.2.(b).

[23] This is a good example of the use of שׁוּב as an auxiliary verb, adding the force of *again* to the verb which follows it; cf. note 15–15 above.

[24] In אֱסֹף־לִי there is one tonal unit. The impf. Qal of אָסַף is יֶאֱסֹף and the imper. is אֱסֹף; but in אֱסָף־לִי the *ḥôlem* of אֱסֹף has to be shortened since it is now in a closed syllable before the tone.

[25] Cf. § 37.2.(b).

[26] § 35.2.(c) notes how the Hiph. form הֶעֱמַדְתָּ undergoes vocalic modification when it is used with *wāw* consec.: וְהַעֲמַדְתָּ, owing to the movement of the tone. The same vocalic modification often takes place for the same reason, when verbal suffixes are added to a Hiph. verbal form. But here, in sentence 11, no vocalic change is made. The usage is not uniform with אָכַל, possibly owing to the influence of the א. וְהַאֲכַלְתִּי and וְהַאֲכַלְתִּים are found and both הַאֲכַלְתִּיךְ and וְהַאֲכַלְתִּיךְ.

B.

1 תֹאכְלוּ מִפְּרִי דַרְכֵיכֶם: 2 ¹אַל־נֹאבְדָה ²בְּנַפְשׁוֹ: 3 וַיִּקְרָא
אֶת־הָעָם לֶאֱכֹל ³וַיֹּאכֵלוּ: 4 וַיֹּאמְרוּ בְּנֵי יִשְׂרָאֵל מִי יַאֲכִלֵנוּ
בָּשָׂר: 5 לֹא־תֹאכְלוּ כָּל־נְבֵלָה לַגֵּר תִּתְּנוּהָ וַאֲכָלָהּ: 6 לֹא
יֵאָכֵל בָּאֵשׁ יִשָּׂרֵף: וַיֹּאכְלוּ הַכְּלָבִים אֶת־בְּשַׂר עֶגְלִי:
7 וַיַּשְׁכֵּם הָאִישׁ בַּבֹּקֶר ⁴וַיַּגֵּד אֶת־כָּל־הַדְּבָרִים הָאֵלֶּה ⁵בְּאָזְנֵי

עֲבָדָיו: 8 אַל־נַקְשִׁיבָה ⁶אֶל־דְּבָרָיו כִּי לֹא ⁷יֶחְדַּל לָנוּ
מִשְׁפָּט מִן־⁸הַכֹּהֵן וְעֵצָה מִן־הֶחָכָם וְדָבָר מִן־הַנָּבִיא:
9 וַיִּקְרְאוּ אֶל־יהוה ⁹וַיֹּאמְרוּ אַל־נָא¹ נֹאבְדָה בְּנֶפֶשׁ הָאִישׁ
הַזֶּה: ¹⁰נִשְׂאָה אֹתוֹ ¹¹וְנַשְׁלִיכֵהוּ בַיָּם ¹²לְמַעַן יֶחְדַּל¹² הַיָּם
מֵרָגְזוֹ:

¹ Or אַל־נָא.

² Cf. note 8 in A above.

³ Note the pausal form with the vowel ṣērê under the tone ; cf. sentence 2 in Heb.–Eng. Exercise of this section of the Grammar.

⁴ In this consec. impf. form the final ṣērê cannot be shortened to sᵉghôl because, while the final syllable is closed, the penultimate syllable is not open, as in וַיָּקָם (cf. §§ 30.2.(b) ; 20.4.(d)) ; but note וַיַּגֶּד־לוֹ in which the vocalic shortening does take place because the whole phrase is one tonal unit, with the tone on the final syllable לוֹ.

⁵ אָזְנֵי is cstr. of the dual form אָזְנַיִם ; hence its first syllable is closed (ʾoz-nê).

⁶ Or לִדְבָרָיו.

⁷ In Jer. 18.18, in a sentence substantially corresponding to this one, the verbal form used is from אָבַד ; that would give יֹאבַד here.

⁸ Likewise in Jer. 18.18 the article is not used with this noun ; it has מִכֹּהֵן and, in the other cases, מֵחָכָם and מִנָּבִיא.

⁹ § 37.2.(b) states that וַיֹּאמֶר is found in pause as וַיֹּאמֵר ; similarly וַתֹּאמֶר and וַתֹּאמֵר ; but in the plur. וַיֹּאמְרוּ and וַתֹּאמְרוּ are found in pause as וַיֹּאמֵרוּ and וַתֹּאמֵרוּ ; cf. note 3 above.

¹⁰ Note the omission of the dagh. forte because of the vocal shᵉwa following the sibilant שׂ and preceding א ; the 1 plur. impf. is נִשָּׂא (cf. § 6 5).

¹¹ Or we may read וְהִשְׁלַכְנֻהוּ.

[12-12] In Jonah 1.11 it is וְיִשְׁתֹּק *that* [the sea] *may be still* which is used ; in 1.15 there is the responsive phrase וַיַּעֲמֹד הַיָּם מִזַּעְפּוֹ *and the sea stood still* (i.e. became calm) *after its raging.* For this use of the verb עָמַד, cf. note 12 in A above.

§ 38.

A.

We shall create (*1 pl. impf. Qal*) *or* he (*or* it) was created (*3 sing. masc. perf. Niph.*). I have filled thee (*1 sing. perf. Pi'el* with *2 sing. masc. suffix*). Call ye (*plur. fem. imper. Qal* without final ה [for קְרֶאןָה] cf. Ruth 1.20). And they found him (*3 pl. masc. impf. consec. Qal* with *3 sing. masc. suffix*). He will cause him to find (*3 sing. masc. impf. Hiph.* with *nûn energicum* and *3 sing. masc. suffix*). We fear (cf. § 19.2.(c)) *or* We feared. Let me be filled *or* I would be filled (*1 sing. cohort. Niph.* ; cf. § 20.2). He will lift me up *or* He will carry me away (*3 sing. masc. impf. Qal* of נָשָׂא, with *1 sing. suffix*). Thou wilt cause to sin *or* She will cause to sin (*2 sing. masc.* or *3 sing. fem. impf. Hiph.*). And you will sin (*2 plur. masc. consec. perf. Qal*). You will sin (*2 plur. masc. impf. Qal*).

B.

1. And Jacob said to his sons : " Gather together[1] that I may tell[2] you what will befall[3] you in days to come."[4] 2. And the king of Israel said : " I hate him for he never prophesies[5] good concerning me[6] but[7] evil." 3. Thus says Yahweh : " I[8] am about to make all the nations quake, and I shall fill[9] this house with glory."[10] 4. When Yahweh thy God brings thee to the land which he swore to give thee,[11] great and fine cities[12] which thou didst not build, houses full of every good thing[13] which thou didst not fill, vineyards and olive-groves which thou didst not plant, and thou eatest and art full[14] ; beware[15] that thou dost not forget Yahweh thy God who brought thee out of the land of Egypt, from a house of slaves. 5. There is a time for every business[16] under heaven : a time to be born[17] and a time to die ; a time to plant

and a time to reap ; a time to kill and a time to heal ; a time to
break down and a time to build ; a time to weep and a time to
laugh ; a time to embrace and a time to refrain[18] from embracing ;
a time to acquire and a time to destroy ; a time to keep and a time
to throw away ; a time to love and a time to hate ; a time for
war and a time for peace. 6. Seek Yahweh when he is to be found,[19]
call upon him while he is near. Let the wicked man forsake[20] his
way and the rebellious man his thoughts[21] ; and let him return
to Yahweh and he will have mercy[22] upon him and to our God
for he will [23]abundantly pardon.[23]

7. אָמַר הַכֹּהֵן הַגָּדוֹל סֵפֶר הַתּוֹרָה מָצָאתִי וַיִּתֵּן אֶת־הַסֵּפֶר
אֶל־הַסֹּפֵר [24]וַיִּקְרָאֵהוּ :

The high priest said : " It is the book of the law that I have
found." So he gave the book to the scribe and he read it.

8. [25]וַיִּמְצָאֵהוּ אִישׁ [25]וַיִּשְׁאָלֵהוּ לֵאמֹר מַה־[26]תְּבַקֵּשׁ :

And a man found him and asked him : " What are you searching
for ?"

[1] Masc. plur. imper. Niph. of אָסַף.

[2] Simple *wāw* with the cohortative : *and let me tell* would be the strict
rendering, or, as in the Key, *that I may tell*, expressing the purpose of their
gathering together. וְהִגַּדְתִּי *and I shall tell you* expresses essentially the
same thing in a somewhat different way.

[3] קָרָא *to call* and קָרָה *to happen, to befall* are often confused. Here we
would expect יִקְרֶה (impf. Qal of קָרָה) and not יִקְרָא. The infin. cstr. of
קָרָא is לִקְרֹא ; but *to meet, to befall* is לִקְרַאת (with suffix לִקְרָאתִי, etc.).

[4] Lit. *in the end* (or *after-part, sequence) of the days*. It is a common
phrase in the prophetical books of the Old Testament. Since the phrase
means simply *in future days, in days to come*, it does not specify whether
the reference is to the near or the distant future.

[5] A frequentative use of the impf. ; cf. § 43.II.2.

[6] עָלַי means *of me, concerning me*. It is not possible to translate עַל
here by *against me*, since that is fitting of evil spoken but not of good.

⁷ כִּי אָם means *but* (exceptive), *except*; it is used after a negative.

⁸ אֲנִי need not be emphatic here; it is necessary because the following participial form does not itself define the subject.

⁹ The perf. consec. form וּמִלֵּאתִי is a normal sequence after a participial clause such as the one which precedes it.

¹⁰ Not בְּכָבוֹד for *with glory*; cf. § 38.6.

¹¹ Note two points: לָךְ here is not *to thee* (fem.), but the pausal form of לְךָ; לָתֵת is the normal form of the infin. constr. of נָתַן with the preposition לְ (תֵּת < תֶּנְת; cf. 34.3.(a)). In לָתֶת־לָךְ the *ṣērê* of לָתֵת is shortened to *seghôl* because the tone is on לָךְ, and the *qāmeṣ* following the preposition is retained by the secondary accent which is marked by *methegh*.

¹² עִיר has plur. עָרִים (cf. § 31.5), with the masc. plur. ending although it is a fem. noun. Note how the qualifying adjectives have fem. endings.

¹³ טוּב *good*, *goods*, *good things*; cf. also Key § 37A, sentence 2.

¹⁴ Or *satisfied*.

¹⁵ The *ṣērê* of הִשָּׁמֶר is shortened because the following לְךָ is treated as virtually monosyllabic and bears the tone.

¹⁶ חֵפֶץ can mean *pleasure*, *delight*, but here it means *matter*, *business*.

¹⁷ This is a better rendering than *to bear children*; לֶדֶת is infin. cstr. of יָלַד *to bear* (cf. יֶלֶד *boy*); cf. § 29.2.2.(b).iii.

¹⁸ Lit. *to be far from*.

¹⁹ An example of the *Niphʿal Tolerativum*; cf. § 22.3.iii.

²⁰ As far as the form of יַעֲזֹב goes, we may give the rendering *The wicked man will* (or *may*) *forsake his way*; but וְיָשֹׁב which follows and has a distinctive jussive form (cf. § 30.1.(b).i,iii) shows that the translation should be as given in the Key.

²¹ Note מַחֲשָׁבָה *thought*, *plan*; cstr. מַחֲשֶׁבֶת (with 1 s. suffix מַחֲשַׁבְתִּי); pl. מַחֲשָׁבוֹת cstr. pl. מַחְשְׁבוֹת.

²² Or *that he may have mercy upon him*; cf. § 20.5.

²³⁻²³ רָפָא means *to heal*. The healing may be of the separation between a sinful man and God, and so we may translate *abundantly pardon*; or the healing may be within the sinful man himself, and we may translate *make completely whole*.

²⁴ *And he read it.* So the narrative in 2 Kings 22.8. It is interesting that, in the parallel narrative in 2 Chr. 34.18, the text is וַיִּקְרָא־בֹו *and he read in it.* The Chronicler believed that the book was the whole of the Pentateuch and not the Book of Deuteronomy (or part of it) only.

²⁵ Note how impfs. in *a* with suffixes follow the analogy of the First Declension (cf. § 27.3.(a)) ; thus יִשְׁמֹר, יִשְׁמְרֵנִי but יִמְצָא, יִמְצָאֵנִי and יִשְׁלַח, יִשְׁלָחֵנִי.

²⁶ For this use of the impf., cf. § 43.II.1.(b).

C.

1 יִשְׁמַע יהוה בְּקָרְאֲךָ ¹לוֹ : 2 מָלֵאתִי ²רוּחַ מִשְׁפָּט וּגְבוּרָה לְהַגִּיד אֶת־יַעֲקֹב אֶת־פִּשְׁעוֹ וּלְיִשְׂרָאֵל אֶת־³חַטָּאתוֹ : 3 וַתִּמָּלֵא הָאָרֶץ חָמָס : 4 ⁴הֲמְצָאתַנִי אֹיְבִי וַיֹּאמֶר מְצָאתִיךָ : 5 מְלֵאת אֶת־הַבַּיִת הַזֶּה ⁵אֶת־כְּבוֹדֶךָ : 6 שָׂנֵאתָ אֶת־כָּל־פֹּעֲלֵי אָוֶן : 7 ⁶וַתִּשָּׂאֵהוּ רוּחַ יהוה וַתַּשְׁלִיכֵהוּ ⁷אָרְצָה : 8 ⁸תֶּאֱהַב אֶת־⁹אֹיְבֶךָ לֹא־תִשְׂנָאֵהוּ בִּלְבָבֶךָ : 9 וַיֹּאמֶר לָהּ הַשְׁקִינִי־נָא מְעַט מַיִם כִּי ¹⁰צָמֵאתִי כִּי ¹¹יֵאָמֵר אִם רָעֵב אֹיִבְךָ ¹²הַאֲכִילֵהוּ וְאִם צָמֵא הוּא הַשְׁקֵהוּ : 10 צִוָּה יוֹסֵף אֶת־עֲבָדָיו ¹³וַיְמַלְאוּ אֶת־כְּלֵיהֶם שֶׁבֶר וַיִּתְּנוּ לָהֶם אֹכְלָה לַדָּרֶךְ וַיִּשְׂאוּ אֶת־שִׁבְרָם עַל־חֲמוֹרֵיהֶם ¹⁴וַיֵּלֵכוּ :

¹ Or אֵלָיו.

² Note that in poetic style Hebrew may omit the article where we might expect it ; so here, not רוּחַ הַמִּשְׁפָּט וְהַגְּבוּרָה *the spirit of judgment and power* but simply רוּחַ מִשְׁפָּט וּגְבוּרָה. In addition, note that רוּחַ is not repeated before the second noun in the genitive.

K

³ Or חֲטָאוֹ (from חָטָא). Cstr. of חַטָּאת is חַטַּאת; pl. חַטָּאוֹת, cstr. חַטֹּאת.

⁴ Note that the interrogative particle הֲ, when it occurs before a word whose first vowel is vocal shᵉwa, requires the pointing הַ. A statement upon the pointing of this interrogative particle is given in § 46.1.

⁵ The use of two accusatives after a verb is well-known in Hebrew; e.g. נָחַל means *to inherit*; the Hiph. הִנְחִיל *to cause* [a person] *to inherit* [something]; as in Josh. 1.6: תַּנְחִיל אֶת־הָעָם הַזֶּה אֶת־הָאָרֶץ *thou wilt cause this people to inherit the land.* Again, פָּשַׁט means *to strip off* (e.g. clothes); the Hiph. הִפְשִׁיט *to strip* [a person of something], as in Gen. 37.23: וַיַּפְשִׁיטוּ אֶת־יוֹסֵף אֶת־כֻּתָּנְתּוֹ *and they stripped Joseph of his coat* (*kuttontō* from כֻּתֹּנֶת or כְּתֹנֶת). Similarly, while מָלֵא, for instance, can take an accus. of respect (cf. § 38.6), the *Pi'ēl* מִלֵּא can take a direct accus. and an accus. of respect; cf. sentence 3 in Heb.–Eng. Exercise in Grammar § 38. This accus. of respect after מָלֵא in the Old Testament is usually indefinite, and, therefore, it does not take the אֶת־ which is used with a definite accusative. But in this sentence the accus. of respect כְּבוֹדֶךָ, is definite, so that אֶת־ is used properly with it. Let it be clearly understood that this אֶת־ is that which is used before a definite accus., and not the preposition meaning *with* (notwithstanding the English *with thy glory*).

⁶ רוּחַ is more often fem. than masc.; but וַיִּשָּׂאֵהוּ and וַיַּשְׁלִיכֵהוּ may be used.

⁷ Pausal form of אַרְצָה. The *Hē Locale* does not take the accent; cf. § 14.5.

⁸ Or וְאָהַבְתָּ. אָהֵב commonly takes the accus., but occasionally it is construed with the prep. לְ.

⁹ אֹיְבֶךָ is pausal form of אֹיִבְךָ; cf. sentence 9. The *ḥireq* in the ordinary form is notable. The common vocalization of nouns of this class with pron.

suffixes is as שָׁמַר, שָׁמְרִי, שָׁמְרָךְ; כֹּהֵן, כְּהֹנִי, כֹּהֲנֶךָ shows the influence of the guttural; אֹיֵב, אֹיְבִי, אֹיִבְךָ shows the influence of the labial בּ or the *yôdh* or both; cf. § 26.2.(b).

[10] Or צָמֵא אָנִי.

[11] For this use of the impf., cf. § 43.II.2.(a).

[12] Instead of the imperatives הַאֲכִילֵהוּ and הַשְׁקֵהוּ, it is possible to use consec. perf. forms וְהַאֲכַלְתָּהוּ and וְהִשְׁקִיתָהוּ. In the first of these forms, ַ ֲ is used rather than ֶ ֱ (perf. Hiph. הֶאֱכִיל; cf. §§ 7.1.(b) and 35.2.(c)). The imper. of הִשְׁקָה is הַשְׁקֵה; הַשְׁקֵהוּ of the text here is the imper. הַשְׁקֵה with 3 s.m. suffix.

[13] Note in the form וַיְמַלְאוּ that dagh. forte has been elided from י and ל (cf. § 6.5).

[14] Or וַיִּסְעוּ (from נָסַע *to pull up the tent-pegs, to break camp, to journey*).

§ 39.

A.

בַּזֹּונוּ	1 plur. pf. Qal of בזז.
קַלּוּ	3 plur. pf. Qal of קלל.
וְחַגֹּתֶם	2 plur. masc. pf. Qal of חגג with *wāw* consec.
אָאֹר	1 sing. impf. Qal of ארר.
וַיָּחָן	3 sing. masc. impf. Qal of חנן with *wāw* consec.
גֹּל	sing. masc. imper. Qal of גלל *or* infin. cstr. Qal.
תֵּרַע	2 sing. masc. *or* 3 sing. fem. impf. Qal of רעע.
בֹּזּוּ	plur. masc. imper. Qal of בזז.
לָקֹב[1]	infin. cstr. Qal of קבב with לְ.
וְנָקַל	3 sing. masc. pf. Niph. of קלל with *wāw* consec.
וּנְמַקֹּתֶם[1]	2 plur. masc. pf. Niph. of מקק with *wāw* consec.

יֻמַּד   3 sing. masc. impf. Niph. of מדד.

הֲשִׁמֹּ֫תָ   2 sing. masc. pf. Hiph. of שמם.

הֵתַמּוּ   3 plur. pf. Hiph. of תמם. For the _ below the ת instead of the more usual *ṣērê*, a vocalic modification which occurs particularly with a guttural or *rêš* but occasionally with other consonants, cf. § 39.3.(b).i.

תִּדֹּם   2 sing. masc. *or* 3 sing. fem. impf. Qal (§ 39.7) of דמם.

אָקֹב[1]   1 sing. impf. Qal (§ 39.7) of קבב.

וַיִּתַּ֫מּוּ   3 plur. masc. impf. Qal (§ 39.7) of תמם with *wāw* consec.

תַּתֵּם   2 sing. masc. *or* 3 sing. fem. impf. Hiph. (§ 39.7) of תמם.

[1] In later editions of the Grammar the corresponding form from the root סבב will be used.

B.

1. As for me, I will cause all my goodness to pass before thee,[1] and I will be gracious to whom[2] I will be gracious and I will show compassion[3] to whom I will show compassion.[3] 2. Men began to increase in number on the earth and daughters were born[4] to them. 3. Even upon the woman with whom I am finding hospitality[5] thou hast brought [6]distress by slaying[6] her son. 4. Then she said to them : " Do not call[7] me Naomi,[8] call me Mara,[9] for Shaddai[10] has dealt very bitterly with me. I went away[11] full,[12] and Yahweh has brought me back empty.[13] Why will you call me Naomi when Yahweh has testified[14] against me and Shaddai has brought distress on me ?" 5. Cursed be thou in the city and cursed be thou in the field ; cursed be thou in thy coming in[15] and cursed be thou in thy going out.[16] 6. And thou art my Lord, a God merciful and gracious, slow[17] to anger and abounding in love and faithfulness. Turn to me and be gracious to me[18] ; make with me a sign for good[19] ; give thy strength to thy servant and save the son of thy maidservant.[20] 7. And I shall pass through the

land of Egypt this night and I shall destroy every firstborn in
the land, both[21] man and beast. And the blood will be your
sign[22] on the houses where you are ; when[23] I see the blood, I shall
pass over you. And this day will be for you a (day of) remembrance[24] ; you will keep[25] it as a festival for Yahweh. You will
keep the festival as a perpetual obligation[26] throughout your
generations. 8. Then I looked[27] and saw ; there was[28] a man with
a measuring line[29] in his hand. And I said to him : " Where
are you going ?" And he said to me : " To measure the city, to
see how broad it is and how long it is."[30]

9. וַיָּשָׁב מֹשֶׁה אֶל־יהוה [31]וַיֹּאמֶר [32]אֲדֹנָי לָמָה [33]הֲרֵעֹתָ לָעָם
הַזֶּה לָמָּה שְׁלַחְתַּנִי אֶל־פַּרְעֹה : [34]הִרְבֵּיתִי לָבוֹא אֶל־פַּרְעֹה
לְדַבֵּר בִּשְׁמֶךָ וְהוּא הֵרַע לָעָם הַזֶּה וְלֹא הִצַּלְתָּ אֶת־עַמֶּךָ :

And Moses returned to Yahweh and said : " My Lord, why hast
thou brought evil on this people ? Why hast thou sent me to
Pharaoh ? I have gone many times to Pharaoh to speak in thy
name and he has done evil to this people and thou hast not saved
thy people."

[1] עַל־פְּנֵי possibly implies closer association than לִפְנֵי, but the difference is not to be forced.

[2] Two points are to be noted : (a) חָנַן to be gracious takes the accus.
of the person to whom the grace or favour is shown, as here ; cf. וַיָּחָן
יהוה אֹתָם And Yahweh was gracious to them (חָנַן ; impf. יָחֹן ; consec.
impf. וַיָּחָן with the final vowel shortened because the final syllable is
closed and the penultimate is open) ; חָנֵּנִי be gracious to me (imper. חֹן
but, when an afformative or verbal suffix is added, the ʿayin radical takes
dagh. forte because the verb is a Double ʿAyin one, so that the form is
חָנֵּנִי) ; (b) the second point to note is that אֲשֶׁר is here, not a relative, but
a correlative ; cf. § 10.4.(c).

[3] רָחַם (which is used in the Piʿel and the Niph.) normally takes the
accus.

⁴ יָלַד *to bear* ; Niph. נוֹלַד *to be born.* The *Piʿēl* is very little used, but מְיַלֶּדֶת is found, *a midwife.* The *Puʿal* is found as here ; it has the same force as the Niph.

⁵ הִתְגּוֹרֵר is *Hithpôʿlēl* of גּוּר and means *to seek hospitality* or, as here, *to find (or receive) hospitality.*

⁶⁻⁶ Lit. *evil to slay* ; *evil* here means *distress* or *calamity.*

⁷ 2 plur. fem. jussive Qal of קָרָא ; the preceding אֲלֵיהֶן shows that it is women who are being addressed.

⁸ The name *Naomi* (*Noʿomi*) is derived from נֹעַם *pleasantness, sweetness* (נָעֵם *to be pleasant*).

⁹ מַר *bitter* ; fem. מָרָה or (Aramaic form) מָרָא. For the vocalization, see § 40.3.

¹⁰ The meaning of the divine name Shaddai has been disputed. It was once thought to be composed of the relative (·שֶׁ) and דַּי *sufficiency* and to mean *the all-sufficient one,* or to go back to שַׁדַּי *my guardian spirit, my lord* (the pron. suff. as in אֲדֹנָי). But the view is now commonly held that the word is related to Accad. *šadû a mountain* and is a form of *šaddaʾû mountain god.* Probably we should use simply the title Shaddai in translation.

¹¹ *Went away* refers to the fact that Naomi had gone from Judah to Moab because of a famine.

¹² *full* has an emphatic place in the order of the sentence ; the meaning is that Naomi, when she went to Moab, had a husband and a family. Of these she had been bereft.

¹³ רֵיקָם *empty* is strictly an adverb ; therefore, unlike מָלֵא, fem. מְלֵאָה, it cannot show change for gender. In form it is parallel to חִנָּם *free, for nothing,* אָמְנָם *truly,* etc.

¹⁴ Suffering was often interpreted as a penalty for sinfulness (cf. § 30, Heb.–Eng. Exer., sentence 8). Therefore, Naomi says that Yahweh had testified against her in the suffering she had endured. To testify in this way is often expressed in Hebrew by the Hiph. of עוּד, viz. הֵעִיד (cf. § 30), but here עָנָה *to answer, to respond* (as a witness) is used.

¹⁵ בֹּאֶךָ is pausal form of בֹּאֲךָ, i.e. infin. cstr. בֹּוא with 2 s.m. suff.

¹⁶ צֵאת is the infin. cstr. of יָצָא; cf. § 29.2.(2).(b).iii. A man's *going out and coming in* refers to his going out to work in the morning and coming home at night and thus means his whole, everyday life.

¹⁷ אֹרֶךְ *length* and the Hiph. of √ ארך, as in הֶאֱרִיךְ יָמִים *he prolonged days, he lived long, he continued to live*, gives a clue to the meanings of √ ארך. But the phrase used here אֶרֶךְ אַפַּיִם must be noted. *Long of* (or *in respect of*) *anger* is not used in Hebrew to describe a man who maintains his anger for a long time, but one who suffers long before he becomes angry ; thus the phrase means *patient, tolerant*. So אֶרֶךְ רוּחַ likewise means *patient* and, notably, אֶרֶךְ אַפַּיִם is contrasted in Prov. 14.29 with קְצַר רוּחַ *short-tempered, impatient*. This use of אֶרֶךְ in turn has influenced the Hiph. usage of the verb ; cf. Job 6.11 אַאֲרִיךְ נַפְשִׁי *I shall be patient*.

¹⁸ Cf. note 2 above.

¹⁹ *For good* here means *for favour* or *blessing*. The meaning is : *Give me a sign of thy favour, give me a token of thy goodness*.

²⁰ *the son of thy maidservant* is a polite periphrasis for the first personal pronoun, as is *thy servant* earlier in the sentence.

²¹ *both . . . and* can be expressed, as here, by מִן . . . וְעַד, by גַּם . . . גַּם or simply by וְ . . . וְ.

²² Lit. *to you* (*Dativus Commodi*) *for sign*.

²³ The Hebrew here can be rendered as *and I shall see*, but English style demands a dependent clause.

²⁴ Lit. *a memorial* ; we may render it, as in the Key, *a* (*day of*) *remembrance* or *a memorable day*.

²⁵ We cannot reproduce in English the cognate verb and noun (in the accus.) of the Hebrew.

²⁶ Lit. *a statute of eternity*, i.e. an obligation which they must perpetually honour and never neglect.

²⁷ Lit. *I lifted up my eyes*.

²⁸ Lit. *and behold*, a phrase which almost defies satisfactory translation into current English usage.

²⁹ Lit. *and in his hand a cord of* (i.e. *for*) *measurement*, a circumstantial clause. Note חֶבֶל *a cord* or *a rope* ; חֹבֵל *a sailor* ; but הֶבֶל *a breath*, or *an idol*.

³⁰ Lit. *how much its breadth* (רֹחַב *breadth*) *is and how much its length* (אֹרֶךְ *length*) *is*.

³¹ For the pausal form וַיֹּאמַר, cf. § 37.2.(b).

³² אֲדֹנִי *my lord* and אֲדֹנָי *my lord* or *my lords* with reference to men ; אֲדֹנָי with reference to God.

³³ The *ṣērê* in הֲרֵעֹתָ is due to the fact that ר cannot be doubled ; the *ḥireq* of the regular form הֲסִבֹּתָ is lengthened in compensation to *ṣērê*.

³⁴ רָבָה means *to be much* ; here the Hiph. הִרְבָּה *to do many times, to multiply* is used as an auxiliary verb before the following infin. cstr. (cf. § 36.3 and notes 15 . . . 15 and 23 of § 37A of the Key).

C.

1 אֹאַר אֶת־¹מְקַלְלֶיךָ : 2 ²יָאֵר יהוה אֶת־פָּנָיו ³עָלֶיךָ ⁴וִיחֻנֶּךָּ : 3 ⁵בְּקָרְאִי ⁶עֲנֵנִי אֱלֹהֵי ⁷יִשׁוּעָתִי חָנֵּנִי ⁸וּשְׁמַעְתָּ אֶת־תְּפִלָּתִי : 4 שַׂמַּח אֶת־נֶפֶשׁ עַבְדְּךָ כִּי אֵלֶיךָ אֲדֹנָי אֶשָּׂא אֶת־נַפְשִׁי : כִּי טוֹב וְצַדִּיק אַתָּה וְחַנּוּן ⁷וְרַחוּם ⁸לַאֲשֶׁר יִקְרָאוּ אֵלֶיךָ : בַּעֲבוּר חַסְדְּךָ שְׁמַע אֶת־תְּפִלָּתִי ⁹וְהִקְשַׁבְתָּ לְקוֹל תַּחֲנוּנָי : ¹⁰כַּמָּה מַעֲשֶׂיךָ אֲדֹנָי בְּחָכְמָה עָשִׂיתָ ¹¹כֻּלָּם ¹²תִּמָּלֵא כָל־הָאָרֶץ אֶת־¹³פְלָאֶיךָ : 5 וַיָּחֶל שָׁאוּל לִבְנוֹת מִזְבֵּחַ לַאדֹנָי וַיֹּאמֶר לַעֲבָדָיו : ¹⁴הַגִּישׁוּ לִי כָל־אִישׁ אֶת־¹⁵שׁוֹרוֹ וּשְׂחַטְתֶּם אֹתוֹ ¹⁶הֵנָּה וַאֲכַלְתֶּם : וְאַל־תֶּחְטְאוּ לַיהוָה לֶאֱכֹל אֹתוֹ עַל־הַדָּם :

¹ The sing. is מְקַלֵּל ; note, therefore, the omission of the *dagh. forte* from the first ל because it is followed by vocal shᵉwa ; cf. § 6.5.

² יָאֵר here is not from the same root as אָאֹר (sentence 1) יָאֵר is the 3 sing. masc. jussive Hiph. of the root אוֹר *to shine* (cf. Voc. § 30) ; but אָאֹר is 1 sing. impf. Qal of the root אָרַר *to curse.*

³ In Num. 6.25 אֵלֶיךָ is used in this context.

⁴ יָחֹן is 3 sing. masc. jussive (or impf.) of חָנַן. When a verbal suffix is added, the *nûn* is written with *dagh. forte* since it is no longer final, and the *ḥôlem* of יָחֹן, being now the pretonic syllable, is shortened to ֵ or ָ (ŏ) ; (cf. § 39.5.(a)). Instead of יְחָנְךָ we may write the form with *nûn energicum* יְחָנֶּךָ.

⁵ עָנָה is *Pē Guttural* and *Lāmedh Hē.* Therefore, in the impf. Qal, the form is יַעֲנֶה (cf. יַעֲמֹד and יִגְלֶה for its vocalization), and in the imper. עֲנֵה ; hence imper. with 1 sing. suffix is עֲנֵנִי.

⁶ In poetic form וּשְׁמַע would often be used instead of the consec. pf. form.

⁷ Or מְרַחֵם (*Piʿēl* ptc.). This verb is very rarely used in the Qal.

⁸ For the use of אֲשֶׁר here, cf. section (b) of note 2 in B above.

⁹ Or וְהַקְשִׁיבָה or וְהַקְשֵׁב ; cf. note 6 above.

¹⁰ Ps. 104.24 is very similar to this sentence. Instead of כַּמָּה it has מָה־רַבּוּ ; this is preferable since it is exclamatory while כַּמָּה is interrogative.

¹¹ כֻּלָּם, without *dagh. lene*, is possible after the preceding open syllable, but possibly כֻּלָּם is to be preferred to make it come in sharply, following a slight pause for emphasis, after the verb. The fem. pl. כֻּלָּן is not found in the Old Testament ; כֻּלָּנָה occurs twice.

¹² Or מָלְאָה, מָלֵא being an intransitive or stative verb (cf. § 19.2.(c)).

¹³ Or נִפְלְאֹתֶיךָ, which is the fem. plur. ptc. Niph. of the root פלא which is found in Niph. and Hiph.

[14] This is the verb used in 1 Sam. 14.34. הִקְרִיבוּ might seem more suitable here with reference to offerings, but it would anticipate the use of שְׁחַטְתֶּם which has ritual connotations (the usual verbs meaning *to slay* being הָרַג and the Hiph. of מוּת).

[15] Hebrew uses the 3 sing. suffix in שׁוֹרוֹ, correlating it with כָּל־אִישׁ and not the second sing. or plur., correlated with the verb, as English often does.

[16] *Here* can be translated into Hebrew by הֵנָּה, as in the Key, or by פֹּה or בָּזֶה ; שָׁם means *there*. אֵיפֹה means *where* ?

§ 40.

A.

1. [1]And in its shadow many nations shall dwell.[1] 2. And I gave them to the priest and his sons [2]as a perpetual obligation.[2] 3. Then the woman came to him and said : " See, thy handmaid[3] has given heed to thy voice, and I have taken[4] my life in my hands." 4. Our end is near, our days are fulfilled. 5. God thou shalt not despise,[5] and a ruler of thy people thou shalt not curse. 6. And they said to him : " [6]Put your hand on your mouth and come[6] with us, and be[7] to us a father and a priest. Is it better[8] for you to be priest to the house of one man or to be priest to a tribe or clan in Israel ?" 7. Then Noah built an altar to Yahweh and took of all the clean beasts[9] and of all the clean birds[9] and offered[10] a burnt-offering on the altar. And Yahweh [11]came to this decision[11] : " I will not again[12] curse the ground because of man, for the nature[13] of man's heart is evil from his youth ; and I will not again[12] destroy[14] every living thing as I have done." And Yahweh blessed Noah and his sons and said to them : " Be fruitful and multiply and fill the earth." 8. All of us, like sheep,[15] have wandered away ; we have all deviated in our own ways[16] ; and Yahweh has made the guilt[17] of all of us fall upon him. 9. Then she said : " One small thing only I ask ; do not repulse me."[18] The King said to her : " Ask it, mother,[19] for I will not repulse thee." Then she said : " Let the young woman be given[20] to thy brother as wife." The king answered his mother with the

words : " Why dost thou ask only for the young woman for my brother ? Ask for him the kingdom, for he is my elder[21] brother." 10. " Thy father made our yoke hard ; but do thou alleviate[22] for us the hard service of thy father and the heavy yoke which he laid upon us, and[23] we shall serve thee." Then the king answered the people harshly[24] and deserted the advice which the old men had given him.[25] He spoke to them according to the advice of the young men and said : " My father[26] made your yoke heavy, and I will add to your yoke."

11. אֵ֫לֶּה הַחֻקִּים וְהַמִּשְׁפָּטִים אֲשֶׁר תִּשְׁמְרוּ לַעֲשׂוֹת בָּאָ֫רֶץ אֲשֶׁר נָתַ֫תִּי לָכֶם לְרִשְׁתָּהּ כָּל־הַיָּמִים אֲשֶׁר־אַתֶּם חַיִּים עַל־הָאֲדָמָה כִּי עַמִּי אַתֶּם׃

These are the statutes and the regulations which you shall observe in the land which I have given you to possess[27] all the days that you live[28] on the land, for you are my people.

1-1 Or the translation might be : *And in his shadow many nations used to dwell.* The context is needed to determine the suitable translation.

2-2 Heb. *for an everlasting statute* ; cf. Key § 39B, note 26.

3 Polite mode of speech ; cf. Key § 39B, note 20.

4 Note carefully וָאָשִׂים, not וָאָשֶׂם (impf. Qal of שִׂים). In the *wāw* consec. impf. " in the *first* pers. sing. alone the retraction of the tone and the reducing of the long vowel in the final syllable are not usual " (G.K. § 49.e). Thus, though we write וַיָּקָם, we should write וָאָקוּם (or וָאָקֻם) : so Hiph. וַיָּקֶם but וָאָקִים (or more generally וָאָקֵם). So in the 1 sing. impf. Hiph. of *all* vbs. the long *î* is almost always retained ; e.g. Am. 2.9 וָאַשְׁמִיד *and I destroyed* (while וַיַּשְׁמֵד, 2 Kings 10.28, for the *third* person, is normal).

5 קָלַל in Pi., *to make light, to belittle, to consider contemptible,* hence *to curse* ; practically synonymous with אָרַר.

6-6 *To put the hand on the mouth* means to keep silence ; cf. Isa. 52.15, as well as Jud. 18.19 on which this sentence is based. *Come* rather than *go* is required in the translation of לֵךְ here.

⁷ For the form וְהָיָה and that of הָיוֹתְךָ later in the sentence, cf. § 33.2.(a),(b).

⁸ Hebrew does not have a comparative ; *better than* can be rendered by טוֹב מִן, but in this sentence טוֹב alone is sufficient ; cf. § 44.1.

⁹ בְּהֵמָה and עוֹף are both collective nouns.

¹⁰ וַיַּעַל should be noted. Impf. Qal of עָלָה *to go up* is יַעֲלֶה (cf. Key § 39C, note 5), apoc. form יַעַל. The pf. Hiph. is הֶעֱלָה ; impf. Hiph. יַעֲלֶה (as Qal), apoc. form יַעַל. Here וַיַּעַל is 3 sing. masc. consec. impf. Hiph. (apocopated form). In place of וַיַּעַל, וַיִּקְרַב might have been used.

¹¹⁻¹¹ Lit. *said in his heart.* That can mean *thought, reflected,* but here rather *resolved, decided.*

¹² הוֹסִיף (root יסף) is used here as an auxiliary verb. It means *to add* ; *to add to do a thing* is *to do it again,* so that the following עוֹד is tautologous. For such auxiliary verbs, cf. §§ 29.4 ; 36.3 ; and the Key § 37A, notes 15–15 and 23, and § 39B, note 34.

¹³ יָצַר means *to form, to shape, to frame* ; *to form in the mind, to devise, to purpose.* יֵצֶר means *form, shape* ; *device, purpose* ; *nature, disposition* (presumably, as the devising and purposing agent). יֵצֶר רַע is common in post-biblical Hebrew to mean man's *evil nature,* St. Paul's *lower law* in our nature.

¹⁴ הִכָּה *to strike,* does not state whether the blow is mortal or not. So it can mean *to strike, to wound* (מַכָּה *a wound*) or *to strike down, to destroy.*

¹⁵ Note the use of the generic article ; cf. § 12.2.(b).i.

¹⁶ Lit. *We have turned each to his own way.*

¹⁷ עָוֹן should be rendered here, not as *iniquity,* but as *guilt* or *punishment.*

¹⁸ Lit. *do not turn away my face.* תָּשֵׁב is 2 sing. masc. jussive Hiph. of שׁוּב. The Hiph. can mean *to cause to return, to bring back, to restore,* or *to turn aside* (trans.), *to turn away* (trans.).

[19] Heb. idiomatically *my mother*.

[20] For the form יִתֵּן, cf. § 34.3.(d). For אֶת־הַנַּעֲרָה after the passive verbal form יֻתַּן, cf. § 40.7.

[21] Cf. note 8 above ; but אָחִי הַגָּדוֹל can also mean *my eldest brother* ; cf. § 44.2.

[22] The מִן following הָקֵל (imper. Hiph. of קלל) emphasizes the effect of the verb : *make light from*, i.e. by taking something away ; so *lighten, alleviate*.

[23] Simple *wāw* and the impf. or, probably, jussive ; it may also be rendered *that we may serve thee*.

[24] קָשָׁה is an adjective (fem. of קָשֶׁה) which has the force of a neuter in other languages. It may be considered to have the value (a) *harsh* (*word*), but is most suitably translated into English by an adverb. Cf. 1 Sam. 20.10 (so LXX) : מִי יַגִּיד לִי אִם יַעַנְךָ אָבִיךָ קָשָׁה *who will tell me if thy father answers thee harshly* ? ; 1 Kings 14.6 : וְאָנֹכִי שָׁלוּחַ אֵלַיִךְ קָשָׁה *Am I sent to thee* (*with news which is*) *hard* (*to bear*) ?

[25] Note the use of the verb יָעַץ and the cognate noun עֵצָה ; lit. *the advice of the old men which they had advised him*.

[26] Note how emphatically אָבִי and וַאֲנִי are placed in the sentence.

[27] Heb. *to possess it*. רֶשֶׁת (with suffix רִשְׁתִּי, etc.) is the cstr. infin. of יָרַשׁ (cf. § 29.2.2.(b).iii and Paradigm).

[28] חַיִּים is plur. of חַי, *alive, living*, from root חיי (which appears in verb form as חָיָה, § 33.2(e)) ; hence dagh. forte in י.

B.

1 נִחֲמוּ עַמִּי דַּבְּרוּ ¹עַל־לְבָבָם ²וְקִרְאוּ אֵלֶיהָ כִּי מָלְאָה ³מִלְחַמְתָּם : 2 רִיבוּ בְאִמְּכֶם רִיבוּ כִּי ⁴הִיא לֹא אִשְׁתִּי וְאָנֹכִי לֹא אִישָׁהּ : 3 תִּפֹּל עַל־⁵הָרֲרֵי יִשְׂרָאֵל אַתָּה וְכָל־הָעַמִּים אֲשֶׁר ⁶אִתָּךְ : 4 נָשָׂא ⁷הַשַּׂר אֶת־עֵינָיו ⁸וַיַּרְא אִישׁ עוֹמֵד לְפָנָיו

וְחַרְבוֹ בְיָדוֹ: וַיֹּאמֶר לוֹ הֲלָנוּ אַתָּה אוֹ ⁹לְאֹיְבֵינוּ ¹⁰וַיַּעַן לֹא
כִּי כְשַׂר ¹¹צְבָא יהוה בָּאתִי: 5 הוֹדִיעֵנִי אֶת־קִצִּי וְאֶת־מִדַּת
יָמַי מַה־הִיא ¹²וְאֵדְעָה כִּי גֵר בָּזֶה אָנִי: 6 שָׁלַח הַמֶּלֶךְ אֶת־
הַמַּלְאָכִים ¹³לִקְרֹא אֶת־הַכֹּהֲנִים וַיָּבֹאוּ כֻלָּם אֶל־¹⁴הַמֶּלֶךְ:
7 וַתֹּאמֶר הַבְּתוּלָה לָאִישׁ ¹⁵יֵעָשֶׂה־לִּי הַדָּבָר הַזֶּה ¹⁶וְהַרְפֵּנִי
מְעַט לְמַעַן אֵלְכָה אָנִי לְבַדִּי ¹⁷וְאֶבְכֶּה עַל־⁵הָרָרֵי יִשְׂרָאֵל:
8 ¹⁸וַיַּסַּע מֹשֶׁה אֶת־בְּנֵי יִשְׂרָאֵל אֶל־הַמִּדְבָּר וַיֵּלְכוּ יָמִים
רַבִּים וְלֹא מָצְאוּ מָיִם: וַיָּבֹאוּ ¹⁹אֶל־מָרָה וְלֹא יָכְלוּ לִשְׁתֹּת
אֶת־הַמַּיִם שָׁם כִּי מָרִים הֵם עַל־כֵּן קָרְאוּ אֶת־שְׁמָהּ מָרָה:
וַיִּצְעֲקוּ הָעָם עַל־מֹשֶׁה לֵאמֹר מַה־²⁰נַּעֲשֶׂה: וַיִּצְעַק הוּא
לַיהוה ²¹וַיַּרְאֵהוּ עֵץ וַיֹּאמֶר הַשְׁלִיכֵהוּ אֶל־הַמַּיִם וַיַּשְׁלִיכֵהוּ
אֶל־הַמַּיִם וַיִּמְתְּקוּ הַמָּיִם:

---

[1] *To their heart*, i.e. kindly, sympathetically, comfortably (AV);
alternatively עַל־לְבָּם (abs. לֵב; cf. § 40.6.(a)).

[2] In poetic form (such as Isa. 40.1f. on which this sentence is based)
a series of imperatives is quite in order. In prose וּקְרָאתֶם would have
been used in place of the third. Characteristic also of poetic form is the
omission of אֶת־ before עַמִּי in the first phrase of the sentence.

[3] Isa. 40.2 has מָלְאָה צְבָאָהּ, using the 3 sing. fem. suffix.

[4] הִיא and אָנֹכִי are placed first in the clauses in which they occur for
emphasis. Besides כִּי לֹא הִיא אִשְׁתִּי might easily be construed as meaning
for not she (but another woman) is my wife. For the form of אִשְׁתִּי, cf. Voc.
§ 29.

[5] A reduplicated form fairly frequently used in poetic passages; הָרֵי
also may be used (cf. § 40.2.(c),3).

[6] Pausal form for אִתְּךָ.

[7] For the vocalization of this noun, cf. § 40.2.(a).

[8] For this form, cf. § 33.1.(d).

[9] Or לְצָרֵינוּ; cf. § 40.2.(a).

¹⁰ For this form, cf. § 33.1.(d), where the verb עָלָה is used to illustrate it.

¹¹ For the *qāmeṣ*, cf. § 38.5.

¹² וְאֵדְעָה is strictly correct for the final clause *that I may know*; וְיָדַעְתִּי would describe the consequence *and I shall know*.

¹³ This is the common form of the cstr. infin. of קָרָא *to call* with לְ ; occasionally לִקְרֹאת is found ; cf. Key § 38B, note 3.

¹⁴ Pausal form is always thus הַמֶּלֶךְ, never הַמֶּלֶךְ.

¹⁵ Or תֵּעָשֶׂה־לִּי זֹאת ; for the *dagh. forte conjunctivum*, cf. § 6.6.

¹⁶ The Hiph. of רָפָה, הִרְפָּה, means *to leave alone, to let be* ; imper. Hiph. is הַרְפֵּה (apoc. form הֶרֶף), with 1 sing. suffix הַרְפֵּנִי *leave me alone*. In Jud. 11.37, on which this sentence is based, הַרְפֵּה מִמֶּנִּי is used ; such a use of מִן is readily intelligible, as emphasizing the *separation* of the woman *from* human society for a period. Instead of the imper. הַרְפֵּנִי, וְהִרְפֵּיתַנִי would be possible.

¹⁷ וְאֶבְכֶּה continues the idea of purpose expressed in אֵלְכָה ; i.e. *that I may go . . . and (that I may) weep. . . .*

¹⁸ הִסִּיעַ is possible, but the impf. consec. Hiph. form וַיַּסַּע is more idiomatic Hebrew. The root is נסע *to pull up* (the tent pegs), *to strike camp, to journey* ; Hiph. הִסִּיעַ *to cause to journey*. Sentence 8 is based on Exod. 15.22–25. As an alternative to וַיַּסַּע, וַיּוֹלֶךְ (3 s.m. impf. consec. Hiph. of הָלַךְ) would be suitable.

¹⁹ Or מָרָתָה (cf. § 14.5).

²⁰ The dagh. forte following מַה־, which is illustrated here is *dagh. forte conjunctivum* (cf. G.K. § 37.1.(b)) ; מַה may go back to מַנְתְּ < מַת, which could be the fem. of *man* meaning *who* ? found in Arabic.

²¹ Note the form וַיִּרְאֵהוּ. The root is רָאָה ; impf. Hiph. is יַרְאֶה ; with 3 sing. masc. suff. יַרְאֵהוּ as here. The Exodus passage has וַיּוֹרֵהוּ ; this

form is from the root ירה, of which the impf. Hiph. is יֹרֶה (cf. § 29) ;
hence וַיֹּורֵהוּ *and he showed him*. The basic meaning of ירה is *to shoot*
(arrows). The Hiph. הֹורָה means *to decide* (orig. from observance of the
flight of arrows), *to instruct, to teach* (cf. the noun תֹּורָה) or, as here, *to show*.
Both verbs in the Hiph. can take the accus. of person and accus. of thing,
as here ; cf. Key § 38C, note 5.

§ 41.

A.

1. Then David said with great longing[1] : " [2]O that I could
have some water to drink[2] from the well of Bethlehem which is
by the gate !" The three[3] warriors went out of the camp of the
Israelites and came to the well of the city and drew water from
it.[4] They carried it away and brought it to David, but [5]he would
not drink[5] it and poured[6] it out to Yahweh with the words[7] :
" Far be it from me to do this. Shall I drink the blood[8] of the
men who went at the risk[9] of their lives ?" So he would not drink
it. 2. Then she said to her : " All that thou sayest to me I will
do." So she went down to[10] the threshing-floor, and did [11]exactly
as her mother-in-law had instructed her."[11] When the man had
eaten and drunk and felt cheerful,[12] he came to lie down at the
end of the grain-heap. In due course[13] she came also and lay
down beside him. Thereupon he said : " Who art thou ?" " I am
Ruth, thy handmaid," she said ; " [14]cover thy handmaid with
thy skirt,[14] for thou art nearest of kin."[15] He said : " Blessed
be[16] thou of the Yahweh, for thou hast [17]shown the depth of[17]
thy love in not running after the young men, poor or rich."
3. Remember thy mercies, O Yahweh, and thine acts of love,
for they have been from of old. Remember not [18]the sins and
faults of my youth,[18] but according to thy love remember me.[19]
Good and upright is Yahweh ; he instructs sinners in the way.
4. [20]Hide not thy face from me,[20] [21]turn not away thy servant in
anger[21] ; thou hast been my help ; leave me not nor forsake me,
O my Saviour God. Should[22] my father and mother forsake me,
Yahweh will take care of me.[23]

¹ Lit. *desired and said*, or *longed and said*. But since his words obviously express the desire and longing, it is preferable in the English translation to make one of the verbs subsidiary, as is done above.

²⁻² Lit. *who will let me drink water* ; so *who will fetch me water*, or as above. מִי־יִתֶּן is a common way of expressing a wish ; cf. Voc. § 34 and § 46.3.(b).

³ Heb. *the three warriors*. This sentence, taken by itself, might seem to call for the translation *Three warriors . . .* ; but the mention of them in 2 Sam. 23.16 (on which this sentence is based), is to be understood as referring to the three mentioned in the preceding verse 13, so that the translation given above is the appropriate one. But an interesting Hebrew usage may be mentioned here. Occasionally in the Old Testament the first reference to a person or thing not yet defined has the article. This is so, for example, in the case of the reference to the burning bush in Exod. 3.2. The reason for the usage probably is that, as the tradition was handed down, the burning bush became so renowned and so well known that the article came to be used even in the first reference to it.

⁴ Literally *there*.

⁵⁻⁵ The literal rendering *was unwilling to drink* is too weak ; what is required is *would not drink* or *refused to drink*.

⁶ The usual Hebrew verb meaning *to pour out* is שָׁפַךְ. The verb used here נָסַךְ means *to pour* (as into a mould) ; hence מַסֵּכָה *a metal image* ; or *to pour out ritually* ; hence נֶסֶךְ *libation*. It is this latter usage which is illustrated here ; David pours out the water on the ground as a holy offering.

⁷ Literally *and said*. English literary style is more complex and flexible than Hebrew, and the translation given here shows it.

⁸ Note the emphatic order of the Hebrew, with the words *the blood of . . .* following immediately after the interrogative particle.

⁹ For this use of the preposition בְּ, cf. § 12.2.(a).ii.

L

[10] Note the absence here from the Hebrew of a preposition such as אֶל־. Presumably הַגֹּרֶן, as used here, is an accus. of " motion to " ; cf. § 24.II.1.

[11-11] Literally *according to all that her mother-in-law had commanded.*

[12] Literally, *his heart was good,* i.e. *he felt satisfied and content, he was comfortably at ease.*

[13] Cf. note 7 above. *And she came,* or *then she came* would be a stodgy translation ; *later* or *in due course* helps the flow of the narrative.

[14-14] Literally, *spread thy skirt over thy handmaid.* The woman's request is that the man should cast the skirt over her and so, symbolically, accept her as a wife.

[15] The Hebrew word גֹּאֵל, often rendered *redeemer,* is used here as a technical term. If a man died childless, it was the duty of his nearest of kin to marry the widow and to give the name of the deceased husband to the first child born of this marriage ; in this way the nearest of kin acted as גֹּאֵל and the name of the deceased was kept alive in the community (cf. Gen. 38.8 ; Deut. 25.6f). It was also the duty of the nearest of kin as גֹּאֵל to recover for the family any family property which had had to be sold because of penury or had been lost to the family in any other way (cf. Ruth 4.3–13).

[16] Or *art.*

[17-17] Literally, *made thy love great* or *abundant.*

[18-18] Or *the sins of my youth and my faults* ; cf. Ps. 25.7 ; Job 13.26.

[19] The לִי following זְכָר־ (shortened form of imper. זְכֹר because it is joined with לִי־אָתָּה in one tonal unit) may be regarded as a method of expressing a direct object which is found in later parts of the Old Testament and is common in Aramaic (cf. Key § 35A, note 13). Otherwise consider לִי as an example of *Dativus Commodi* (cf. § 12.2.(c).i).

[20-20] God is said to *hide his face* when he *forsakes* anyone or gives no evident sign of his blessing and care ; God *makes his face to shine* upon a man when he returns to him to bless him and to make his presence known.

²¹⁻²¹ In modern English we may say : *do not repel* (or *repulse*) *thy servant in anger* (cf. Key § 40A, note 18).

²² This seems a better rendering than *when* (so A.V.) An alternative translation would be : *Though my father and mother were to forsake me, yet Yahweh would take care of me.*

²³ The usual rendering *will take me up* might suggest lifting up a child, to carry it when it is exhausted. But Isa. 52.12 and 58.8 speak of Yahweh going before his people as leader and gathering up and caring for stragglers as rearguard. For this second sense it is the verb אסף which is used. It is that meaning which is given to the verb in the translation above ; *if my father and mother leave me in the lurch, Yahweh will gather me up and care for me.*

B.

1 שָׁאַל אֲדֹנִי אֶת־עֲבָדָיו ¹הֲיֵשׁ לָכֶם אָב אוֹ אָח : וַנֹּאמֶר
לַאדֹנִי יֶשׁ־לָנוּ אָב זָקֵן וְאָח קָטֹן בֶּן־זְקֻנָיו הוּא לְבַדּוֹ ²יִוָּתֵר
³לְאִמּוֹ וְאָבִיו אֲהֵבוֹ : וַתֹּאמֶר לָנוּ הוֹרִידֻהוּ אֵלָי וְאָשִׂימָה
אֶת־עֵינִי עָלָיו : וַנֹּאמֶר לַאדֹנִי לֹא ⁴יֻכַל הַיֶּלֶד לַעֲזֹב אֶת־
אָבִיו ⁵כִּי אִם יַעֲזֹב אֶת־אָבִיו יָמוּת אָבִיו: וַתֹּאמֶר לַעֲבָדֶיךָ
אִם לֹא יֵרֵד אֲחִיכֶם הַקָּטֹן אִתְּכֶם לֹא תֹסִיפוּ לִרְאוֹת אֶת־
פָּנָי : וַיְהִי ⁶בְּשׁוּבֵנוּ אֶל־בֵּית ⁷אָבִינוּ וַנַּגֶּד־לוֹ אֶת־כָּל־אֲשֶׁר
אָמַרְתָּ לָנוּ : וַיֹּאמֶר לָנוּ שׁוּבוּ מִצְרַיְמָה וּשְׁבַרְתֶּם לָנוּ מְעַט
אֹכֶל : וַנֹּאמֶר לֹא לֹא ⁸יֻכְלְנוּ לָשׁוּב אִם יֵרֵד אָחִינוּ הַקָּטֹן
אִתָּנוּ נָשׁוּב אֲנַחְנוּ כִּי לֹא ⁸יֻכְלְנוּ לִרְאוֹת אֶת־פְּנֵי הָאִישׁ
⁹וְאָחִינוּ הַקָּטֹן אֵינֶנּוּ אִתָּנוּ⁹: וְעַתָּה ¹⁰מָצְאָה אֹתָנוּ הָרָעָה
הַזֹּאת : אֵיךְ יָכֹלְתִּי לָשׁוּב עַתָּה אֶל־אָבִי ⁹וְהַיֶּלֶד אֵינֶנּוּ אִתִּי⁹:
¹¹אֵשְׁבָה־נָּא אֲנִי¹¹ תַּחְתָּיו ¹²עֶבֶד לַאדֹנִי :

---

¹ For the pointing of יֵשׁ, cf. Key § 29B, note 13.

² The root שאר, which in the Niph. means *to be left, to remain, to survive*, is given in Vocabulary § 29. This verb is often used in the sense of being a

survivor after a calamity. It is possible to use it here, but the root יָתַר is preferable. In Vocabulary § 39 יֶתֶר, *remainder* is given; the Niph. of יָתַר means *to remain, to be left* and should be used here since the words *he alone is left to his mother* means *he is the only child now at home with his mother.*

³ אֵם *mother* is from a Double ʿ*Ayin* root, so that the forms with suffixes are אִמִּי, אִמְּךָ, etc.; cf. § 40.1, 6.(a).

⁴ Or יוּכַל.

⁵⁻⁵ Gen. 44.22 has the very short text וְעָזַב אֶת־אָבִיו וָמֵת in which the first clause must be translated as a subsidiary one; i.e. *if he leaves his father, he* (his father) *will die.*

⁶ Gen. 44.24 has כִּי עָלִינוּ *when we went up.* Hebrew usage speaks of *going up* from Egypt to Palestine and *going down* from Palestine to Egypt.

⁷ Gen. 44.24 has the polite form of speech with עַבְדְּךָ inserted before אָבִי which it reads in place of our אָבִינוּ.

⁸ Or נוּכַל, the impf. form; cf. § 29.4.

⁹⁻⁹ *Unless our young brother is with us* is really a circumstantial clause (as is *if the boy is not with me* later in the exercise), so that the neatest and most idiomatic way of translating it is that given in the text. For אַיִן, cf. the footnote to § 31.4. יֵשׁ means *there is,* e.g. יֵשׁ־לִי כֶּסֶף *I have money* (there is to me money): אַיִן (cstr. אֵין) means *there is not.*

¹⁰ מָצָא *to find* can be used, in such a sentence as this, meaning *to happen to.* Otherwise use קָרָה but note that it takes an accus. after it, not the preposition לְ.

¹¹⁻¹¹ Or יֵשֶׁב־נָא עַבְדְּךָ with the polite 3rd person usage in place of the 1st person.

¹² עֶבֶד is sufficient here; cf. Gen. 44.33. Otherwise לְעֶבֶד may be used, but not כְּעֶבֶד which means *like a servant.*

§ 42.

A.

1. When[1] David and his men came[2] to the city, [3]they found it destroyed[3] by fire ; and their wives, their sons and their daughters had been taken captive.[4] 2. The crown of old men is grandchildren and the glory[5] of children is their fathers. 3. Happy[6] are those who dwell in thy house. 4. And he took[7] the daughter of Pharaoh and brought her to the city of David [8]until he had finished building[8] his house. 5. And he lay[9] with his fathers and was buried in the city of his father. 6. When[10] Joseph's brothers saw that their father was dead, they said : " It may be that Joseph will hate us[11] ; in that case he will certainly requite[12] us for all the harm[13] we [once] did to him." So they approached Joseph with the words : " Thy father gave [us] this instruction before his death : ' Thus shall you speak to Joseph : Pray forgive[14] the wrongdoing of thy brothers and their sin, for they treated thee badly. Forgive now the wrongdoing of the servants of thy father's God.' " Joseph wept as they spoke to him ; and his brothers also came and fell before him and said : " Behold we are thy servants." 7. And they said to Samson's wife : " Entice[15] thy husband that he may tell us the riddle, lest[15] we burn thee and thy father's house with fire. Have you called us that you may take away our possessions ?"[16] Then Samson's wife [17]wept over him[17] and said : " Thou hatest me and dost not love me ; thou hast propounded the riddle to my people,[18] but thou hast not told[19] it to me." And he said to her : " Listen. I have not told it to my own father and mother. [20]Am I to tell it[20] to thee ?" 8. And Yahweh said to Moses : " Stretch out thy hand to the heavens, that darkness may fall upon the land of Egypt." So Moses stretched out[21] his hand to the heavens, and there was darkness in all the land of Egypt for three days.[22] They could not see one another,[23] and [24]no man left his home[24] for three days ; but for all the Israelites there was light in their dwellings.

9. ‏וְעַתָּה לֵךְ וְאָנֹכִי אֶהְיֶה עִם־פִּיךָ [25]וְהוֹרֵיתִיךָ אֲשֶׁר תְּדַבֵּר‎:

And now go, and I, on my part, will be with thy mouth and will teach thee what thou shalt speak.

10. וַהֲקִמֹתִי אֶת־בְּרִיתִי אִתָּךְ²⁶ וּבָאתָ אֶל־הַתֵּבָה אַתָּה
וּבָנֶיךָ וְאִשְׁתְּךָ וּנְשֵׁי־בָנֶיךָ ²⁶אִתָּךְ :

And I will establish my covenant with thee, and thou shalt enter
into the ark, thou and thy sons and thy wife and thy sons' wives
with thee.

¹ Cf. Key § 39B, note 23, and § 41A, note 1.

² Note how the verb is singular, because it is construed with the first
element (דָּוִד) of a composite subject ; וַיָּבֹאוּ also could be used.

³⁻³ Literally *and behold it was burned with fire*. The ptc. שְׂרוּפָה calls
attention to the condition in which the city was found, not to the fact that
it had been burned down.

⁴ In contrast to the use of שְׂרוּפָה (see note 3 above), the verbal form
נִשְׁבּוּ records the fact that the women and children had been taken captive.

⁵ Or *pride*.

⁶ Literally, *the happinesses of the dwellers in thy house*.

⁷ Or *married* (cf. 1 Kings 3.1).

⁸⁻⁸ Literally, *up to [the time] he had finished to build*. כַּלֹּתוֹ is cstr.
nfin. *Piʿēl* of כָּלָה with 3 s.m. suffix and it is followed by another cstr.
infin. לִבְנוֹת. עַד־אֲשֶׁר כִּלָּה לִבְנוֹת would also have been possible.

⁹ I.e. was buried. Since, however, that is the meaning of the next verb
וַיִּקָּבֵר, it may well be that the first clause here had a somewhat different
sense : e.g. *he lay down in death, like all his forefathers and. . . .*

¹⁰ Cf. note 1 above.

¹¹ The literal rendering of this clause probably assumes a lacuna :
If Joseph should hate us (i.e. show hostility to us), *[what are we to do ?]* ;
he will certainly. . . . The translation given above expresses the sense of
the words in less literal form. It should be noted that לוּ, as used in conditional clauses, commonly refers to the past and to something which
cannot be fulfilled in the future ; cf. § 46.3.(a).

¹² That is, *pay us out, square accounts with us* ; *take his revenge* is also
possible, but probably too strong an expression for the purpose.

13 *The evil we have done to him* is a much less suitable rendering in view of the high position to which Joseph had attained in Egypt. *Harm* or *injury* is more suitable than *evil*.

14 The precative force is strong here with the use of the two particles אָנָּא and נָא. An English equivalent might be, *Please, for my sake, forgive.* . . . Note the form of the 2 s.m. imper. Qal of נָשָׂא. As a *Lāmedh 'Aleph* it would be נְשָׂא (cf. § 38.1.(a).ii), but as a *Pē Nûn* with impf. in *a* the נ is dropped (cf. § 34.2.(a)) ; hence שָׂא, cf. § 41.1.(i).

15 S.f. imper. *Pi'ēl* of פָּתָה. The phrase *lest we burn* which follows would be more vigorously expressed by, *or we will burn.* . . .

16 For the pointing of the interrogative particle with *pathaḥ* before vocal shᵉwa, cf. § 46.1.(b). יָרַשׁ *to possess* has two meanings in the Hiph. (הוֹרִישׁ) : (*a*) *to cause to possess* ; (*b*) *to dispossess*. It is the latter value which is exemplified here.

17–17 The value of עַל־ in this phrase is difficult to express. She did not weep over him in sympathy. Rather she wept (and wailed) *at him* in peevish complaint. *She lamented to him* or *bewailed her lot to him* may catch the sense.

18 Lit. *the sons of my people.* The use of *sons* here is comparable with that in בְּנֵי אָדָם *human beings* ; cf. בֶּן־בָּקָר *a bullock, an ox, a calf.*

19 Or *expounded*, as contrasted with *propounded*.

20–20 The Hebrew words here may be rendered as : *To thee I shall tell it.* But the context demands that they be interpreted as a question, even although there is no interrogative particle.

21 יֵט is from נָטָה ; impf. יִטֶּה (< יִנְטֶה) ; apoc. impf. יֵט. Cf. § 41.1.(4).

22 שָׁלֹשׁ (m.) is *three* ; fem. שְׁלֹשָׁה, cstr. שְׁלֹשֶׁת· שְׁלֹשָׁה יָמִים and שְׁלֹשֶׁת יָמִים may be used meaning *three days*. The peculiarities of this usage will be studied in § 45.

23 Literally, *each his brother* ; cf. § 33.4.

24–24 Lit. *they did not arise, each from his place.* . . .

²⁵ 1 sing. pf. consec. Hiph. of ירה with 2 sing. masc. suffix.

²⁶ Pausal form for אִתְּךָ.

B.

1 כַּבֵּד אֶת־אָבִיךָ וְאֶת־אִמֶּךָ כַּאֲשֶׁר צִוְּךָ אֱלֹהֶיךָ:
2 וַתְּדַבֵּרְנָה בְנֹתָיו ¹אִשָּׁה אֶל־אֲחֹתָהּ¹ לֵאמֹר: ¹לְכִי נַשְׁקָה
אֶת־אָבִינוּ יָיִן ²וַיֵּשְׁתְּ וַיִּשְׁכָּר: 3 וַתּוֹסֶף אִשְׁתּוֹ ³לָלֶדֶת בֵּן
וַיִּגְדַּל ⁴הוּא וַיֶּאֱהַב אֶת־יוֹלְדָיו בְּכָל־לְבָבוֹ ⁵וַיֶּרֶב לְהֵיטִיב
לְאֶחָיו וּלְאַחְיֹתָיו: 4 ⁶וַיֵּשְׁבוּ אֶת־נְשֵׁי אֹיְבֵיהֶם ⁷וַיָּבֹזּוּ אֶת־
בָּתֵּיהֶם וַיֵּלְכוּ ⁸לְדַרְכֶּם וְלֹא ⁹הֵמִיתוּ כָל־אִישׁ: 5 וַתֵּשֶׁב בִּתּוֹ
בְּבֵית אָבִיהָ ¹⁰שְׁנָתַיִם: 6 ¹⁰יוֹמַיִם לֹא ¹¹פָּתַח אָבִיו אֶת־פִּיו:
7 עֲזָבֻנִי אָבִי וְאִמִּי: 8 יִהְיֶה שְׁמוֹ בְּפִי תָמִיד: 9 מָצָאתִי
בְּבֵיתְךָ כְּלֵי כֶסֶף וּכְלֵי זָהָב: 10 ¹²אַשְׁרֵי אֲנָשֶׁיךָ:

¹⁻¹ For such reciprocal usages, cf. § 33.4. Note how there follows in direct speech the individualizing sing. לְכִי (s.f. imper. Qal of הָלַךְ) and, immediately after it, the plur. נַשְׁקָה.

² The vocalization found in the form יֵשְׁתְּ (3 s.m. apoc. impf. Qal of שָׁתָה) is one which occurs very infrequently; cf. § 33.1.(a).iii,iv.

³ Or וַתֵּלֶד. For the cstr. infin. form לֶדֶת, cf. § 29.2.(2).(b).iii, and for the construction of וַתּוֹסֶף לָלֶדֶת, cf. § 29.4.

⁴ הוּא may, but need not, be inserted here because of the change of subject.

⁵ וַיֶּרֶב is 3 s.m. impf. consec. Hiph. of רָבָה (Hiph. pf. הִרְבָּה; impf. יַרְבֶּה, apoc. form יֶרֶב > יַרְבְּ); for the verbal construction here, cf. note 3 above.

⁶ Or שָׁבוּ, but such unconnected perfects are used more often in English than in Hebrew.

⁷ Or וַיִּשְׁלוּ (from שָׁלַל).

⁸ Hebrew idiomatically לְדַרְכָּם, not בְּדַרְכָּם.

⁹ Or הָרְגוּ.

¹⁰ For such duals, cf. § 13.6.(a).

¹¹ The use of יִפְתַּח is possible here instead of the perf. ; its use would emphasize the *continued* state of silence.

¹² For the form אַשְׁרֵי, cf. note A6 above.

§ 43.

A.

1. Yahweh is my shepherd,[1] I shall not lack.[2] 2. Every man used to do what was right in his own eyes. 3. Thy servant was a shepherd to his father, in charge of the flock.[3] Whenever[4] a[5] lion came and picked off a sheep from the flock, I went out after it and attacked[6] it and rescued [the sheep] from its mouth. 4. But the poor man had nothing except[7] one little ewe lamb which he possessed.[8] He had reared it, and it had grown up together with him and his sons ; it ate of his morsel and drank from his cup and lay in his bosom and became like a daughter to him. 5. Yahweh knows the way of righteous men[9] ; but the way of wicked men[9] shall perish. 6. As he looked, he noticed a well in the field, [10]with flocks of sheep lying there beside it[10] ; for from that well the flocks were watered.[11] 7. And Yahweh opened the mouth of the ass and it said to Balaam : " What have I done to thee that thou hast beaten me three[12] times ?" Balaam said to the ass : " Because thou hast dealt severely with me ; if[13] I had a sword in my hand, I would kill thee this very moment." But the ass said to Balaam : " Am I not thine ass on which thou hast ridden from thy youth until this day ? Have I ever been in the habit of behaving like this to thee ?" And he said : " No." 8. My people did not listen to my voice and Israel would have none of me.[14] So I let them go from me in the stubbornness of their hearts and they lived by their own devices. Would that my people would listen to me ! Would that Israel would walk[15] in my ways ! 9. It happened that, as the king of Israel was passing along the city wall, a woman cried out to him, saying : " Save[16] me, my lord." And he said : " [17]If Yahweh will not save thee,

from what source[18] am I to save thee ?[17] From the threshing-floor
or the wine-vat ?'' Then the king said to her : '' What is the
matter with thee ?'' And she replied : '' This woman said to me :
' Give thy son and we shall eat[19] him today, and my son we shall
eat tomorrow '.'' When[20] the king heard the words of the woman,
he tore his clothes (he was passing along the wall at the time[21]) ;
when the people looked, they caught sight of the sackcloth on his
body.

10. זֹאת הַבְּרִית אֲשֶׁר אֶכְרֹת [22]אֶת־בֵּית יִשְׂרָאֵל אַחֲרֵי הַיָּמִים
הָהֵם נְאֻם־יהוה: [23]נָתַתִּי אֶת־תּוֹרָתִי בְּקִרְבָּם וְעַל־לִבָּם
[24]אֶכְתֲּבֶנָּה וְהָיִיתִי לָהֶם לֵאלֹהִים וְהֵמָּה יִהְיוּ־לִי לְעָם:

This is the covenant that I will make with the house of Israel
after those days, saith Yahweh. I will put my law within them
and on their hearts I will write it ; and I will be their God and
they shall be my people.

[1] רָעָה to shepherd, to pasture has, as its Qal ptc. form, רֹעֶה ; with
1 sing. suffix, רֹעִי, as here.

[2] The verb can also have reference to the present : *I lack nothing.*

[3] שֶׂה is a *nomen unitatis*, meaning *a sheep* ; צֹאן is a collective noun,
meaning *sheep* ; עֵדֶר means *flock* (of sheep).

[4] In this sentence the consec. pf. forms, being equivalent in force to
simple impfs., may be rendered fittingly as frequentatives (cf. § 43.II.2) ;
that effect is gained in the translation by the use of *whenever.*

[5] Heb. *the lion*, possibly a generic use of the article ; cf. Key § 12A,
note 10.

[6] וְהִכְּתִיו is 1 sing. consec. pf. Hiph. of נכה with the 3 sing. masc.
pron. suffix. For translation *destroyed it* may be used as an alternative to
attacked it.

[7] This is an example of the use of כִּי אִם after a negative, meaning
but or *except.*

[8] Or *had acquired.*

⁹ In poetic form the article is quite often omitted in cases where it would be used in prose passages. Thus צַדִּיקִים may be rendered here as *the righteous* and רְשָׁעִים as *the wicked.*

¹⁰⁻¹⁰ Literally *and behold flocks of sheep were lying there beside it.*

¹¹ Probably the subject of יַשְׁקוּ should be taken to be the 3 plur. of indefinite or general reference (cf. § 40.7) so that the passive may be used in English translation.

¹² Obviously the demonstrative זֶה is not in agreement with the noun פְּעָמִים, but is, as used here, an unchanging proclitic ; cf. זֶה פַעֲמַיִם *twice.* For the use of the numeral here, cf. § 45.1.(c) and Key § 42A, note 22.

¹³ For לוּ, cf. § 46.3.(a) and (b). Alternative translations are : *If I had had a sword in my hand, I should have killed thee by now* or *Would that I had a sword in my hand ; in that case I would kill thee.*

¹⁴ Literally *was not willing for me* ; i.e. *did not want me, would not have me.*

¹⁵ The Piʻel of הָלַךְ is not in common use like the Qal. It means *walk*, not in the physical sense of locomotion, but of *walking in a way of life*, so that *live* often expresses its meaning.

¹⁶ הוֹשִׁיעָה is the emphatic 2 s.m. imper. Hiph. of יָשַׁע.

¹⁷⁻¹⁷ This is the translation which is commonly adopted here (cf. 2 Kings 6.27 in AV and RSV). But it is possible to make two sentences of this compound sentence by regarding the initial אִם־לֹא as introducing a strong asseveration (cf. § 46.3.(d)) thus : *Surely Yahweh will save thee. From what source am I to save thee ?*

¹⁸ Literally *whence* (interrogative).

¹⁹ Or *that we may eat. . . .*

²⁰ Nothing is gained here in English translation by reading *And it came to pass,* or *And it happened* at the beginning of the sentence.

²¹ The use of brackets in the English translation to enclose a clause indicates that while it is obviously a circumstantial clause in the Hebrew text, it is parenthetical as it stands in the narrative.

²² אֶת־ here is the preposition *with*, not the sign of the definite accusative.

²³ Not *I have given*, but an example of the prophetic perfect : *I will give, I will put* ; cf. § 43.I.2.(d).

²⁴ The normal form would be אֶכְתְּבֶנָּה, but in Jer. 31.33, which is the source of this sentence, a composite sheʷa is found (Kittel, *Biblia Hebraica*, 3rd edit., has אֶכְתֲּבֶנָּה). For forms with *nûn energicum*, cf. § 27.6.

B.

1 כַּאֲשֶׁר יְעַנּוּם הָאֹיְבִים כֵּן יִרְבּוּ : 2 יִקַּח אֶת־הָאֹהֶל וְנָטָהוּ מִחוּץ ¹לַמַּחֲנֶה : 3 לֹא יֵעָשֶׂה כֵן בְּאַרְצֵנוּ : 4 ²כַּאֲשֶׁר אָבַדְתִּי אָבָדְתִּי : 5 אָז ³יָשִׁיר מֹשֶׁה וּבְנֵי יִשְׂרָאֵל אֶת־הַשִּׁירָה הַזֹּאת לֵאלֹהֵיהֶם : 6 אֲשֶׁר יְחַזֵּק אֶת־לְבָבוֹ ⁴וְעָבַר אֶת־תּוֹרָתִי יוּמַת הוּא : 7 הָאָרֶץ עֹמֶדֶת לְעוֹלָם : 8 מָצְאוּ נְעָרוֹת יֹצְאוֹת לִשְׁאֹב מַיִם : 9 אֶת־כָּל־⁵זֹאת אֶתֵּן לְךָ אִם ⁶תִּפֹּל אַרְצָה וְהִשְׁתַּחֲוִיתָ⁶ לְפָנָי : 10 ⁷יָדַע הַצַּדִּיק⁷ אֶת־נֶפֶשׁ בְּהֶמְתּוֹ : 11 לְעוֹלָם סָמַךְ יהוה אֶת־כָּל־⁸הַנֹּפְלִים : 12 עוֹד הוּא מְדַבֵּר ⁹וַיָּבוֹא⁹ אֶחָד מֵעֲבָדָיו⁹ וַיֹּאמֶר ¹⁰נִדְמֵינוּ כֻלָּנוּ : 13 בָּנֶיךָ וּבְנֹתֶיךָ אֹכְלִים וְשֹׁתִים בְּבֵית אֲחִיהֶם ¹¹הַגָּדוֹל : ¹²וְהִנֵּה בָּאָה¹² רוּחַ גְּדוֹלָה ¹³מִן־הַמִּדְבָּר וַתִּגַּע בַּבַּיִת וַיִּפֹּל עַל־כָּל־הַיֹּשְׁבִים בְּתוֹכוֹ וַיָּמֻתוּ :

¹ Notice how Hebrew expresses *outside* adjectivally : not חוּץ alone, or even מָחוּץ (= *outside* adverbially) but מָחוּץ לְ *on the outside relative to*, i.e. *outside*.

² So Esther 4.16 ; cf. Gen. 43.14. This is an expression of resignation in which כַּאֲשֶׁר, not אִם, is used.

³ The verb is here in the sing., being construed with the first element (מֹשֶׁה) in the subject ; cf. Key § 42A, note 2. For this use of the impf. יָשִׁיר, cf. § 43.II.1.(a).

⁴ It would be possible also to use לַעֲבֹר, i.e. *by transgressing.*

⁵ In such a phrase זאת alone is used without the article.

⁶⁻⁶ *Fall down* cannot be translated here by תִּפֹּל alone, but תִּכְרַע may be used. For the form וְהִשְׁתַּחֲוִיתָ, cf. § 32.4.

⁷⁻⁷ The ptc. יֹדֵעַ also may be used. For *a righteous man*, as used here, Hebrew uses הַצַּדִּיק.

⁸ Or הַנִּכְשָׁלִים.

⁹⁻⁹ Or וְאָחָד מֵעֲבָדָיו בָּא.

¹⁰ The verb דָּמָה can mean *to cease* or *to cause to cease, to destroy.* The Niph. נִדְמָה means *to be destroyed, to be ruined,* or the curious English usage *to be undone.*

¹¹ Or הַבְּכוֹר *the firstborn.*

¹²⁻¹² Or וַתָּבוֹא.

¹³ Or מֵעֵבֶר *from across.*

§ 44.

A.

1. Take away¹ my life, for I am no better than my fathers. 2. What is sweeter than honey, and what² is stronger than a lion ? 3. Yahweh loves the gates of Zion more than all the dwellings of Jacob. 4. Better is the day of death than the day of one's birth.³ 5. There was no man among the Israelites better than he ; ⁴he stood head and shoulders above⁴ all the people. 6. The fairest⁵ among women. 7. Listen !⁶ To obey⁷ is better than sacrifice, and to pay heed than the fat of rams. 8. Death will be preferable⁸ to life for all who survive of this evil family. 9. When Joseph saw that his father was laying his right hand on the head of Ephraim, ⁹he thought it wrong⁹ ; and he took hold of his father's hand to transfer it from the head of Ephraim to the head of Manasseh. And he¹⁰ said to his father : " ¹¹That is not right,¹¹ father,¹² for this one is the firstborn ; lay thy right hand on his head." But his father refused and said : " I know that, son. And I know that

he also will become a people ; he also will become great. But his younger brother will become greater than he, and his posterity[13] will fill[14] the nations." 10. When I see the heavens, the work of thy fingers, the moon and the stars which thou hast established,[15] what is man that thou rememberest him, or a human being that thou carest[16] for him? Thou hast made him a little less than God,[17] crowning[18] him with glory and honour.

11. ‏וְעַתָּה יהוה קַח־נָא אֶת־נַפְשִׁי מִמֶּנִּי כִּי טוֹב מוֹתִי מֵחַיָּי‎ :

And now, Yahweh, take away my life from me, for [19]it is better for me to die than to live.[19]

12. ‏אֶעֱשֶׂה אוֹתְךָ לְגוֹי עָצוּם ²⁰וָרָב מִמֶּנּוּ‎ :

I shall make thee into a more powerful and numerous nation than it.

[1] ‏קַח‎ imper. Qal of ‏לָקַח‎ ; cf. § 34.3.(b).

[2] The pointing of ‏מָה‎ before gutturals is given in § 10.3. There it is said that, before gutturals pointed with qāmeṣ, the form of the interrogative is ‏מֶה‎. In actual usage the pointing of ‏מָה‎ is more complicated than is given in the table in § 10.3 ; the form ‏מֶה‎ is found before ‏ע‎ and ‏ח‎ pointed with other vowels than qāmeṣ, as in the case of ‏עָו‎ here. Cf. 1 Sam. 20.1 : *What have I done ? What is my iniquity ? What is my sin ? :*
‏מֶה עָשִׂיתִי מֶה־עֲוֹנִי וּמֶה חַטָּאתִי‎

[3] ‏הִוָּלְדוֹ‎ is the cstr. infin. Niph. of ‏יָלַד‎ with the 3 sing. masc. suffix, *one's being born.* Strictly this pronominal suffix has no antecedent in the earlier part of the sentence.

[4-4] Lit. *from his shoulder* (and) *upwards he was taller than all the people.*

[5] Or ‏הַיָּפָה‎ may be taken as a vocative : *O thou fairest among women.*
" The person addressed is naturally definite to the mind, and the so-called vocative often has the article : cf. 1 Kings 18.26 ‏הַבַּעַל עֲנֵנוּ‎ ' O Baal, answer us '. Jud. 6.12 ‏יהוה עִמְּךָ גִּבּוֹר הֶחָיִל‎ ' Yahweh is with thee, O man of valour ' "—the article in the second illustration is used with the noun that is in the absolute (*Syntax*, § 21.(f). *Grammar*, § 14.4, rule 1).

[6] Literally : *Behold.*

⁷ שָׁמַע, followed by a direct accus., means *to hear*; שָׁמַע אֶל ־ *to listen*; שָׁמַע בְּ *to obey*. Here the infin. cstr. is used absolutely; *to hear* is not adequate; *to listen* or *to obey* is needed.

⁸ Literally: (*to be*) *chosen rather than life*, in which case the following לְ is to be rendered as *by*; cf. § 22.4,5.

⁹⁻⁹ Literally: *it was evil in his eyes*. That could mean *he was displeased* or *annoyed*, but probably a sense of wrongdoing and injustice is expressed by these words here rather than displeasure; *he thought it wrong* may give the meaning; even *he objected*, his objection being expressed first in action and then in words.

¹⁰ Heb. explicitly *Joseph*.

¹¹⁻¹¹ *Not so* is a possible rendering; but כֵּן can mean *right* as well as *so*, so that the two renderings are possible. They are, of course, closely related. *Not so* means *not in this way*, the reason being because *it is not the right way*.

¹² Heb. idiomatically *my father*; cf. *my son* which occurs a little later.

¹³ Literally, *seed*.

¹⁴ Literally, *will be the filling of the nations*. מְלֹא is the cstr. infin. of מָלֵא used gerundially.

¹⁵ כּוֹנַנְתָּ is the pausal form of כּוֹנַנְתְּ, 2 s.m. of כּוֹנֵן, which is 3 s.m. perf. *Pô'lēl* of כּוּן; cf. § 30.4.

¹⁶ פָּקַד has various meanings: (*a*) *to review, to inspect*; (*b*) construed with עַל ־ *to punish*; (*c*) *to care for*; cf. פְּקוּדָה *providence*.

¹⁷ The term אֱלֹהִים can be rendered here as *God*, but sometimes *angels* has been given. The meaning doubtless is that man is less than *divine*; he is by nature human, a creature. He has great powers, even the power of procreation; but it is presumption on his part to think he can break the bonds of his finite limitations.

¹⁸ It is possible to regard וַתְּחַסְּרֵהוּ as the main verb and the following impf. תְּעַטְּרֵהוּ as subsidiary, as is done in the translation given above. Or,

in view of the order of the words in the second clause, we may translate it :
yet thou crownest him. . . .

[19-19] Literally, *my death is better than my life.*

[20] Cf. § 11.II.(e).

B.

1 וַיְהִי הַנָּחָשׁ עָרוּם מִכָּל־חַיַּת הַשָּׂדֶה אֲשֶׁר עָשָׂה אֱלֹהִים:
2 הָרַג אֲנָשִׁים צַדִּיקִים מִמֶּנּוּ : 3 [2]אַתָּה חָכָם מִדָּנִאֵל : 4 טוֹב
[3]הַכֶּלֶב הַחַי מִן־[3]הָאֲרִי הַמֵּת : 5 וַיְהִי הָאִישׁ הַהוּא גָּדוֹל
מִכָּל־בְּנֵי קֶדֶם : 6 וַיֶּאֱהַב אֶת־יוֹסֵף [4]מִכָּל־בָּנָיו[4] כִּי בֶן־
זְקֻנִים הוּא־לוֹ : 7 וַיִּשָּׂא אֶת־עֵינָיו וַיַּרְא אֶת־אָחִיו [5]בֶּן־אִמּוֹ[5]
וַיֹּאמֶר הֲזֶה אֲחִיכֶם הַקָּטֹן אֲשֶׁר אֲמַרְתֶּם אֵלָי : 8 וְלוּ [6]שְׁתֵּי
בָנוֹת וַתְּהִי הַקְּטַנָּה[7] יָפָה מִן־הַגְּדוֹלָה : 9 גְּדוֹלֵי הָעִיר : 10 לֹא
נִשְׁאַר־לוֹ כִּי אִם קָטֹן[7] בָּנָיו : 11 [8]לֹא קָצְרָה יַד יהוה
מֵהוֹשִׁיעַ[8] וְלֹא כָבְדָה אָזְנוֹ מִשְּׁמוֹעַ : 12 נָתַן אֲדֹנִי אֶת־כָּל־
אֲשֶׁר־לוֹ בְּיָדִי : לֹא גָדוֹל הוּא בַּבַּיִת הַזֶּה מִמֶּנִּי וְאֵיךְ אֶעֱשֶׂה
אֶת־הָרָעָה הַגְּדוֹלָה הַזֹּאת :

[1] In Gen. 3.1 this appears as וְהַנָּחָשׁ הָיָה which is the order of words
often used when a new subject is introduced (cf. Job 1.1 אִישׁ הָיָה בְאֶרֶץ־
עוּץ אִיּוֹב שְׁמוֹ). But the more common construction, beginning with וַיְהִי, is
used here, since this sentence has been isolated from its context for the
purpose of this exercise and only the context can tell us whether or not this
sentence introduces a new subject.

[2] אַתָּה חָכָם puts emphasis on the person addressed ; חָכָם אַתָּה puts
emphasis upon his wisdom. Either order may be used here.

[3] Two examples of the use in Hebrew of the generic article ; cf.
§ 12.2.(b).i.

[4-4] *More than all his sons* might be taken to mean *more than all his sons
in the aggregate.* That is not what this use of כָּל־ conveys ; *more than any
other of his sons* would be more accurate. The precise point is that Joseph
was his father's favourite.

⁵⁻⁵ בֶּן־אִמּוֹ, used in apposition to אָחִיו, means a full brother. A man in ancient Israel might have more than one wife ; hence the reason for the addition of the phrase בֶּן־אִמּוֹ in such a case as this.

⁶ For the form שְׁתֵּי, cf. § 42 Voc. ; a note upon it is to be found in § 45.1.(b).ii. The absol. form שְׁתַּיִם also could be used here ; cf. 2 Kings 2.24 שְׁתַּיִם דֻּבִּים two bears (from דֹּב, cf. חֹק in § 40.1,2.(a),6.(a)—here fem.).

⁷ קָטוֹן is very common, but it is not inflected (except that once, 2 Chr. 21.17, it appears in the construct—קְטוֹן בָּנָיו the youngest of his sons). The fem., the plur., and the suffixed forms are supplied by קָטָן, for declension of which see § 40.5.

⁸⁻⁸ Lit. Yahweh's hand is not short away from saving, i.e. is not short (or so short) so that he cannot save, or is not too short to save.

§ 45.

A.

1. And he said to his father : " My two sons¹ thou mayest² kill if I do not bring him³ to thee." 2. And he took a present for his brother, two hundred she-goats,⁴ twenty rams, and thirty milch⁵ camels with their colts.⁶ 3. So it came about that in the six hundred and first year of⁷ his life, in the second month, on the twenty-seventh day of⁷ the month, the earth was dry. 4. In the thirty-seventh year, in the twelfth month, on the twenty-seventh day of⁷ the month, the king of Babylon released⁸ the king of Judah from the prison house. 5. And the⁹ three warriors broke through the camp of the enemy and drew some water and brought it to him ; but he would not drink it.¹⁰ 6. And five of you will pursue a hundred, and a hundred of you will pursue ten thousand. 7. Then he said to them : " Come out, the three of you."¹¹ And they came out, the three of them.¹¹ 8. Now this man was the head of the thirty and he wielded his spear against three hundred ¹²and slew them¹² ; and he had a reputation¹³ among the thirty. He was honoured among the thirty and became a leader of them, but he did not become a member of¹⁴ the three. 9. Then the king gathered Judah and ¹⁵set over them¹⁵ commanders of thousands

M

and commanders of hundreds, and mustered[16] those from[17] twenty years of age and upward, and found them to be three hundred thousand picked men able to handle[18] spear and shield. Besides, he hired from Israel a hundred thousand warriors[19] for[20] a hundred talents of silver. 10. Then the king answered and said : " Bring sacrifices and thank-offerings to the house of Yahweh." So the people brought sacrifices and thank-offerings ; the number of the sacrifices which they brought was seventy oxen, a hundred rams, two hundred lambs ; all these they brought[21] to Yahweh.

11. ‎[22]‎וַיְחִי אַחֲרֵי־זֹאת מֵאָה וְאַרְבָּעִים שָׁנָה ‎[23]‎וַיַּרְא אֶת־בָּנָיו וְאֶת־בְּנֵי בָנָיו אַרְבָּעָה ‎[24]‎דֹרוֹת :

And he lived after this one hundred and forty years, and saw his sons and grandsons, four generations.

12. ‎[25]‎וַיִּמְלָךְ־שָׁם שֶׁבַע שָׁנִים וְשִׁשָּׁה חֳדָשִׁים וּשְׁלֹשִׁים וְשָׁלוֹשׁ שָׁנָה מָלַךְ בִּירוּשָׁלָ͏ִם :

And he reigned there seven years and six months, and thirty-three years he reigned in Jerusalem.

[1] Not " two of my sons " ; see Note 4 of Exercise 15C.

[2] Hiph. of מוּת. This is the concessive or permissive use of the impf. (§ 43.II.4)—not quite so strong as the imper. slay (הָמֵת or הֲמִיתָה) which is the rendering of A.V. and R.V. The impf., of course, is also used where may implies indefiniteness : cf. Exod. 5.11 קְחוּ לָכֶם תֶּבֶן מֵאֲשֶׁר תִּמְצָאוּ '' get you straw wherever (lit. from what) you may (or can) find it.''

[3] 1 sing. impf. Hiph. of בּוֹא with 3 sing. masc. suff. and nûn energ. (Gen. 42.37). The pf. (= fut. pf.) would also have been possible here— הֲבִיאֹתִיו ; see the similar sentence in Gen. 43.9.

[4] Note that in this enumeration the noun comes first in the Hebrew text, as in an inventory ; but very frequently the numeral precedes.

[5] Hiph. ptc. fem. pl. of ינק (Grammar, p. 273, col. 4) ; giving suck (lit. causing to suck). The sing. takes the form מֵינֶקֶת not מֵינִיקָה (nurse) ; see § 25.4.(a),(b).

[6] Note the use of the more familiar *masc.* pronom. suffix referring to a *fem.* subject. This irregularity is occasionally found ; e.g. Is. 3.16 the women of Zion בְּרַגְלֵיהֶם תְּעַכַּסְנָה *make a tinkling with their feet* (where the pronom. suffix is masc., though the vb. is fem.).

[7] לְ is customarily used in dates before the second substantive (*e.g.* month, year, life, reign, captivity, etc.) : *e.g.* 2 Kings 25.27 (cf. sentence 4 of this Exercise) " in the 37th year *of* the captivity of Jehoiachin " לְגָלוּת יְהוֹיָכִין (*qāmeṣ* in גָלוּת unchangeable), " on the 27th day *of* the month " לַחֹדֶשׁ. When the word שָׁנָה appears, it is sometimes in the absolute, sometimes in the construct, and sometimes the MSS. vary. *E.g.* 1 Kings 16.10 בִּשְׁנַת עֶשְׂרִים וָשֶׁבַע לְאָסָא *in the 27th year of Asa*, 2 Kings 17.6 בִּשְׁנַת הַתְּשִׁיעִית לְהוֹשֵׁעַ *in the 9th year of Hoshea.* So 2 Kings 25.1 בִּשְׁנַת הַתְּשִׁיעִית לְמָלְכוֹ *in the 9th year of his reign* (constr. inf. of מָלַךְ with suffix) ; but Jer. 52.4, in practically the same sentence, בַּשָּׁנָה. The construct, where it occurs, is to be explained on the analogy of נְהַר פְּרָת *the river Euphrates* and בְּתוּלַת יִשְׂרָאֵל *the virgin Israel*, where the absolute is a noun of nearer definition.

[8] Literally *lifted up the head of.* This phrase in Hebrew can mean *to show favour, to grant a request* (i.e. to lift up the head of a petitioner) or *to forgive.* In this sentence *forgive* is not a suitable word, but *release* will serve. In Gen. 40 there is a play on the double sense of this phrase : in 40.13 the butler's head is to be lifted up, i.e. he is to be restored to his office ; in 40.20 the baker's head is lifted up (by hanging, v. 22 ; or lifted from off him, by decapitation, v. 19).

[9] Not *three of the mighty men.* Cf. note 1 of this section.

[10] Plur. suffix, agreeing with מַיִם.

[11] שְׁלֹשֶׁת takes pron. suffixes on the analogy of קְטֹרֶת ; cf. § 25.4.

[12-12] Hebrew has simply the noun חָלָל *slain* used as a collective. It is used proleptically in this sentence. We cannot say : *he wielded his spear against three hundred slain men* ; we may say : *he wielded . . . hundred men, slaying them* ; or we may translate as in the Key.

[13] Literally *name*.

[14] Literally *he did not come as far as the three, he did not reach the three, he did not attain to a place among the three.*

[15-15] Or *placed them under commanders . . .* or *assigned them to commanders. . . .*

[16] *Reviewed, mustered,* or *paraded* seems to give the sense. Those of military age were separated and numbered (cf. 2 Chron. 25.5f).

[17] A double preposition used with reference to a *terminus a quo*. When לְמִן is used with reference to a date in the past, it means from that date forward ; when to a place, it means from that place to another (which is defined) ; cf. Deut. 9.7 לְמִן־הַיּוֹם אֲשֶׁר־יָצָאתָ מֵאֶרֶץ מִצְרַיִם עַד־בֹּאֲכֶם עַד־הַמָּקוֹם הַזֶּה *from the day when you left the land of Egypt until you reached this place* ; Judges 20.1 וַיֵּצְאוּ כָּל־בְּנֵי יִשְׂרָאֵל וַתִּקָּהֵל הָעֵדָה כְּאִישׁ אֶחָד לְמִדָּן וְעַד בְּאֵר שֶׁבַע *and all the Israelites came out and the congregation assembled as one man from Dan to Beersheba* ; cf. also לְמֵאִישׁ וְעַד־בְּהֵמָה *both man and beast* and לְמִקָּטֹן וְעַד־גָּדוֹל *both great and small.*

[18] Literally *holding, grasping.*

[19] גִּבּוֹר חַיִל probably should be rendered *warrior* or *trained soldier*. אִישׁ חַיִל does not have reference so narrowly to military qualities but seems to include in its reference qualities of character and social standing. Such a man, of course, would also be a leader in war.

[20] *Bêth pretii* ; cf. § 12.2.(a).ii.

[21] Literally, *brought near*, i.e. *offered*.

[22] From חָיָה *to live* ; for it and הָיָה *to become, to be*, cf. § 33.2.

[23] For this form, cf. § 33.1.(d).

[24] דֹּרוֹת, in spite of its fem. termination, is *masc.*, because the *sing.* is masc., cf. § 13.5.(f) ; hence אַרְבָּעָה is in the *fem.*, cf. § 45.1.(c).i.

[25] The ordinary impf. Qal form is יִמְלֹךְ but it is united with the following word שָׁם in one accentual unit, with the accent on שָׁם, so that the *hôlem* in the preceding closed syllable has to be shortened.

B.

1 הָלְכוּ עִמּוֹ חֲמֵשֶׁת אֶחָיו וּשְׁלֹשׁ אֲחִיֹתָיו ¹אֶל־בֵּית אֲבִיהֶם:
2 מָלְכָה הַמַּלְכָּה שִׁשִּׁים וְאַרְבַּע שָׁנָה וַתָּמָת ²בַּת־שְׁמֹנִים
וּשְׁתַּיִם שָׁנָה וְלָהּ אַרְבָּעָה בָנִים וְחָמֵשׁ בָּנוֹת וְאִישָׁהּ מֵת
בְּאַרְבָּעִים וּשְׁתַּיִם שָׁנָה ³לְחַיָּיו ⁴וּבְעֶשְׂרִים וְאַרְבַּע שָׁנָה
⁵לְמָלְכָה: 3 וַיִּוָּלְדוּ לוֹ ⁶שְׁלֹשֶׁת בָּנִים ⁶וּשְׁבַע בָּנוֹת וַיְהִי
⁷מִקְנֵהוּ שֵׁשֶׁת ⁸אֲלָפִים צֹאן וְאַרְבַּעַת אֲלָפִים גְּמַלִּים וּשְׁבַע
מֵאוֹת ⁹חֲמוֹרִים: 4 יְמֵי שְׁנֵי חַיֵּי ¹⁰אַרְבַּע שָׁנִים וְשִׁבְעִים שָׁנָה¹⁰:
5 ¹¹הָיוּ בְּאַרְצוֹ ¹²מֵאָה עֶשְׂרִים וְשֶׁבַע¹² עָרִים וּבְאַחַת
¹³הֶעָרִים ¹⁴הָאֵלֶּה שְׁתַּיִם־עֶשְׂרֵה ¹⁵רְבָבוֹת אָדָם: 6 טוֹב הַחֲצִי
מִן־הַכֹּל: 7 וַיֹּאמְרוּ אִישׁ אֶל־¹⁶רֵעֵהוּ נִשְׁבְּעָה ¹⁷שָׁנִינוּ בְּשֵׁם
אֱלֹהֵינוּ וַיִּשָּׁבְעוּ שְׁנֵיהֶם:

¹ אֶל־ and ל־ and are both found after the verbs הָלַךְ, בּוֹא and שׁוּב, אֶל־ being the commoner of the two. In addition, quite often the simple accus. is used (*i.e.* without any prepos.) : *e.g.* 2 Sam. 13.8 וַתֵּלֶךְ בֵּית אָחִיהָ *she went to her brother's house*, 2 Sam. 4.7 וַיָּבֹאוּ הַבַּיִת *and they came into the house* (cf. § 24.II.1). The He locale is also common (though very rarely as a construct, § 14.5 ; cf. Gen. 44.14 וַיָּבֹא בֵּיתָה יוֹסֵף *and he went into the house of Joseph*), Gen. 24.32 וַיָּבֹא הַבַּיְתָה *and he went into the house*, 2 Sam. 17.17 לָבוֹא הָעִירָה *to come into the city*, Gen. 44.13 וַיָּשֻׁבוּ הָעִירָה *and they returned to the city.*

² Note that " so many years old " is rendered by *son* or *daughter of so many years.* Cf. Deut. 34.7 מֹשֶׁה בֶּן־מֵאָה וְעֶשְׂרִים שָׁנָה בְּמֹתוֹ *Moses was one hundred and twenty years old when he died* : 2 Kings 15.2 בֶּן־שֵׁשׁ עֶשְׂרֵה שָׁנָה הָיָה בְמָלְכוֹ *he was sixteen years old when he began to reign* (cstr. inf.). Gen. 17.17 שָׂרָה בַּת־תִּשְׁעִים שָׁנָה *Sarah who is ninety years old.* In 2 Kings 15.2 occurs חֲמִשִּׁים וּשְׁתַּיִם שָׁנָה *fifty-two years* ; so 2 Kings

10.14 אַרְבָּעִים וּשְׁנַיִם אִישׁ *forty-two men.* It is interesting to note, however, that with the same number in 2 Kings 2.24 the construct of *two* is
used, אַרְבָּעִים וּשְׁנֵי יְלָדִים *forty-two lads.*

³ For לְ here and with מַלְכָּה, see note 7 in section A of this Exercise.

⁴ Or וּבִשְׁנַת עֶשְׂרִים וְאַרְבַּע שָׁנָה לְמָלְכָה. For this construction, with
the repetition of שָׁנָה, cf. 2 Kings 15.1,8,17.

⁵ Cstr. infin. of מָלַךְ with 3 s.f. suffix. This is the common usage in
the Old Testament, being preferred to the use of מַלְכוּת ; cf. 2 Kings
24.12 ; 25.1 ; etc.

⁶ If the absol. forms שְׁלֹשָׁה and שֶׁבַע are used here, the vocalization
of the conjunction is with pretonic *qāmeṣ* ; וְשֶׁבַע. Cf. § 11.II.(e).

⁷ The general word for *cattle.* רְכֻשׁ might also have been used, רְכוּשׁ,
property, often including cattle.

⁸ In Job 1.3 the construct אַלְפֵי is used ; but this is much rarer than
the absolute. The sing. is also used, cf. Isa. 37.36 מֵאָה וּשְׁמֹנִים וַחֲמִשָּׁה
אֶלֶף 185,000—also when it is followed by a substantive ; cf. 2 Sam. 24.9
חֲמֵשׁ־מֵאוֹת אֶלֶף אִישׁ 500,000 men.

⁹ Or אֲתֹנוֹת if *she-asses.*

¹⁰⁻¹⁰ For the repetition of שָׁנָה, cf. Gen. 12.4 בֶּן־חָמֵשׁ שָׁנִים וְשִׁבְעִים שָׁנָה
seventy-five years old, and note 4 above.

¹¹ Cf. the sentence in Gen. 47.9a, where the vb. is omitted. In the
similar sentence Gen. 47.28b, the vb. appears (וַיְהִיוּ (M.T. וַיְהִי)), and
47.9b—a little dissimilar—also adds הָיוּ.

¹²⁻¹² This same number, one hundred and twenty-seven, appears in
Esth. 1.1 ; 8.9 (a late book) in the order *seven and twenty and a hundred*
(מֵאָה) ; cf. the similar order in Gen. 47.28, Exod. 6.16,18 (P), where
hundred is in the constr. מְאַת. In the lists in Ezra 2 and Neh. 7 the order
is usually as above, with the *hundred(s)* first, and with no *wāw* before the
tens.

¹³ So Deut. 19.5,11 ; also 2 Sam. 2.1 אַחַת עָרֵי יְהוּדָה *one of the cities of Judah*. In Deut. 4.42, however, אַחַת מִן־הֶעָרִים, cf. Gen. 2.21 אַחַת מִצַּלְעֹתָיו *one of his ribs*.

¹⁴ הָאֵלֶּה rather than הָהֵם ; cf. Deut. 19.5 ; 1 Kings 9.13.

¹⁵ For this, in Jonah 4.11 the later Aramaizing form רִבּוֹ appears. The number might also have been written מֵאָה וְעֶשְׂרִים אֶלֶף. Cf. Isa. 37.36, quoted in note 8.

¹⁶ Or אָחִיו (§ 33.4).

¹⁷ Not שְׁנֵינוּ, although the שׁ is pretonic, because the absolute is שְׁנַיִם.

§ 46.

A.

1. Whither shall I go from thy spirit ? 2. Whence¹ shall come my help ? 3. Then he wept² ; and this is what he said as he went along³ : " Would that I⁴ had died instead of thee,⁵ my son." 4. Thou shalt go without fail⁶ to my father's house and get a wife for my son. 5. I will certainly not take⁷ anything which is thine. 6. Which is the better for you—that seventy men should rule⁸ over you or that one man should rule over you ? 7. A man had⁹ a vineyard beside the king's palace in Samaria. The king said to him : " Give me¹⁰ thy vineyard, that I may have it¹¹ as a garden, for it is close by my house ; and I will give¹² thee instead a better vineyard than it is ; or, ¹³if thou prefer it,¹³ I will pay thee in money¹⁴ the price of thy vineyard." But the man said : " Far be it from me to give¹⁵ the inheritance of my fathers to thee." 8. Then the prophet approached the king of Israel and said to him : " Go and regain thy strength,¹⁶ and make inquiry¹⁷ and see what thou must¹⁸ do ; for at ¹⁹this time next year¹⁹ the king of Syria will come and attack thee." And the servants²⁰ of the king of Syria said to him : " Their god is a god of the hills ; therefore, they have been too strong for us.²¹ But if we join battle with them on the plain, we shall certainly²² be stronger than they." 9. Nevertheless, as I live, the glory of Yahweh shall fill all the earth. ²⁵For none²³ of the men who saw²⁴ my glory and the wonders

I performed in Egypt and in the wilderness and refused to listen
to my voice shall ever see the land[25] which I sware (to give) to their
fathers ; and none that despises[26] me shall see it.

10. וַיִּשָּׁבַע לָהּ שָׁאוּל בַּיהוה לֵאמֹר [27]חַי־יהוה אִם־[28]יִקְּרֵךְ
[29]עָוֹן [30]בַּדָּבָר הַזֶּה: וַתֹּאמֶר הָאִשָּׁה אֶת־מִי [31]אַעֲלֶה־[32]לָּךְ
וַיֹּאמֶר אֶת־שְׁמוּאֵל [33]הַעֲלִי־לִי: [34]וַתֵּרֶא הָאִשָּׁה אֶת־
[35]שְׁמוּאֵל וַתִּזְעַק בְּקוֹל גָּדוֹל וַיֹּאמֶר לָהּ הַמֶּלֶךְ אַל־[36]תִּירָאִי
כִּי מָה רָאִית וַתֹּאמֶר הָאִשָּׁה [37]אֱלֹהִים רָאִיתִי עֹלִים מִן־
הָאָרֶץ :

And Saul swore to her by Yahweh in these words : " As Yahweh
liveth, no harm shall ever come to thee in this matter." Then the
woman said : " Whom shall I bring up for thee ? " " Bring me
up Samuel," he said. When the woman saw Samuel, she cried
out aloud ; but the king said to her : " Have no fear. But what
didst thou see ? " The woman said : " I saw a god rising out of
the earth."

[1] This אַיִן, which is to be distinguished from the negative אַיִן (cstr.
אֵין) meaning (there) is not, no (cf. § 31.4 footnote), is never found alone,
but always in the combination מֵאַיִן whence ? (interrog.). The interrogative
אַיֵּה where ? is the lengthened form of אַי (cf. הִנֵּה from הֵן) ; אַי is never
found by itself, but only with pronom. suffixes, e.g. אַיּוֹ where is he ? אַיָּם
where are they ? The form אֵי is found four times (e.g. Gen. 4.9 אֵי אָחִיךָ
where is thy brother ?) ; in every other case it is accompanied by the enclitic
זֶה where, then ? (even in indirect quotations, e.g. 1 Sam. 9.18 הַגִּידָה־נָּא לִי
אֵי־זֶה בֵּית הָרֹאֶה tell me, I pray thee, where the seer's house is), or by
מִזֶּה, e.g. Job 2.2 אֵי מִזֶּה תָּבֹא whence comest thou ? Jon. 1.8 אֵי־מִזֶּה עַם
אָתָּה : whence, as regards people, art thou ? i.e. of what people art thou ?

[2] וַיֵּבֶךְ ; see § 33.1.(a).iv.

[3] לְכָתּוֹ, not לְכָתּוֹ (§ 29.2.(2).(b).iii)—inf. cstr. of הָלַךְ with 3 sing. masc.
suffix. If בְּלֶכְתּוֹ here means, not when he went away, but as he went on his

way, another form of Hebrew expression might have been used : וַיֵּלֶךְ

הָלוֹךְ וְאָמוֹר lit. *he went, going and saying*, i.e. *he went, saying as he went*, or

and, as he went along, he said. Cf. *Syntax*, § 86.

⁴ Note the emphatic use of the pers. pron. אֲנִי here.

⁵ For suffixes to תַּחַת, cf. § 36.4.(a).i.

⁶ אִם לֹא, at the beginning of this sentence, makes it a strong adjuration

or asseveration, after an implicit verb of swearing. The usage is explained

in § 46.3.(d). *Without fail* is used in the translation to give the force of

expression required.

⁷ This is an example of אִם introducing a strong negation after an

implicit verb of swearing ; cf. § 46.3.(d).

⁸ הֲמָשֹׁל is not, of course, the Hiph. (which it could not be), but the

inf. cstr. Qal of מָשַׁל with the interrog. הֲ. Note the order in both these

clauses—the בָּכֶם immediately after the vb., and the subj. of the inf.

cstr. after that.

⁹ הָיָה, rather than וַיְהִי, is sometimes used at the beginning of a story,

possibly with the sense of : *It once happened*, or, here, *A certain man*

happened to have a vineyard ; cf. Job 1.1 ; contrast Ruth 1.1.

¹⁰ תְּנָה־לִּי emphatic 2 sing. masc. imper. Qal of נָתַן (cf. § 34.3.(a))

followed by the indirect object expressed by לִּי with *dagh. forte conjunctivum*

(cf. § 6.6).

¹¹ Literally, *that it may be to me for a garden*. This use of לְ before גַּן

has often been illustrated.

¹² Or *and let me give thee*.

¹³⁻¹³ Literally, *if it be good in thine eyes* or *if it seem good to thee*.

¹⁴ כֶּסֶף and מְחִיר־כַּרְמְךָ may be in apposition : *money, the price of*

your vineyard, so that the general, undefined word *money* is followed by a

phrase of nearer definition. Otherwise, כֶּסֶף may be taken as an accus.

of respect, as in the translation.

[15] Literally *from my giving*. This use of מָן with a cstr. infin. after such an introductory phrase as חָלִילָה לִּי is as readily intelligible as the use of it after יָרֵא *to fear*, e.g. יָרֵא מִגֶּשֶׁת אֵלָיו *he feared to approach him*.

[16] The exact force of the Hithpa'el of חזק is sometimes difficult to determine. Possible meanings are : *show thy strength, make thyself strong, exert thy strength*, so *be resolute, take courage, brace thyself*. This sentence is taken from 1 Kings 20.22 f. and the call is made to the king to build up his forces against the expected renewed attack on Israel by the king of Syria ; thus *strengthen your forces* may convey the meaning.

[17] Literally *know and see* (imperatives). *Know* must be used here in the sense of *get to know, learn*, i.e. consult all sources of information and review the situation as it exists ; and *see* in the sense of *consider, give attention to*. In other words, the king is to take all appropriate measures required to meet the expected emergency by investigating at once the needs which are likely to arise and the steps to be taken to meet the needs.

[18] *What thou must do* (or *what action thou must take*) is to be preferred to *what thou shalt do*.

[19-19] Lit. *at the turn of the year*. This is an idiomatic Hebrew phrase. 2 Sam. 11.1 makes it plain that, in the time of the United Kingdom in Israel, there was a season of the year when war was waged. This probably remained long after that time, so that *at the return of the year* probably means *at this time next year*.

[20] *The servants of a king* may be *his subjects* or *his household slaves*, but the term here may be used to indicate his advisers or, as we might say, his cabinet ministers.

[21] In the case of the preposition מָן with suffixes, note that the forms of the preposition with the 3 s.m. suffix and with the 1 plur. suffix are similar : (מִן/מֶן/הוּ) מִמֶּנּוּ and (מִן/מֶן/נוּ) מִמֶּנּוּ respectively.

[22] For the effect of this use of אִם לֹא, cf. note 6 above and § 46.3.(d).

[23] Hebrew commonly negatives the verb in such a sentence as this, but it is usually more fitting in English to apply the negative force to the subject.

[24] The participle as such has no defined temporal value ; the context in which it is used must define it. Here the reference is clearly to the past.

[25-25] Lit. *For all the men who saw . . . listen to my voice—(I swear) if they shall see the land . . .* i.e. they shall never see it. Cf. note 23 above.

[26] Or *despised* ; cf. note 24 above.

[27] Note the phrase חַי־יהוה וְחֵי נַפְשְׁךָ (1 Sam. 20.3 ; 25.26) *as Yahweh liveth and as thy soul (i.e. thou) liveth.* " It is evidently only a rabbinical refinement which makes the pronunciation חַי distinctive of an oath by God (or of God by himself)." G.K., p. 270, footnote 1. Cf. *Syntax*, § 119.

[28] 3 s.m. impf. Qal (יִקְרֶה) of קָרָה, with 2 s. *fem.* suffix (referring to the witch, 1 Sam. 28.10). The *daghesh forte*, which seems surprising, is the *dagh. f. dirimens* (§ 6.6), a device to secure the more audible enunciation of the shᵉwa. It is used occasionally with ק, ר, נ, מ, ל (as here), and the sibilants : cf. עִנְּבֵי (for עִנְבֵי, cstr. pl. of עֵנָב grape), קַשְּׁתוֹתָם Ps. 37.15 (*their bows*, from קֶשֶׁת *a bow* : note the ending ם ָ, § 16.3.(a).v) ; הַצְּפִינוֹ Exod. 2.3 (for הַצְפִּינוֹ *to hide him*, Hiph. of צפן) is similar to יִקְרֵךְ here in that the shᵉwa of the form without *dagh. forte dirimens* is normally silent.

[29] עָוֺן (as sometimes also חֲטָא) may mean *punishment*, as well as *iniquity, guilt.*

[30] Besides meaning *word,* דָּבָר not seldom means *matter* (here *in this matter*), *affair, thing.* See Key § 32B, note 4.

[31] 1 s. impf. Hiph. of עָלָה (pf. הֶעֱלָה) : the corresponding part of the Qal would be אֶעֱלֶה.

[32] Note the *dagh. forte conjunctivum* ; see note 10 above.

[33] Fem. sing. imper. Hiph. ; masc. (הַעֲלֵה >) הַעַל, always found in this form (§ 33.1.(c)).

[34] Cf. § 33.1.(d).

[35] Perhaps the true reading here (cf. 1 Sam. 28.12) is שָׁאוּל, which is found in four Greek MSS. " When she *looked at Saul.*" So W. O. E. Oesterley, *Immortality and the Unseen World*, pp. 68 f.

[36] 2 s.f. jussive of יֵרָא (§ 29.2.(2).(a)).

[37] Notice the order—the emphatic אֱלֹהִים put first : *it was a god that I saw.* אֱלֹהִים a superhuman being or beings : cf. Ps. 8.6 וַתְּחַסְּרֵהוּ מְּעַט מֵאֱלֹהִים *and thou* (Yahweh) *didst make him to lack* (Pi. of חָסֵר) *little of the* (superhuman or) *divine beings* (not God, which makes no sense, as God [Yahweh] is being addressed). In the Samuel passage the word is applied to the shade of Samuel : this might seem to imply that at this time the dead, or at least the great dead, like Samuel, were regarded as superhuman or divine, so that a form of ancestor worship may have been practised.

B.

1 וַיֹּאמֶר אֵלֶיהָ בִּתִּי הֲתֵלְכִי עִם־הָאִישׁ הַזֶּה אִם תֵּשְׁבִי ¹עִמָּדִי וַתֹּאמֶר אֲהָהּ אָבִי לֹא ²אוּכַל לָשֶׁבֶת עִמָּךְ : 2 אָנָה אֶבְרַח ³מִפָּנֶיךָ : 3 הַאַתָּה בְּנִי אִם־לֹא : 4 מִי־יִתֵּן מוּתֵנוּ בְיַד־אֱלֹהֵינוּ ⁴בְּאֶרֶץ בָּבֶל ⁵בְּשִׁבְתֵּנוּ ⁶וּבְכִינוּ עַל־⁶מֵימֶיהָ : 5 נִשְׁבַּעְתִּי בְאַפִּי אִם־⁷תְּבֹאוּן אֶל־מְנוּחָתִי : 6 לֹא־יָמוּשׁ סֵפֶר הַתּוֹרָה הַזֶּה מִפִּיךָ וְהָגִיתָ בּוֹ יוֹמָם וָלַיְלָה לְמַעַן תִּשְׁמֹר לַעֲשׂוֹת כְּכָל־הַכָּתוּב בּוֹ ⁸וּדְבַרְתָּ ⁹בּוֹ לְבָנֶיךָ אַחֲרֶיךָ בְּשִׁבְתְּךָ ¹⁰בְּבֵיתֶךָ ¹¹וּבְלֶכְתְּךָ בַדֶּרֶךְ : 7 לֹא ¹²יִיעַף אֱלֹהִים וְלֹא יִיגָע אִם תַּאֲמִינוּ בּוֹ אֵיךְ תֹּאמְרוּ ¹³נִסְתְּרָה דַרְכִּי מֵאֱלֹהָי :

[1] Or עִמִּי or אִתִּי (§ 40.6.(b)). Both עִם and אֶת־ are used with יָשַׁב ; cf. Gen. 29.19 שְׁבָה עִמָּדִי 1 Sam. 22.23 שְׁבָה אִתִּי *abide with me* (שְׁבָה emphatic form of imper. שֵׁב, § 29.2.(2).(b).iii).

[2] Impf. Qal of יָכֹל (cf. § 41.2.(4)). יָכֹל is usually followed by לְ ; cf. § 19 Heb.–Eng. Exercise, 2 ; but contrast Num. 22.38 : הֲיָכוֹל אוּכַל דַּבֵּר מְאוּמָה *Have I any power to speak anything ?*

[3] In Ps. 139.7 the last words are transposed, doubtless simply for the sake of varying the more customary order of the first clause אָנָה אֵלֵךְ מֵרוּחֶךָ.

⁴ The absolute בָּאָרֶץ might seem more natural, as a pure apposition. But Hebrew prefers to say " the land *of* Egypt, Canaan ", etc. ; *i.e.* the construct may sometimes express apposition with the following word : cf. 1 Sam. 28.7 אֵשֶׁת בַּעֲלַת־אוֹב *a woman, possessor of a soothsaying spirit* (see Key § 45A, note 7, and *Syntax*, § 28 Rem. 6).

⁵ " The constructions of the infinitive with a preposition are almost always continued in the further course of the narrative by means of the *finite verb, i.e.* by an independent sentence, not by a co-ordinate infinitive " (G.K. § 114.(r)). The tense of the second vb. takes the sequence which it would take if the first vb. were finite : *e.g.* Gen. 39.18 *and it came to pass* כַּהֲרִימִי קוֹלִי וָאֶקְרָא *as I lifted up my voice and cried* (exactly = כַּאֲשֶׁר עַד־בֹּאִי וְלָקַחְתִּי 2 Kings 18.32 so ;(רוּם) Hiph. of : הֲרִימֹתִי קוֹלִי וָאֶקְרָא אֶתְכֶם *until I shall come and take you* (= עַד־אֲשֶׁר אָבוֹא וְלָקַחְתִּי), עַל־רָדְפוֹ אָחִיו וְשִׁחֵת רַחֲמָיו Am. 1.11 (*on account of his pursuing, i.e.*) *because he pursued his brother and destroyed his compassion* (the *wāw* consec with the pf.—Piʿel—implies a preceding *impf.* in the *frequentative* sense ; cf. § 43.II.2, יִרְדֹּף *repeatedly* pursued). The latter construction has been followed in the translated sentence—" when we *used to* sit and weep " כִּי נֵשֵׁב וּבָכִינוּ (or כַּאֲשֶׁר). If the sitting and weeping referred to a single occasion, we should write בְּשִׁבְתֵּנוּ וַנִּבְכֶּה.

⁶ For the reduplicated form of מֵי (cstr. of מַיִם *waters*) with pron. suffixes, see § 42.

⁷ The ending וּן with the so-called *nûn paragogicum* (cf. Ps. 95.11 יְבֹאוּן) is occasionally found. It may express emphasis, and it bears the tone. It is found with the 2 and 3 pl. masc. ; also, but seldom, with the 2 sing. fem. (יִן). In pause the preceding vowel is lengthened, *e.g.* Exod. 15.14 יִרְגָּזוּן *they tremble.*

⁸ *Wāw* consec. with pf. after the preceding impf. following לְמַעַן.

⁹ For בְּ in the sense of *about, concerning*, after דִּבֶּר (Pi.), cf. Deut.

3.26 ; 6.7 ; 11.19, 1 Sam. 19.3. More commonly the object *about* which one speaks is indicated by עַל.

[10] In Deut. 6.7 ; 11.19 this is written בְּבֵיתֶךָ with dagh. forte in the initial בְּ. With the previous word בְּשִׁבְתְּךָ finishing in an open syllable, this dagh. forte could have been omitted, but it may have been inserted to avoid two aspirate ב's together in בְּבֵיתֶךָ.

[11] See Note 3 in section A of this Exercise.

[12] *Never* is suggested by the impf.—not *at any time*.

[13] Isaiah 40.27 thus construes דֶּרֶךְ as a fem. noun, but it is more often masc.

INDEX OF SCRIPTURE PASSAGES QUOTED

(In any reference (e.g. 37A.2) the first number refers to the section in the Key (corresponding to the one in the Grammar similarly numbered), the letter to a division of the section, and the second number to the note within the division. Only passages from the Old Testament which are quoted in the Key are included in this list ; passages merely referred to are not included).

Genesis

2.5	31C.2.
3.5	27C.4, 31C.4.
3.23	20A.14.
4.9	46A.1.
12.11,13	31C.1.
15.18	22B.14.
17.17	45B.2.
18.14	32B.4.
20.3	34B.30 . . . 30.
20.11	31C.2.
21.8	36C.2.
22.7f	32A.15.
24.2	36C.4.
24.6	36C.4.
24.23	25A.11.
24.32	45B.1.
26.11	17B.11.
26.28	22B.14.
27.3	31C.1.
27.18	32A.15.
27.42	36C.2.
30.31	32B.4.
31.14	31A.16.
37.23	38C.5.
39.9	32B.4.
39.18	46B.5.
41.42	27A.2.
42.1	25A.11.
42.21	34B.30 . . . 30.
44.9	37A.4.
44.13	45B.1.
44.14	45B.1.
50.2	32A.1 . . . 1.

Exodus

3.7	22C.9 . . . 9.
3.12	36C.7.
15.9	26B.3.
16.6	27C.4.
21.17	17B.11.
21.28	36C.2.
27.20	32A.1 . . . 1.

Numbers

12.1f	31A.16.
22.38	32B.4.
26.10	32B.8.

Deuteronomy

2.7	32B.4.
6.8	19B.4.
9.7	45A.17.
10.21	13B.2 . . . 2.
22.2	37A.4.
23.4	33A.7 . . . 7.
26.16	13B.2 . . . 2.
28.67	32A.11.
34.7	45B.2.

Joshua

1.6	38C.5.
10.13	37A.12.
23.14	20B.4.

Judges

8.22	26B.6.
20.1	45A.17.

1 Samuel

1.23	32A.11.	6.15
9.18	46A.1.	29.13
		31.8

2 Samuel

4.7	45B.1.	
11.1	46A.19 . . . 19.	11.8
11.11	31A.8.	14.7,8
12.10	36C.1.	
13.8	45B.1.	
17.17	45B.1.	2.26f
17.19	32B.4.	
19.1	32A.11.	
		1.11

1 Kings

2.21	36C.2.	2.15
8.44	30C.1.	5.4f
8.48	30C.1.	
13.31	27C.4.	1.8
14.5	32B.17.	1.15
16.10	45A.7.	
20.25	31A.8.	
		2.3

2 Kings

2.24	45B.2.	
4.6	37A.12.	4.7
7.4	37A.4.	24.6
10.4	45B.2.	27.8
15.2	45B.2.	75.11
17.6	45A.7.	
18.32	46B.5.	
25.1	45A.7.	14.29
25.5	31A.5.	26.24
25.27	45A.7.	

Isaiah

		2.2
1.15	19C.3.	6.11
5.3	22B.14.	29.14
11.12b	27C.3 . . . 3.	
24.2	20A.15.	
48.8	33A.7 . . . 7.	8.5

Jeremiah

	33A.7 . . . 7.
	27C.14.
	27C.3 . . . 3.

Hosea

	34B.30 . . . 30.
	31C.8 . . .8, 9 . . . 9.

Joel

	36C.1.

Amos

	46B.5.
	37A.12.
	27C.14.

Jonah

	46A.1.
	37B.12 . . . 12.

Zephaniah

	31C.14, 27C.14.

Psalms

	32A.11.
	27C.14.
	27C.14.
	35B.1.

Proverbs

	39B.17.
	32B.17.

Job

	46A.1.
	39B.17.
	27A.2.

Nehemiah

	37A.12.

INDEX OF SUBJECTS

(In any reference (e.g. 37A.2) the first number refers to the section in the Key (corresponding to the one in the Grammar similarly numbered), the letter to a division of the section, and the second number to the note within the division. Where a subject has been dealt with in the Grammar, reference is made to what is said on it in the Key only when it amplifies or further illustrates what is said in the Grammar.)

Accusative, 36C.2 ; anticipatory, 26A.8 . . . 8, 33B.15 ; *motion to*, 45A.17.

Accusatives, use of two, 37C.5.

Adverbial Infin., 29B.9, 30B.2 . . . 2, 34B.28 . . . 28.

Age, indication of, 45B.2.

Apodosis, 37A.4.

Apposition, 18B.12, 46B.4.

Article, notable Hebrew use of, 41A.3 ; omission of, 15C.10 . . . 10, 22B.2b, 22C.1,2, 25B.1, 30B.1 . . . 1, 32A.3, 37B.8, 37C.2 ; generic, 12A.6, 12B.2, 18C.2, 40A.15, 44B.3.

Assimilation of נ, 24A.5.

Athnah, 19C.4.

Casus pendens, 22B.6, 26A.12 . . .12.

Circumflex, use of, on pure long vowels, § 3B.

Circumstantial clause, 16C.4 . . . 4, 18B.8,13, 20A.8, 26A.7 . . . 7, 32B.20, 36C.8, 41B.9 . . . 9.

Collective singulars, 13A.3, 15D.8, 22B.14, 26B.3, 31A.5, 40A.9.

Compound subjects, 31A.16.

Construct-genitive relationship, 18B.11, 25A.11.

Daghesh forte dirimens, 46A.28 ; *daghesh lene*, elision of, 14A.4,11, 14B.5, 15C.2 . . . 2, 16C.6.

Dative of Advantage, 12A.9, 20B.16, 30B.19, 36C.11.

Gentilic endings, 35A.18.

Hiding the face, 24A.8 . . . 8.

Hiph'il, permissive or concessive use, 45A.2.

Hireq for pathah, 23B.2.

Imperatives, series of, 30B.14, 31C.13, 37A.10, 40B.2.

Impf., frequentative use of, 38B.5 ; modal use, 29B.16 ; 1 sing. *wāw* consec., 40A.4 ; Impfs., a series of *wāw* consec., 30B.5 and 20 . . . 20, 33B.17, 35A.19.

Methegh, 22B.1, 22B.9, 27C.5, 31C.5.

Modal use of Impf., 29B.16.

Motion to, 45A.17.

Negatives, use of Hebrew, 15C.3, 17B.12.

Niph'al, consec. impf., 22B.12 ; ptc. 36B.23 ; cstr. infin., 36C.2.

Nouns used in dual and plural, 29C.4., 35A.1.

Nûn paragogicum, 46B.7.

Omission of *daghesh forte*, 23B.15.

Optative in Hebrew, 32A.11.

Order in a sentence, 22C.7 . . . 7 and 9 . . . 9, 23A.15, 23B.14 . . . 14, 29B.2, 30B.4 . . . 4, 39B.11, 44B.1.

Participle, futural use of, 20B.4, 26B.5, 30B.23, 46A.24 ; expressing continuity, 23A.6.

Polite mode of address, 33A.15, 33C.9, 39B.20, 40A.3, 41A.14 . . . 14.

187

N

Prepositions, compound, 20A.6, 22B.7, 30C.2, 32A.8, 45A.17.

Proleptic use, 45A.12 . . . 12.

Pronouns used for emphasis, 23B.7 and 9.

Singular used where English uses plural, 23B.13.

Tone, movement of, 37A.26.

Vocative use of *my father*, etc., 32A.15, 44A.5.

Wāw consec. impf., 1st sing., 40A.4 ; consec. impfs., a series of, 30B.5 and 20 . . . 20, 33B.17, 35A.19 ; consec. pf. verb after a temporal clause 27C.4.

188

INDEX OF HEBREW WORDS AND FORMS

(In any reference (e.g. 37A.2) the first number refers to the section in the Key (corresponding to the one in the Grammar similarly numbered), the letter to a division of the section, and the second number to the note within the division. In this index reference is made to Hebrew words only when the Key adds something to what is said in the Grammar concerning their form or use.)

אָבָה 37A.2, 43A.14.

הָאָדָם 20A.11.

אָדוֹן 31C.13, 37A.18 . . . 18, 39B.32.

אַחֲרִית הַיָּמִים 38B.4.

אַיֵּה ,(אֵי)אַי 46A.1.

אֹיֵב 38C.9.

אַיִן (אֵין) 31C.2.

אֱלֹהִים 46A.37.

אֱלֹהִים with article, 9A.1.

אֶלֶף 45B.8.

אִם in oaths, 31A.8.

אִם interrog., 31A.8.

אִם־לֹא 43A.17 . . . 17, 46A.6.

אָמַר 35A.17 . . . 17, 36C.6, 37B.9.

אָמַר followed by לְ and infin. cstr. 18B.1.

אָסַף 35B.13.

יֹסֵף and אָסַף 32A.2 and 10, 37A.24, 41A.23.

אֶרֶךְ, אֹרֶךְ 39B.17.

אֶרֶץ 10A.5.

אֲשֶׁר relative 32A.7.

אֲשֶׁר omitted 35B.8.

אֲשֶׁר correlative 11B.8, 17B.7, 30C.3.

אֶת־ 16B.4.

בְּ 36B.20, 37A.8, 46B.9.

בֶּגֶד 31C11.

צֵאתְךָ וּבוֹאֶךָ 30B.10 . . . 10, 39B.16

בּוֹשׁ 33A.7 . . . 7.

בָּטַח בְּ 22C.8.

בֶּן־אִמּוֹ 44B.5 . . . 5.

בְּנֵי״ 20A.4, 42A.18.

בִּקֵּשׁ 17C.2 . . . 2, 27C.14.

בֶּרֶךְ 36B.13.

בַּת״ 45B.2.

גָּאַל 41A.15.

גִּבּוֹר חַיִל 14A.9 . . . 9, 45A.19.

189

גַּם . . . גַּם 39B.21.

וְגַם 32B.14, 33A.7 . . . 7, 33B.9 and
10 . . . 10.

גַּ ת 34C.1.

דָּבָר 32B.4.

דָּם 17B.2, 22C.3.

דָּמָה 43B.10.

דֶּרֶךְ 30C.1.

דָּרַשׁ 17C.2 . . . 2, 27C.14.

הָלַךְ 46A.3.

הָלַךְ (Hithpa'el) + לִפְנֵי 23B.8.

וְ range of meaning 14A.8, 17C.2 . . .
2 ; with the jussive, 32A.1 . . . 1 ;
with cohortative to express purpose, 20B.11.

זֶה enclitic and proclitic, 29B.27,
43A.12.

זָכַר (Hiph.), 24A.9 . . . 9.

חוּץ 43B.1.

חָזַק Hithpa. 46A.16.

חַטָּאת 38C.3.

חַי'', חֵי'' 46A.27.

חַיִּים 22B.2.

חַיִל 31A.4, 45A.19.

(גִּבּוֹר) חַיִל 14A.9 . . .9, 45A.19.

חָכָם 13A.7.

חֲלִילָה 37A.19, 46A.15.

חָנַן 39B.2, 39C.4.

חֶסֶד 34B.26, 36B.14.

בְּיַד 18B.15.

יָדַע range of meaning, 29C.18,
46A.17 ; (ptc.) 20A.12.

יהוה 20B.10.

יָכוֹל 46B.2.

יָלַד 39B.4.

יצא Hiph. 34B.21.

יָצַר, יֵצֶר 40A.13.

ירה Hiph. 40B.21.

יַרְכָּה 27C.3 . . . 3.

יֵשׁ(וְשׁ־) 25A.11, 29B.13.

יתר Niph. 41B.2.

כְּ 20A.15.

כבד (Pi'el) 24B.13.

כִּבֵּס 36B.16.

כִּי 24A.16.

כלה (Pi'el) 42A.8 . . . 8.

כָּנָף 27C.3 . . . 3, 31C.1.

190

כָּרַת בְּרִית 22B.14.

כָּשַׁל 29B.20.

לְ *according to, in respect of,* 34B.10 ; *as, for,* 19B.4, 20A.2, 35A.11, 16 ; with a following noun as an alternative to a direct object, 35A.13 ; *by* after a passive verbal form, 44A.8.

לֹא . . . אִישׁ 15C.3.

לֹא . . . כֵּן 44A.11 . . . 11.

לָבַשׁ 27A.2.

לחם (Niph.), 24B.5, 36B.9.

לְמִן 45A.17.

לָקַח 36B.10.

מְאֹד 20A.7, 20B.3.

מְאוּמָה 32B.4.

מַה־ 40B.20, 44A.2.

מַחֲשָׁבָה 38B.21.

מְעַט 36B.1.

מַעֲלָל 22B.10.

מִצְרִי 23A.4.

מִצְרַיִם 27C.8.

מִשְׁפָּט 26A.11.

נָא 27C.7, 30B.5, 42A.14.

נָטָה 34B.7.

נוּחַ (Hiph.) 31C.10, 33A.20.

נָכְרִי (נכר√) 32B.17.

נָסַךְ 41A.6.

נסע (Hiph.) 40B.18.

נָשָׂא רֹאשׁ 45A.8.

נָתַן, infin. cstr. תֵּת 35A.8, 37B.11.

סתר (Hiph.) etc. *to hide* 31A.2, 32B.6.

עַבְדֵי הַמֶּלֶךְ 46A.20.

עָבַר 35B.3.

עוּד (Hiph.) 30B.26.

עוֹלָם 25B.5 . . . 5, 36C.1, 39B.26.

עַל־ 34C.4 . . . 4, 37B.6, 42A.17 . . . 17.

עָלָה 40A.10.

עַל־פִּי 29B.15.

עָמַד 37A.12.

עָמַד לִפְנֵי 17B.5.

פֶּה ,לְפִי 33A.27.

פָּנִים 25A.3,16 ; with a pl. verb, 33A.19.

פָּקַד 44A.16.

פָּקַד עַל־ 20A.16.

פַּר, שַׁר, etc. 24B.2.

צִוָּה 33B.2.

קוֹל 19B.1.

קָטָן ,קָטֹן 44B.7.

קָרָא 12A.1.

קָרָה ,קָרָא 38B.3.

קָשָׁה used with force of Eng. adverb, 40A.24.

רָבָה 39B.34, 42B.5.

רֵיקָם 39B.13.

רָם 13A.8.

רַע, meaning of 13A.1.

רַע בְּעֵינָיו 44A.9 . . . 9.

רָפָא 38B.23.

רָפָה (Hiph.) 40B.16.

שׁאר (Niph.) 41B.2.

שֶׁבֶר 35A.31.

שַׁדַּי 39B.10.

שָׁלוֹם 37A.21.

שָׁמַע 44A.7.

שמר (imper. Niph.), 22B.13, 32A.9.

תָּמִים 33A.1.

תֵּת (לָתֵת־לְךָ) 29B.4.